D1421467

MARRIAGE MINUTES

Robert and
Cheryl Moeller

MARRIAGE MINUTES

Inspirational
Readings to Share
with Your Spouse

MOODY PRESS
CHICAGO

ISBN: 0-8024-2146-6

5 7 9 10 8 6 4

Printed in the United States of America

To Rob, Melissa, Brent, Andrew, and Megan.
Heaven gave us its very best when it gave
us you five for our children.

and

To Cathryn Marie Webster,
our favorite sister from Tennessee.

ACKNOWLEDGMENTS

Marriage Minutes is in reality the result of marriage years. Our marriage is the product of so many people who have loved, supported, and mentored us as a couple throughout our nearly two decades together.

Our heartfelt thanks go to our parents, our pastors, and our professors who, whether they were aware of it or not, have been instilling in us throughout our lives the values, examples, and wisdom needed to produce something God desires from every couple—a Christian marriage.

To Jim Bell, Bill Soderberg, Cheryl Dunlop, Saralyn Temple, Danielle Essex, Linda Haskins, and all the other wonderful people at Moody Press, thank you for believing in this project. To Bob Neff, Bruce Everhart, Wayne Shepherd, Jon Gauger, Andrew Bee, Chris Wright, and all the outstanding staff and management of the Moody Broadcasting Network, thank you for your support and production of the daily radio broadcast of "The Marriage Minute." And to Rick Pierce and Jim Jenks in the Moody Conference Ministries department, thank you for your partnership in sponsoring the "For Better, For Worse, For Keeps" marriage seminar. To Dr. Joe Stowell, president of the Moody Bible Institute, thank you for allowing us the opportunity to work together with your outstanding institution. Your leadership, vision, and humility of spirit have made the Institute truly a joy to be in partnership with in all these endeavors.

To Jan Dennis, our good friend and literary representative, thank you for your integrity, helpfulness, and sense of humor. To Brian Ogne, Roger Johnson, and Steve Schoenwetter and all the tremendous people at Timber-lee Christian Center in East Troy, Wisconsin, thanks for offering us the needed solitude necessary to complete this project. You have been more than kind to us over and over again. To Keith Wells and the thoroughly helpful staff of the Rolfing Library on the Campus of Trinity International University in Deerfield, Illinois, thank you for making your lovely fa-

cility and considerable resources available to us throughout the project. To the wonderful staff and congregation of First Evangelical Free Church of Chicago, thank you for your support of us in seeing this project through to its finish.

God bless you, everyone.

INTRODUCTION

*W*hen we first aired our daily one minute radio program, *The Marriage Minute*, we wondered if sixty seconds was enough time to help anyone. After all, how much can you do to encourage couples to keep their vows, deal with sin in their lives, and call on God to give them fresh love for each other in the same amount of time advertisers use to sell aspirin, new cars, and low-fat yogurt?

What we discovered surprised even us. One minute can change a lifetime. By day after day presenting God's Word in a focused, get-to-the-point fashion, over time the cumulative impact of persistent encouragement and challenge is for God to change hearts and lives. Walls of resistance, apathy, and misunderstanding eventually give way under the steady stream of loving but straightforward reminders of God's power-filled plans for our marriages.

It's in that same spirit we offer this one year devotional guide for couples. The format is similar to *The Marriage Minute*. Each day contains a short portion of Scripture, a one sentence spiritual insight, and approximately one minute of illustration and application of truth for our marriages.

Our expectation is that over time, as you and your spouse work your way through the book, things are going to change in your relationship. Your confidence in God, your determination to honor your vows, and your desire to draw near your spouse is going to increase.

How can we make such a prediction? Certainly not because of any insight or wisdom of our own. We don't have the slightest power to change your marriage. Rather it's the inherent power that comes from dwelling in God's Word and calling on God in prayer. Not only has our Lord promised that His Word will never return empty, He has also promised our honest seeking in prayer will never go unanswered: "Call to me and I will answer you and tell you great and unsearchable things you do not know" (Jeremiah 33:3).

If yours is already a strong, intimate, and growing marriage, you'll find encouragement to stay the course. Hopefully all the healthy things you now believe and practice in your marriage and life will be reinforced. The warnings and exhortations to avoid wrong choices and sinful attitudes can be used to help those close to you looking for help and a breakthrough in their own marriage.

If you are a believer, but your spouse is not one yet, this devotional guide can show you principles and attitudes that can help draw your spouse to the Savior. Above all else make certain the husband or wife you love so much is surrounded by the prayers of others. Assault heaven's doors with prayer for your beloved spouse until the day arrives when you two truly become one in Christ.

Several entries deal with anger. We make no apology for this. We have found this to be the number one problem of married couples we counsel with. Unresolved anger, bitterness, and even emotional abuse are found in too many relationships today. Anger ranges from the mildly sarcastic to the openly hateful. God never intended marriage to go down that road. It's time to bring such painful and destructive emotions to the Cross where Christ can set one or both of you free to love each other.

If destructive anger is not your problem but it is your spouse's downfall, you'll at least gain insight into your spouse's struggle and the road to freedom for you both. Most of all, you and other believers need to call on the name of the Lord for your spouse's repentance and healing.

Finally, if you are a couple in serious trouble, this book could be of great help. No problem in marriage is too big for our God Almighty. Through Jesus you can start over again, learn to love each other once more, and discover God's magnificent plan for your relationship. All of heaven is on the side of your marriage succeeding.

So take heart. God is at work today. Come together each day as a couple with hearts open to God and each other. May God use this simple devotional guide to point you to the Word of God and

prayer as the true hope for your marriage. God has a plan for your marriage that is above and beyond what you could ever imagine. What is God preparing to do in your marriage? Heaven only knows, but that's what is so encouraging. The God of heaven is in charge.

Now to him who is able to do immeasurably more than all we ask or imagine, according to his power that is at work within us, to him be glory in the church and in Christ Jesus throughout all generations, for ever and ever! Amen. (Ephesians 3:20–21)

With love,
Bob and Cheryl

MARRIAGE MINUTE TRUTH:

CALLING ON THE LORD IS PRAYER IN ITS MOST BASIC FORM

Primary Passage:
This is what the Lord says, he who made the earth, the Lord who formed it and established it—the Lord is his name: "Call to me and I will answer you and tell you great and unsearchable things you do not know."
Jeremiah 33:2–3

The English satirist Samuel Johnson once remarked that few things clear our minds as quickly as the prospect of being hung. Desperate situations seem to give us clarity of thought and action. When it comes to discovering the true nature of prayer, this has certainly been true in our experience. As we have faced desperate, seemingly impossible circumstances, we have learned to call out to God. This is prayer that comes from the bottom of our soul. This is prayer that drops away high-sounding or eloquent words. This is prayer that basically says, "O God, if you don't show up, we're finished."

As one insightful pastor observed, "God is attracted to weakness." When we find ourselves helpless and hopeless and call unto God in sincerity and truth, He answers. He can't help but answer. He is drawn to our needy and humble spirit. He is attracted by our sense of utter helplessness and dependence. Regardless of the problem you two are facing at the moment, could we urge you to call out to God?

MARRIAGE MINUTE TRUTH:

ONE REASON BEHIND TROUBLE IN OUR MARRIAGE MIGHT BE PRIDE

. . . .

Primary Passage:
God opposes the proud but gives grace to the humble.
James 4:6

. . . .

*O*ur financial plans collapse. We suffer unexpected setbacks in our career. We have a house that won't sell. How can we explain such difficulties in life? They may have any number of causes. But one overlooked explanation is our pride. The Bible teaches that God opposes the proud. When pride enters our hearts, He blocks our advance, frustrates our plans, and lets us spin our wheels. It all adds up to God saying, "I'm not letting you go anywhere until you humble yourselves before Me."

We went through one particularly difficult period of life where we couldn't understand why one calamity seemed to pile on another. At the end of this incredibly hard time we realized God had been working to break us. God was telling us it was time to pray. Only when we began to seek Him together in brokenness and humility did the light break through in our lives once again.

We would never suggest all trouble in anyone's life is caused by pride. But if we're not praying and seeking God with all of our hearts, pride may very well have slipped into our lives. The remedy is to humble ourselves before God this very hour. Seek His forgiveness. The choice between God's opposition and God's grace is clear to us. Which do you want?

MARRIAGE MINUTE TRUTH:

GOD IS AVAILABLE TO YOU BOTH THIS VERY MOMENT

Primary Passage:
Come near to God and he will come near to you.
James 4:8

One of the more anxious experiences of our married lives occurred when one of our small children wandered away from us at a Fourth of July parade. In the press of the crowds, floats, and excitement, he simply slipped away from us. We searched frantically for him for the next ninety minutes. Tears of gratitude and joy flowed freely when we were reunited with him at the police station. Though he was only three years old, he had started walking down a busy street in the direction in which our van was parked. His desire was to find us, and as a result we were able to find him.

Perhaps you two are feeling that God is distant from you today. You feel lost, perhaps even abandoned by God, and you are wondering how to find your way home. It begins with a simple biblical principle: Draw near to God and He will draw near to you. He is available to both of you this very moment. The very integrity of the Word of God promises that if you come near to God He will reciprocate. In a spirit of prayer call on God to meet you. Open your heart to the love and embrace He desires to give you. His heart has been longing for you two to be reunited. Allow that to happen right now.

MARRIAGE MINUTE TRUTH:

HOPE IS ONLY AS RELIABLE
AS THE PERSON YOU TRUST IN

Primary Passage:
*When neither sun nor stars appeared for many days and the
storm continued raging, we finally gave up all hope of being saved.*
Acts 27:20

*H*ope is a powerful force.

Consider the case of Florence Chadwick. Chuck Swindoll tells
the story of how on July 4, 1952, she waded into the water off
Catalina Island in the Pacific Ocean. Her goal was an ambitious
one. She was planning to swim the entire distance between the
off-shore island and the coast of California.

The water was bone-numbing cold that morning. Sharks had to
be driven off several times with rifle fire. The fog restricted visibil-
ity to just the waves immediately ahead of her. Almost fifteen
hours later an exhausted human being was pulled from the water—one-half mile short of the California coast. She was later
quoted as saying, "If I could have seen the land I might have made
it." An almost superhuman achievement was frustrated by the lack
of just one element . . . hope. Hope is only as effective as the object
or person you trust in. Who is your hope in for this coming year?
If you place your hope in the risen Christ, He will get you
through the days of fog and despair. You won't be disappointed.

MARRIAGE MINUTE TRUTH:

SERVANTS OF GOD HAVE EVERY REASON TO BE FILLED WITH HOPE

Primary Passage:
Last night an angel of the God whose I am and whom I serve stood beside me and said, "Do not be afraid, Paul. You must stand trial before Caesar; and God has graciously given you the lives of all who sail with you." So keep up your courage, men, for I have faith in God that it will happen just as he told me.
Acts 27:23–25

*T*he apostle Paul once found himself in a terrifying storm at sea in a ship filled with criminals, mutinous sailors, and ruthless Roman soldiers. The sailors were about to abandon ship, the soldiers were about to spear all the prisoners, and the boat seemed about to break up like a matchbox underneath a truck tire. The despair and gloom on that ship was so thick you could cut it with a chain saw and stack it.

Notice Paul's response. He told everyone to keep up their courage because God had assured him no one would drown. Why did Paul, at this time a prisoner, get a word from God when no one else did? Because he belonged to God.

Can you two say that? Can you say that your entire marriage belongs to the heavenly Father? If so, you are servants of God. And if you are His servants, you have every reason to be filled with hope for this coming year. Not sure? Get on your knees and trust your lives and marriage to Him today.

MARRIAGE MINUTE TRUTH:

TAKE HEART—THERE'S A CLOUD OF WITNESSES CHEERING YOU ON

....

Primary Passage:
*Therefore, since we are surrounded by such a great cloud
of witnesses, let us throw off everything that hinders and
the sin that so easily entangles, and let us run with
perseverance the race marked out for us.*
Hebrews 12:1

....

*C*louds can become a pilot's worst enemy. They can quickly leave him disoriented. It's possible to end up flying upside down and not realize it. That's where the term "flying by the seat of your pants" originated. Early aviators had to check to see if they were still resting on the seat of the plane; if they weren't, they knew they were flying upside down.

As a Christian couple you should welcome one kind of clouds as dear friends. These clouds won't disorient you or cause you to stray off course. They are the "cloud of witnesses" who have gone before us to heaven, the saints of the ages who now stand in the presence of Jesus Christ. Let the example of Elijah, who was depressed and discouraged to the point of quitting, spur you on to get up from exhaustion and serve God. Let David, who suffered the loss of his moral integrity with Bathsheba, encourage you that God can forgive you of your worst failures. Let the entire "cloud of witnesses" found in Hebrews 11 and other places in God's Word cheer you on. They are doing the "wave" for you right now. Isn't that encouraging?

MARRIAGE MINUTE TRUTH:

YOU CAN TAKE COURAGE FROM THOSE WHO SERVED GOD IN THE PAST

. . . .

Primary Passage:
*For everything that was written in the past was written
to teach us, so that through endurance and the
encouragement of the Scriptures we might have hope.*
Romans 15:4

. . . .

*L*et's say Jane Christian is struggling in her Christian walk. Early in her life she fell into sin. She compromised herself in her search for love and security. Later she became a Christian but has always felt that she was a second-rate person because of her past.

Now imagine Mary Magdalene standing on the bright shore of heaven. She shouts in a joyous voice, "Jane, listen to me. You need to understand how much Jesus loves you and what His forgiveness can do in your life. I ought to know. My past was whispered all over the inns of Palestine. But then I met Jesus. I confessed my sin and believed in the life He said I could have in Him. Listen, Jane, out of all the people on earth He gave me the honor of meeting Him first when He rose from the dead."

If you find yourself discouraged and plagued by accusations from your past, go back to the Scriptures. Reread the stories of those who have served God before you. God had the final word in their lives. He forgave their past and fit them for heaven. Those stories were written for you both.

MARRIAGE MINUTE TRUTH:

LIVE THE CHRISTIAN LIFE AS A RACE TO BE WON

Primary Passage:
*However, I consider my life worth nothing to me, if only
I may finish the race and complete the task the
Lord Jesus has given me—the task of testifying
to the gospel of God's grace.*
Acts 20:24

*S*everal years ago a European female athlete was running the final yards of the Olympic marathon. Due to oxygen deprivation and fatigue she became dizzy and disoriented. She entered the crowded stadium like a drunk staggering down a dark alley after midnight. The crowd drew its breath. It was a painful and confusing scene on the track.

In a moment of high drama someone from the sidelines rushed out and pointed her toward the finish line. She stumbled across the finish line and collapsed. The crowd rose in a deafening roar of approval for her bravery and determination to finish the race.

Living consistently and effectively for Christ is not a 100 meter dash; instead, it's a twenty, forty, sixty, or even ninety year marathon. The good news is that we have an Advocate, a Coach, a Friend who will come alongside when we are dizzy and disoriented. He is committed to us finishing the race as victors. Like Paul, our goal should be to finish the task God has set before us. Whether we sprint or stumble across the finish line, He will see that we finish.

MARRIAGE MINUTE TRUTH:

PURITY IS A CHOICE WE MUST MAKE EACH DAY OF OUR LIVES

Primary Passage:
I will set before my eyes no vile thing.
Psalm 101:3

*D*o you have a habit of watching television programs or videos that trouble your thought life? If so, how can you find the freedom to say no to viewing those things that undercut your life of purity and peace of mind?

The strength to change is found in God's Word. David in the Psalms made a commitment that you can make as well: "I will set before my eyes no vile thing." The apostle Paul instructs you to flee temptation. The disciple John assures you, "The one who is in you is greater than the one who is in the world" (1 John 4:4).

Armed with the wisdom and power of God's Word, you now take action to change your television habits. To start, you resolve to quit watching television altogether for a season of time. Instead you read, spend time with your children, and get involved in serving others. When you accidentally encounter objectionable programs, say in a doctor's office, you simply get up and take a walk or read a magazine until you're called.

You have placed your will on the side of God's will and taken action. The result is freedom. Who gets the credit? God. Who took the responsibility to make changes? You did. That's "throwing off the sin that hinders and entangles you."

MARRIAGE MINUTE TRUTH:

REVIVAL OFTEN BEGINS WITH PEOPLE WHO HAVE RUN FROM GOD

Primary Passage:
*The word of the Lord came to Jonah son of Amittai: "Go
to the great city of Nineveh and preach against it, because
its wickedness has come up before me." But Jonah ran
away from the Lord and headed for Tarshish.*
Jonah 1:1–3

The book of Jonah is the story of revival. It's the saga of a man who was called to preach to a foreign people he feared and possibly even hated. His first instinct was to run from the call of God.

It's not difficult to see why. Nineveh was the capital of ancient Assyria, much of what is called Iraq today. Assyria had something of a bad reputation. Its armies were known to lead their conquered captives into exile by hooking them through the mouths like fish on a stringer.

God specifically directed Jonah to go to Nineveh and warn them of impending destruction if they did not repent of their sins. Instead, Jonah turned 180 degrees straight away from God's will and took the first ship to Tarshish (located in modern day Spain). But God had other plans for Jonah. He was about to take a rebellious prophet and turn him into a fearless preacher.

Revival often begins with God dealing in the lives of His followers who are in rebellion. What about you and your spouse? Is there some area of your lives where you have gone west when God told you to go east? Then you're a candidate for revival. Repent of your stubbornness and disobedience. Then follow God to Nineveh. There's no telling what He may do with your lives.

MARRIAGE MINUTE TRUTH:

REVIVALS OFTEN OCCUR WITH OUT WARNING

Primary Passage:
Jonah obeyed the word of the Lord and went to Nineveh.
Jonah 3:3

*R*evival occurs when we stop running from God and obey Him instead. The conviction to repent and obey God may come without warning and in a place no one suspects. For Jonah it occurred in the belly of a fish. Throughout history, revival has happened in the most unlikely ways.

It was a cold February morning when students gathered for a scheduled chapel service in a small southern college town. There were a few hymns, a few prayers, and a few students fighting to stay awake. But this day the boredom was about to be interrupted by a visit from God Himself. As the college president later explained to baffled reporters, "You may not believe what I'm going to tell you, but about 10:30 A.M. Jesus Christ walked into Hughes Auditorium. There's no other way to explain it."

It began when a student told how he had hidden deep sin in his life. He confessed it publicly and asked those he had hurt most deeply to forgive him. He was soon joined by another student, then another, then another. The chapel service ended five days later.

Are you open to personal revival in your life? Pray for it. Ask God to renew your heart and love for Him. Confess your deepest sins. Then be prepared. Revival may be closer than you imagine.

REVIVAL LEADS TO DRAMATIC CHANGES IN OUR LIVES

Primary Passage:
When my life was ebbing away, I remembered you, Lord,
and my prayer rose to you, to your holy temple.
Jonah 2:7

A revival is a period of time in which God becomes so real to people they can neither run nor hide from Him. When a revival came to our campus there was no fainting, ecstatic dancing, or anyone entering a trance. Rather students simply and quietly opened their lives to God and let Him reveal to them where they were living in disobedience and sin.

This resulted in numerous individuals seeking out others to confess their wrongdoing. Roommates who had once hated each other now publicly embraced. Teachers who had harbored deep resentment against fellow faculty members admitted it and were reconciled.

Jonah underwent a personal revival inside the belly of the fish that had swallowed him. There in the dark, smelly intestines of a whale, Jonah saw the foolishness of his rebellion. He came to the realization that he was drowning in his own sin.

God wants to make dramatic changes in all our lives and marriages. He wants us to see our sins for what they are. He wants us to experience a personal reawakening of our love for Christ. When that occurs we will be motivated to confess our sins, be reconciled to each other, and tell of the wonderful thing God has done in our lives.

MARRIAGE MINUTE TRUTH:

GOD LOVES US ENOUGH TO DISCIPLINE US

. . . .

Primary Passage:
*Moreover, we have all had human fathers who
disciplined us and we respected them for it. How much
more should we submit to the Father of our spirits and
live! Our fathers disciplined us for a little while as they
thought best; but God disciplines us for our good, that we
may share in his holiness.*
Hebrews 12:9–10

. . . .

*G*od is willing to go to extraordinary lengths to demonstrate His love for us. That includes allowing us to experience just enough trouble, distress, or suffering to bring us to our senses.

One of the more effective fathers we know once received a call from his high school son who was at the police station. He needed one hundred dollars to post bond to get out of jail. He had been arrested after he and a friend had shot out some street lights.

"Son, I always told you that you wouldn't need my help to get into jail," replied the father. "Therefore you don't need my help getting out either. Good-bye." He hung up the phone. He knew a night in jail could help get his son back on track.

God's love is like that toward us. He will do whatever it takes to bring us back to our moral and spiritual senses. He will discipline us—not for revenge, but for instruction. He will apply just enough pressure to teach us a needed lesson. Will we receive it or resent it?

MARRIAGE MINUTE TRUTH:

UNBELIEVERS CAN SPOT INCONSISTENCIES IN OUR LIVES

Primary Passage:
*Then the sailors said to each other, "Come, let us cast
lots to find out who is responsible for this calamity."
They cast lots and the lot fell on Jonah.*
Jonah 1:7

*O*ften unbelievers can see more clearly the discrepancies in our lives than we can. Although they may not hold our values or belief system, they can sense when our behavior is out of sync with our profession of faith. When Jonah was discovered to be running from God, the pagan sailors were terrified. "What have you done?" they demanded. It was no doubt superstition that caused them to ask the question. Due to the terrible storm at sea the sailors could see that Jonah had infuriated his God. But from God's perspective, Jonah had seriously compromised his faith in front of pagans and unbelievers.

We too need to show great care in how we live in front of unbelievers. Though they may not share our faith or values, they nonetheless know hypocrisy when they see it. Let's resolve to love and treat one another in our marriages in a way that validates our profession of faith in Christ. Let's conduct our business dealings in a way that glorifies God. Above all, let's be ready to admit when our actions or words have been inconsistent with our faith. If unbelievers can spot hypocrisy, they can also spot genuine integrity and humility. Let's verify the truth of what we believe by how we behave.

MARRIAGE MINUTE TRUTH:

EVEN BELIEVERS WILL HAVE TO GIVE AN ACCOUNT TO CHRIST

. . . .

Primary Passage:
*For we will all stand before God's judgment seat. . . . So
then, each of us will give an account of himself to God.*
Romans 14:10, 12

. . . .

*C*an believers lose their salvation?"

That's a hotly debated question in some theological circles. Our answer to that particular question would be "No." But if you were to ask us, "Can believers lose their sense of intimacy and close relationship with God?" our answer would be, "Yes, most definitely." Unfortunately, some who hold to the position of the eternal security of the believer attempt to misuse the doctrine. "As long as I'm saved it doesn't matter how I live," they reason. "I'm going to heaven and that's all that counts." What they fail to consider is that the Scriptures clearly teach that one day we will give an account before Christ of how we lived.

Are we prepared to look into the loving eyes of Jesus and say, "So what if I wasted my life? I was saved and that's all that matters." We need to daily remind ourselves that someday we will give an account to Christ. When that occurs, we will be grateful for every step of obedience we ever took and every sin we decided to forsake.

MARRIAGE MINUTE TRUTH:

OUR LIFE'S WORK WILL BE JUDGED WITH FIRE

Primary Passage:
*For no one can lay any foundation other than the one
already laid, which is Jesus Christ. If any man builds on
this foundation using gold, silver, costly stones, wood, hay
or straw, his work will be shown for what it is, because the
Day will bring it to light. It will be revealed with fire,
and the fire will test the quality of each man's work.*
1 Corinthians 3:11–13

Ask anyone who has been through a fire and he will tell you two things: (1) He is immensely grateful that he and his family are alive, but (2) the sense of loss is overwhelming. With the loss of pictures, books, and furniture, it's just as if someone pushed the erase button on the family's past. Hopefully you will never experience that type of loss on earth or in heaven. One day we will all stand before the judgment seat of Christ. This is not the same judgment seat unbelievers will face, but instead this judgment is to test the quality of our life's work. The fire of God's holiness will test the mettle of our obedience on earth. Will your work emerge gleaming with purity and wisdom? Or will it be consumed in waste and foolishness? Don't wait for that day to find out. Begin living obedient, loving, and sacrificial lives for Jesus. Those precious qualities are fireproof.

MARRIAGE MINUTE TRUTH:

GOD WILL REWARD US ACCORDING TO HOW WE LIVED OUR LIVES

Primary Passage:
*His master replied, "Well done, good and faithful
servant! You have been faithful with a few things; I will
put you in charge of many things. Come and share your
master's happiness!"*
Matthew 25:21

*G*eneral Waynewright was commander of the American forces in the Pacific when they were overrun by the Japanese forces at the beginning of World War II. Faced with overwhelming forces and no hope of reinforcements, he was left with no alternative but to surrender. When MacArthur returned to the Philippines and liberated the POW camp that had held Waynewright, he found the general gaunt and still grieving over his decision to surrender.

MacArthur embraced him and would hear none of Waynewright's apologies. The valor, the heroism, and the sacrifice Waynewright had shown had saved the lives of countless soldiers.

As a couple you may have endured seasons of defeat and discouragement. But take courage. God knows your heart. He has witnessed your faithfulness. He knows your sacrifices. If you remain faithful, when Christ returns to earth, you will hear the words, "Well done, good and faithful servant! You have been faithful with a few things; I will put you in charge of many things. Come and share your master's happiness!"

MARRIAGE MINUTE TRUTH:

PRESERVING FRIENDSHIPS REQUIRES SPEAKING THE TRUTH

. . . .

Primary Passage:
*Dear friends, let us love one another, for love comes
from God. Everyone who loves has been born
of God and knows God.*
1 John 4:7

. . . .

*A*sk yourselves the question, "How many significant friendships have disappeared from our lives in the last three to ten years?" Take an inventory of the people you have lost touch with whom you once considered close friends or important acquaintances.

We did that exercise one year and ended up disturbed by the number of people who have come and gone from our lives. How did it happen? It was mainly our fault. We had moved five times in twelve years. People just couldn't keep up with us. Another obstacle was children. For many years we were so preoccupied with diapers, midnight feedings, vaccinations, and sometimes colic that we didn't have much energy left to invest in friendships.

But there was one other disturbing discovery. Some relationships had withered away because we had failed to address tensions or conflicts. It was easier just to let things slide. And slide they did—right out of our lives. Commit yourselves today to loving your friends enough to discuss hurts, misunderstandings, and sin. It may be awkward to pursue such a discussion, but it's one way to prevent a disappearing act.

MARRIAGE MINUTE TRUTH:

OUR CHILDREN ARE AT GREAT RISK IN THIS CURRENT SOCIETY

. . . .

Primary Passage:
Train a child in the way he should go, and when
he is old he will not turn from it.
Proverbs 22:6

. . . .

In his powerful book, *Honest to God*, pastor Bill Hybels paints a picture of the social transformations that have occurred in the last fifty years. He points out that in the 1940s the top offenses committed by public school students were talking, chewing gum, making noises, running in the halls, getting out of turn in line, wearing improper clothing, and not putting paper in the waste-basket. By 1982 much had changed. The top offenses now were rape, robbery, assault, burglary, arson, bombing, murder, and sui-cide. Our kids are at risk. This next year we must make it a top priority to give them our time and attention.

We need to assume primary responsibility for teaching them right from wrong. We must also take our rightful place as the guardians of their welfare until they reach adulthood. The hour has come for us to put aside lesser interests and distractions to give of ourselves to our children as we never have. No sacrifice is too great in order to nurture and protect the precious gifts God has entrusted to us.

It's now or never.

MARRIAGE MINUTE TRUTH:

WE NEED TO LET OUR CHILDREN BE CHILDREN

. . . .

Primary Passage:
*[Jesus] said to them, "Let the little children come
to me, and do not hinder them, for the kingdom
of God belongs to such as these."*
Mark 10:14

. . . .

*I*t's a toddler eat toddler world out there," one author observed. A child development expert sees eight year olds suffering from acute anxiety, and nine and ten year olds having lost all sense of what it means to be a child. A local newspaper reports the problem of burnout among elementary age boys who played a 180-game season in on a traveling baseball team.

Why such excess? Parents today are pushing their children to achieve in sports, music, and academics at earlier and earlier ages. A first-grade teacher told of an angry mother screaming at her because the teacher had given her son a "satisfactory" on his report card. "How is he ever going to get into M.I.T. if you give him a satisfactory!" she demanded.

Jesus loved children. He actually got upset when others tried to keep the boys and girls from getting to Him. He valued them for just who they were—not as future stock traders, NBA forwards, or Harvard graduates, but as little human beings filled with innocence and trust. Let's give our children the gift they're entitled to this next year—a childhood.

MARRIAGE MINUTE TRUTH:

STAY AS FAR AS YOU
CAN FROM INFIDELITY

Primary Passage:
*Now then, my sons, listen to me; do not turn aside from
what I say. Keep to a path far from [the adulteress],
do not go near the door of her house . . .*
Proverbs 5:7–8

*C*harles Spurgeon, the great English preacher of the nineteenth century, used to tell the story of a man who wanted to hire a buggy driver. He asked each applicant the same question: "How close do you think you can drive my carriage to the edge of a cliff without falling off?"

Driver after driver boasted of his daring and driving prowess. Yet none of them was offered the position. Finally one applicant appeared who considered the question, then gave a very different answer. "Sir, as your carriage driver it would be my business to keep you as far away from the edge of the cliff as possible," he said. "I have no intention of seeing how close to the edge I can come." He was hired on the spot.

The question in a marriage relationship should not be "How close can I come to infidelity without crossing the line?" Instead it should be "How can I put safeguards in place that will prevent me from even coming close to adultery?"

Enter into a covenant today that you will both live your lives as far from the edge as humanly possible.

MARRIAGE MINUTE TRUTH:

UNFAITHFULNESS WILL COST YOU MORE THAN YOU CAN IMAGINE

Primary Passage:
. . . lest you give your best strength to others and your
years to one who is cruel, lest strangers feast on your
wealth and your toil enrich another man's house.
Proverbs 5:9–10

I'm losing control of this process," lamented a wealthy businessman. "And I don't like it." Divorce attorneys were actively engaged in dividing up all the couple's lifetime assets.

Accustomed to being in control of companies and employees, he never dreamed that the day would come that someone else would decide who got the money he wrongly believed belonged only to him. But after he filed for a divorce following his admission to a lengthy affair, his wife went out and hired an attorney who was better than his attorney. His big gamble—to get rid of his first wife, marry his lover, and walk away with most of their wealth—had suddenly gone bad. He really should have seen it coming. The writer of Proverbs points out that adultery inevitably leads to moral, emotional, and even financial bankruptcy.

The devil will tempt us to believe things that simply aren't true. He will tell us we can break our promises, engage in an illicit relationship, and still come out ahead. That may momentarily appear to be the case, but God will still judge sin. He will punish us for our deceit, unfaithfulness, and greed. Scripture tells us when we break our promises we lose control of our future. It's a losing market. God will guarantee it.

MARRIAGE MINUTE TRUTH:

GOD'S WILL IS FOR PEACE TO REIGN IN YOUR MARRIAGE

. . . .

Primary Passage:
*Let us therefore make every effort to do what leads
to peace and to mutual edification.*
Romans 14:19

. . . .

*W*hich of these statements is more dangerous to a marriage? "I'm so mad at you I can hardly speak to you." "Do whatever you like. I don't care anymore."

If you guessed the second answer, you're right. Although open conflict may be more immediately painful and unpleasant, a state of apathy and withdrawal is even worse in the long run.

Gifted author Willard Harley believes that all marriages move between three states: intimacy, conflict, and withdrawal. Intimacy involves focusing on each other's needs and avoiding behaviors that irritate, annoy, or wound the other person. Conflict happens when we fail to meet each other's needs and engage in upsetting behavior or speech. Withdrawal occurs when one or both spouses emotionally disengage from the relationship. Given time, that withdrawal can lead to separation or even divorce.

We were never designed to live in a state of permanent conflict or withdrawal from our spouses. If that's where your marriage is today, you need to do the hard work of facing your issues and re-solving your conflicts. The reward will be an intimate marriage that honors God and makes life worthwhile.

MARRIAGE MINUTE TRUTH:

MEN COMMUNICATE AS THE BY-PRODUCT OF AN ACTIVITY, BUT WOMEN SEE COMMUNICATION ITSELF AS THE ACTIVITY

. . . .

Primary Passage:
*For wisdom will enter your heart, and knowledge will be
pleasant to your soul. Discretion will protect you, and
understanding will guard you.*
Proverbs 2:10–11

. . . .

An afternoon at the beach one summer afforded an opportunity to see just how differently men and women communicate with one another. The men chose sides for a vigorous game of sand volleyball (complete with power serves and killer spikes over the net). Bodies covered with sweat, high fives, and competition to the death were the order of the day.

The women, however, took advantage of some available inner tubes and floated out into the water. There they formed a large floating circle and locked arms with one another. They spent more than an hour floating out from shore laughing, talking, and whispering with one another. It was a splendid picture of the differences in how men and women communicate. As one marriage expert has pointed out, men feel much more comfortable talking as the by-product of some activity. Women, on the other hand, see communication itself as the activity.

When it comes to our marriages we need to appreciate the different ways husbands and wives communicate. We need to understand, honor, and appreciate our differences. That's true wisdom. It also makes for great communication.

MARRIAGE MINUTE TRUTH:

HUSBANDS NEED THEIR WIVES TO BE THEIR CLOSE COMPANIONS

Primary Passage:
*I grieve for you, Jonathan my brother; you were very
dear to me. Your love for me was wonderful, more
wonderful than that of women.*
2 Samuel 1:26

*W*ives, can we tell you a secret?

Your husband needs a friend, a buddy, a companion. He probably won't tell you that, but just consider his life before the two of you married. Chances are when he was still single he did things with other single guys: went to baseball games, worked on his car, or perhaps played flag football on Sunday afternoons.

Once you got married his friends likely began to drop away one by one. Why? Because he devoted more and more of his attention to you, the children, and earning a living. Although he might still have one or two good friends, chances are better that he has none. He may have become what one writer described as "The Friendless American Male." Has his need for a buddy disappeared? No. He chose you as his life companion. If the two of you are not close, he has probably just learned to do without. You as his wife have a major opportunity here—to become his best friend, his companion. How important is it that you become that soul mate? A study was done of four hundred divorced men who were engaged to remarry. When asked the number one trait that drew them to their new fiancé the top answer was, "She's my best friend."

MARRIAGE MINUTE TRUTH:

THERE'S A DIFFERENCE
BETWEEN AFFECTION AND SEX

Primary Passage:
Let him kiss me with the kisses of his mouth—
for your love is more delightful than wine.
Song of Songs 1:2

*I*t was the most famous question ever posed by the well-known advice columnist. She asked her loyal female readership, "If you had a choice between making love with your husband, or simply having him hug you and show affection, which would you prefer?"

The response was nothing short of an avalanche. The overwhelming consensus of the female respondents was they would prefer affection over sex. Does that mean wives don't have sexual needs? Of course not. It does illustrate the significant difference in how men and women experience intimacy.

Generally speaking, a wife cannot experience true sexual satisfaction if she doesn't first experience affection. Affection appears to be the key to intimacy in the female soul.

We recommend that husbands demonstrate genuine unselfish love and affection throughout the day. As someone has said, "Good sex begins in the kitchen." Men need to take time to hug their wives, kiss them good-bye when they part each morning, and kiss them hello when they come back together at the end of the day. Whether it's a loving word, a gesture, or a touch, affection is the language of love for most women. Husbands, let's become fluent in it.

MARRIAGE MINUTE TRUTH:

KEEPING YOUR VOWS
YIELDS LONG-TERM BLESSINGS

. . . .

Primary Passage:
*You will eat the fruit of your labor; blessings and
prosperity will be yours. Your wife will be like a fruitful
vine within your house; your sons will be like
olive shoots around your table. Thus is the man
blessed who fears the Lord.*
Psalm 128:2–4

. . . .

*W*hy should two twenty-eight-year-old young adults be forced to keep a fifty-year contract known as marriage? Think of all the changes both will go through in the next five decades. They will change houses, cars, music tastes, not to mention careers, interests, and vocations several times. Why shouldn't they be given the option to change spouses several times as they go through the predictable passages of life? There's no arguing young marrieds will experience numerous life changes along the way. That's precisely the point of marriage vows. They provide the stability, continuity, and companionship needed to successfully navigate the churning and changing waters of life.

When we are secure in our lifelong commitment to each other we can face whatever comes our way with confidence and poise. To spend a lifetime together is a tremendous accomplishment and a tremendous privilege. If you keep your vows today you will bless God tomorrow for the wisdom to stay together.

Don't settle for anything less than a lifetime commitment to love your spouse.

MARRIAGE MINUTE TRUTH:

LOVE IS MUCH MORE WHAT WE DO THAN WHAT WE SAY

Primary Passage:
*Dear friends, since God so loved us, we also ought to
love one another. No one has ever seen God; but if we
love one another, God lives in us and his love
is made complete in us.*
1 John 4:11–12

One of the more popular cults in the world today teaches that God dropped a number of golden tablets to earth to show us the way to live. Contrast that with biblical Christianity that teaches God sent a Person, not a tablet, to show us His love. One religion is content to say God sent His ideas to earth, the other that He gave His only begotten Son.

If God is truly a God of love, then I am convinced the latter religion is true. A loving God would never content Himself simply to pass on to us knowledge. Scripture tells us He stopped at nothing less than giving us His Son.

We can apply this same test to our marriages. Are you content to simply offer your spouse your ideas, advice, and opinions? Or do you go beyond that to actually give of yourself to your mate? True love demands that we live unselfish, sacrificial, and caring lives. It requires that we ask the question, "What does the other person need from me right now?" and that we attempt to lovingly meet that need. Is your love talk or action?

MARRIAGE MINUTE TRUTH:

HUSBANDS TALK AS THE RESULT OF A SHARED ACTIVITY

Primary Passage:
Let your conversation be always full of grace,
seasoned with salt, so that you may know
how to answer everyone.
Colossians 4:6

A common complaint of wives is that their husbands don't talk enough or tell their feelings. Rather than trying to force your husband to sit down and have a conversation, why not choose an activity you both enjoy? Try exercising, walking, riding bikes, or cleaning up together, and watch how he does open up.

Why? As Lois Davidzt Liederman points out, men communicate as the result of a shared activity. Once you understand this truth, you can begin looking for opportunities to do jobs together with your husband. When he says, "Dear, would you like to come out while I change the oil?" or, "Honey, there's a game on tonight; do you want to watch it with me?" or even, "I'm going to the hardware store. Want to ride along with me while I pick up some things?" there's your chance.

Rather than responding, "No, I've got laundry to do," put things down and go with him. We can almost guarantee that he'll talk to you during the trip. That will be your opportunity to tell him what's on your heart as well. You may soon find that the communication gap you thought existed between you and your husband has just disappeared.

MARRIAGE MINUTE TRUTH:

WHAT YOUR CHILDREN REALLY WANT FROM YOU IS A LOVING AND STABLE MARRIAGE

. . . .

Primary Passage:
*Isaac brought her into the tent of his mother Sarah,
and he married Rebekah. So she became his wife,
and he loved her; and Isaac was comforted
after his mother's death.*
Genesis 24:67

. . . .

The statistics tell a tragic story. Two out of three children between birth and age eighteen will spend at least a portion of their growing up years in a single-parent family. The University of California tested fifth and sixth graders to see what causes them the most anxiety. The top answers: having parents separate or divorce, parents arguing with each other, and parents who don't spend enough time with their children. In a survey of high school students at graduation, 80 percent said that a happy and successful marriage is one of the most important goals in life.

It's obvious that children in our time are desperately looking for love, security, and stability. The primary source for those life-stabilizing elements is not to be found in their school, or their church youth group, but in your home.

No two people on earth are better positioned to offer your children what they so deeply need. Give them the gift that's right for Christmas, their birthday, and even graduation. Like Isaac of old, love the person you married.

MARRIAGE MINUTE TRUTH:

CHILDREN NEVER GET OVER A DIVORCE

Primary Passage:
*Has not the Lord made them one? In flesh and spirit
they are his. And why one? Because he was seeking
godly offspring. So guard yourself in your spirit, and do
not break faith with the wife of your youth.*
Malachi 2:15

*I*n January 1992, *Newsweek* magazine reported the long-term effects of growing up in a fragmented family: "Two-thirds of the girls, many of whom had seemingly sailed through the crisis of divorce, suddenly became deeply anxious as young adults, unable to make lasting commitments and fearful of betrayal in intimate relationships. Many boys, who were more overtly troubled in the post-divorce years, failed to develop a sense of independence, confidence or purpose. They drifted in and out of college and from job to job."

Even secular research has validated what we secretly suspected all along—children never get over a divorce. Oh, there's no question that many successfully cope with the breakup and go on to lead normal and productive lives. But deep inside they carry the hurt for a lifetime. For some it even gets worse with the passing of the years.

Spouses, consider carefully the cost to your children and grandchildren of the breakup of your home. It's simply too high.

Make the effort to resolve your conflicts and preserve your home.

Generations of children yet unborn will someday thank you.

MARRIAGE MINUTE TRUTH:

OUR SPOUSE IS TO BE OUR SOLE SOURCE OF SEXUAL SATISFACTION

· ·

Primary Passage:
Drink water from your own cistern,
running water from your own well.
Proverbs 5:15

· ·

*O*ne evening I happened across a late night talk show as a popular Hollywood actress was making her entrance. The talk show host was known for his affectionate welcome to his attractive female guests. This night was no exception.

As the two embraced, their light affection suddenly became much more. She wrapped her arms around his neck. He responded by turning up the heat in his own embrace. The audience screamed its approval as this unexpected sensual scene was played out. When they finally did let go, both had trouble regaining their composure. He was out of breath, and her face was flushed. What was particularly sad is that she was married at the time.

February is often thought of as the month of love and sexual romance. Indeed Scripture celebrates both love and sexual romance and encourages us to drink deeply of both. But we are not to do so with just any casual partner or any attractive person we meet. The writer of Proverbs advises us to drink water from our own well. He's referring to our spouse as the exclusive source of our sexual satisfaction. All other sources are polluted with fraud, exploitation, and embarrassment. The lessons of Scripture are clear: drink deeply of love, but from only one glass.

MARRIAGE MINUTE TRUTH:

SEX IS THE PRIVATE CELEBRATION OF AN EXCLUSIVE RELATIONSHIP

Primary Passage:
Should your springs overflow in the streets,
your streams of water in the public squares?
Let them be yours alone, never to be shared
with strangers.
Proverbs 5:16

There is at last count somewhere between fifty-three and one hundred sexually transmitted diseases at work in our society. They range in severity from the irritating and uncomfortable to the life threatening and fatal. All these diseases have one thing in common—they are spread by people having more than one sexual partner. The ancient Hebrews described such foolish promiscuity in poetic terms, "Should your springs overflow in the streets?"

The writer is asking a rhetorical question, one in which the question provides its own answer.

Pure drinking water was a scarce and precious commodity in ancient days. People understood the need to guard it and keep it unpolluted at all costs. To allow it to spill out into the streets and run among filth, rubbish, and mud was unthinkable. The writer makes the point that God has given both of you a pure, clean, and life-giving source of sexual enjoyment and satisfaction in your marriage relationship. Keep it contained within its proper boundaries and it will remain a clear and beautiful source of intimacy and joy for a lifetime.

MARRIAGE MINUTE TRUTH:

WE ARE TO EXULT IN OUR SPOUSE'S SEXUAL LOVE FOR A LIFETIME

. . . .

Primary Passage:
*May your fountain be blessed, and may
you rejoice in the wife of your youth.*
Proverbs 5:18

. . . .

*S*everal years ago Bob attended the World Series Championship parade in the town he grew up in. After twenty-seven years the team finally had won it all. The air that day was absolutely charged with electricity, jubilation, and anticipation. Fans by the tens of thousands turned out to throw confetti, wave handkerchiefs, and shout for their hometown heroes. It was a day of pure exultation. That's a picture of how we are to celebrate our sexual relationship with our spouse. Scriptures tell us to "rejoice in the wife of your youth."

But is that the case in your marriage? There's no question that all married relationships go through cycles. There are periods of intensity and passion followed by seasons of isolation and apathy. That's simply the normal ebb and flow of life. Yet God designed married sexual love to survive both the good and bad seasons of a relationship. How long has it been since you truly exulted and rejoiced for the gift of your partner? If you've gotten into the pattern of boredom, critical comments, and lack of interest, it's time to go back to the parade. You both are champions, and God has given you a gift to cheer and celebrate.

MARRIAGE MINUTE TRUTH:

THE PHYSICAL LOVE OF OUR SPOUSE IS AN INTOXICATING EXPERIENCE

....

Primary Passage:
*A loving doe, a graceful deer—may her
breasts satisfy you always, may you ever
be captivated by her love.*
Proverbs 5:19

....

*M*any people have the mistaken notion that the Bible is embarrassed by the subject of sex. They somehow believe it's a topic more suited to the supermarket tabloids than the Scriptures.

Where did such an idea ever come from? Certainly not from God. He's the one who inspired and guided writers to write every single word in both the Old and New Testament. If He had wanted to edit out every reference to sex, He certainly could have done so. Instead, the writer of Proverbs describes feminine beauty as both a graceful and a loving attraction. He goes on to encourage a husband to be satisfied, even captivated ("made drunk" in the original Hebrew) by his wife's body and love.

This is no description of cheap sensuality or pornographic imagery. This is a description in tender and discreet terms of the powerful and sacred gift of sexual love between a husband and wife. It's a depiction of the divine approval upon the act of sexual enjoyment within the covenant of marriage. Enjoy the intoxicating love of your spouse—it's a gift from heaven.

MARRIAGE MINUTE TRUTH:

THERE'S NO GOOD
REASON FOR ADULTERY

Primary Passage:
Why be captivated, my son, by an adulteress?
Why embrace the bosom of another man's wife?
Proverbs 5:20

He was to be the future king, the hope of a nation. She was to one day be the queen, the pride of all the empire. Together Charles and Diana possessed all the wealth, fame, and adulation one couple could absorb in a lifetime.

Yet when her gold flag-draped casket was carried out of Westminster Cathedral, the entire world wept tears of grief and disbelief. How could the most publicized storybook romance of the century turn, almost overnight, into one of the saddest endings in the history of the British monarchy? At the risk of oversimplifying confusing and complex factors that led to the premature death of Princess Diana, the answer lies in just one word—adultery. Had Charles and Diana been faithful to each other and preserved their marriage, it's highly doubtful that she would have died in a Paris tunnel.

You've read and seen the story for yourself. If adultery could destroy the world's most famous couple, what could it do to our lives? There simply is no good reason for adultery, while there are a thousand and one good reasons to avoid it. One of those reasons is now marked by a simple grave in the English countryside.

MARRIAGE MINUTE TRUTH:

A WIFE NEEDS ROMANTIC ATTENTION FROM HER HUSBAND HER ENTIRE LIFE

Primary Passage:
Let him kiss me with the kisses of his mouth—
for your love is more delightful than wine.
Song of Songs 1:2

I entered the hospital room of a woman in her early fifties, and she immediately tried to hide the book she was reading. She could have spared the effort; I had caught a quick glimpse of the book's cover. It was another popular romance novel published by a large New York house that caters exclusively to women.

The publishers have made millions because they understand that, regardless of her age, a woman never loses her need or desire for romance. Unfortunately many husbands don't understand or appreciate this basic fact of life. That's because they are wired more for sexual fulfillment than romantic imagination.

Yet for husbands to truly love their wives they need to understand their wives' need for romance. Husbands need to commit themselves to courting their wives for a lifetime. It didn't end the day they stepped up to the wedding altar or into the honeymoon suite. But, husband, if that sounds too difficult, remember this: continued courtship behavior on your part is more likely to elicit "honeymoon-suite" behavior on her part. The husband who takes the time and effort to date his wife their entire marriage will end up with a relationship on the best-seller list.

Best of all—it won't be fiction.

MARRIAGE MINUTE TRUTH:

LOVE PROPERLY BLINDS US TO OUR PARTNER'S IMPERFECTIONS

. . . .

Primary Passage:
*Until the day breaks and the shadows flee, I will go to
the mountain of myrrh and to the hill of incense. All
beautiful you are, my darling; there is no flaw in you.*
Song of Songs 4:6–7

. . . .

*O*h, Denise, I've just met this wonderful guy. He is so perfect.
I mean, everything about him, he is just so right."

"David, you've got to see her. She's the most beautiful woman
I've ever met. She's a perfect 10."

Remember when you first fell in love with the person you
married? Chances are you described him or her in similar terms
to your friends. Your partner was essentially flawless. Infatuation
blinded both of you to obvious imperfections—a nose too long, a
voice too high, or even a laugh that could be a little irritating. At
the time it didn't matter. You were in love and even found the
other person's faults endearing.

Perhaps now you find it hard to get your mind off your mate's
receding hairline or the extra pounds he or she has added. So
what has happened? The person you fell in love with is still there.
You can find that person in your spouse again. But first it's time
to give up the critical, fault-finding attitudes that are hurting your
marriage. Commit yourself to looking at your mate through the
eyes of love once more. Trust us, if you take that step you'll like
what you see.

MARRIAGE MINUTE TRUTH:

HUSBANDS NEED RESPONSIVE WIVES TO EXPERIENCE FULFILLMENT

. . . .

Primary Passage:
Awake, north wind, and come, south wind!
Blow on my garden, that its fragrance may spread
abroad. Let my lover come into his garden
and taste its choice fruits.
Song of Songs 4:16

. . . .

*T*here are many ways to hurt your husband deeply. One is to act irritated, inconvenienced, or even bored when he makes sexual advances toward you. To a large degree it is your response to his overtures that affirms or negates his sense of manhood and value.

"All right, if you insist."

"I'm not really in the mood tonight."

"Why don't we discuss the problems we're having with our son first? I'm much more interested in him at the moment."

All of the above send a loud and clear message to your husband that you're not interested in sexual intimacy. He's left feeling wounded, hurt, even humiliated. The sensitive and loving wife will realize that her husband's overtures, unexpected and ill timed as they sometimes are, are still an opportunity for her to demonstrate an unselfish and caring attitude toward him. When you affirm your husband's desire to "come to his garden and taste its choice fruits," it will be interpreted by him as a deep affirmation of his manhood. In the end it will yield a rich harvest for both of you.

MARRIAGE MINUTE TRUTH:

WIVES CAN NEVER RECEIVE TOO MANY COMPLIMENTS

Primary Passage:
*You have stolen my heart, my sister, my bride; you have
stolen my heart with one glance of your eyes,
with one jewel of your necklace.*
Song of Songs 4:9

He was ninety-three years old. Still somewhat spry and very alert, he pointed across the living room to his wife of more than sixty years. "There she is, my sweetheart," he said. "We're still on our honeymoon. She's the most wonderful wife a man could ever have." His wife blushed for a moment, but didn't argue.

In all our years of counseling troubled couples, we've yet to hear a wife turn to us and say, "I can't stand it any longer. Tell him to stop giving me so many compliments or I'm going to leave him." As you might guess we've heard just the opposite complaint—a lack of compliments—more times than we can count.

Why is it that women have such a deep need for verbal compliments? For much the same reason men crave respect and admiration. It's simply the way God designed us. Time doesn't dim the need of a wife to hear beautiful words from her husband. The important thing is that we be sincere, loving, and consistent. Begin today with a small, simple compliment. Tell her another tomorrow morning, the next day, and the next. It will soon become a habit—one your wife will never ask you to kick.

MARRIAGE MINUTE TRUTH:

LOVE IS THE MOST IMPORTANT THING IN ALL THE WORLD

Primary Passage:
*If I speak in the tongues of men and of angels,
but have not love, I am only a resounding
gong or a clanging cymbal.*
1 Corinthians 13:1

*W*hat if God had only announced that He loved us? Say, perhaps, He wrote it in bright flaming letters in the nighttime sky. Or thundered it across the face of the earth in sonic boom echoes. Or what if He had even appeared in a celestial vision to the entire earth at one time?

No doubt people would have been deeply affected, moved, and even awestruck by such a divine revelation. But what good would it have done any of us who were trapped in our sins and wickedness? God would still be obligated by virtue of His holiness to condemn all of us to an eternity of punishment.

That's why God's announcement of love went beyond *saying* to *doing*. In John 3:16 we learn, "For God so loved the world that he gave his one and only Son, that whoever believes in him shall not perish but have eternal life." He not only said He loved us, but He gave His precious and beloved Son to die a most horrible death on our behalf.

How are you acting as a couple in your love for others? What about your coworker whose wife has cancer? The neighbor who just lost his job? Your teenage daughter who sits alone in her room feeling insecure about herself? To be more than just "clanging cymbals" we need to get up off the couch and surround some lonely or hurting person with the music of caring love.

MARRIAGE MINUTE TRUTH:

CORRECT DOCTRINE WITHOUT GENUINE LOVE IS STERILE KNOWLEDGE

Primary Passage:
*If I have the gift of prophecy and can fathom all
mysteries and all knowledge, and if I have a faith that
can move mountains, but have not love, I am nothing.*
1 Corinthians 13:2

*S*he stood trembling and ashamed. The glare of the religious teachers pierced her soul with pain. She was pushed and dragged through the streets until she stood face-to-face with the great prophet Himself.

"Teacher, this woman was caught in the act of adultery. In the Law Moses commanded us to stone such women. Now what do you say?" (John 8:4–5). The prophet stood quietly and pondered His response. He then stooped over and wrote on the ground with His finger. The angry leaders continued to press their demand for an answer. At last He stood and addressed them, "If any of one of you is without sin, let him be the first to throw a stone at her" (John 8:7). Once again He stooped down and wrote with His finger.

One by one the crowd began to dissipate, the older ones first. The religious leaders had immense knowledge, but Jesus possessed perfect doctrine. The difference? He added genuine love to correct facts. The result was the healing and salvation of others, including a woman taken in adultery.

How about us? Do we love as much as we know?

MARRIAGE MINUTE TRUTH:

SACRIFICE WITHOUT LOVE ACCOMPLISHES NOTHING

Primary Passage:
*If I give all I possess to the poor and surrender my body
to the flames, but have not love, I gain nothing.*
1 Corinthians 13:3

He was the founder of one of the world's great relief agencies. The organization he poured his life into has saved countless lives by distributing food, medical supplies, and clothing. Regimes otherwise hostile to the Western democracies have welcomed his agency into their borders with open arms.

Yet, long after his death, his daughter appeared on national radio to tell of her father's neglect and lack of concern for her and her mother. Such irony. In his effort to save the world he lost his own family.

The apostle Paul is quite candid about the nature of true love. It doesn't matter if someone is involved day and night in the rescue of needy people or even if he dies a martyr's death. If a person lacks love, his sacrifice will amount to nothing.

God is far more concerned with motives than He is with results. That's why the Bible says it's more important to do what is just and right than it is to sacrifice. By that standard it's more important to show attention to your children than to arrive at the scene of a hurricane with help. It's right for us to love sacrifice as long as we don't sacrifice love.

MARRIAGE MINUTE TRUTH:

LOVE WILL ALWAYS LEAVE AN ENDURING LEGACY

Primary Passage:
And now these three remain: faith, hope and love.
But the greatest of these is love.
1 Corinthians 13:13

The evangelist Dwight L. Moody was a man of great humility. He had a special love for children. When he moved to Chicago he began work among the poorest of the poor. Because he worked in such a rough and dangerous section of the city he was nicknamed "Crazy Moody" by local pastors. Over time his name and influence spread as thousands of children came to his Sunday school class.

Once, when he was asked to address a group of workers, he gave a short and awkward speech. At the end of his message, a well-educated clergyman stood up and criticized him for his lack of organization and thought. Many men would have defended themselves in such a situation. Instead Moody thanked the man and promised to work on his preaching.

When Moody died it's estimated he had preached to 100 million people worldwide. His life touched an entire generation and more. As for the educated pastor who humiliated Moody in front of others? We aren't even told his name. What was the essential difference between the two men? Love. Remember what lasts and what doesn't. Let love and humility become the enduring legacy of your marriage.

MARRIAGE MINUTE TRUTH:

WE NEED TO DISMISS
THE MYTHS OF ROMANCE

. . . .

Primary Passage:
*My lover spoke and said to me, "Arise, my darling,
my beautiful one, and come with me. See! The
winter is past; the rains are over and gone."*
Song of Songs 2:10–11

. . . .

*A*re the following statements true or false?

1. Romance is primarily for the unmarried.
2. Romance lasts only during courtship.
3. Romance requires great expense and effort.
4. Only women need romance in a relationship.
5. Romance should lead to sex.
6. Romance isn't a spiritual concept.
7. Romance grows weaker with age.

The correct answer to all the above statements is false.

Romance is a gift every married couple can give each other for a lifetime. Nor does it have to cost a great deal—imagination is far more important than price. Men, as well as women, can enjoy romance. It doesn't have to lead to sexual intercourse to be meaningful. It's a gift from God and it affects our inner selves; therefore, it has a spiritual dimension as well. Finally, it can last a lifetime if we make the effort.

How did you two score? This is one exam you're allowed to take again.

MARRIAGE MINUTE TRUTH:

IF YOU WANT TO FEEL ROMANTIC, ACT ROMANTIC

. . . .

Primary Passage:
*So Jacob served seven years to get Rachel, but
they seemed like only a few days to
him because of his love for her.*
Genesis 29:20

. . . .

We encourage couples to experiment with the ninety-second hug. Here's how it works: for ninety seconds, one minute and a half, the two of you stand and hug each other.

Although wives often welcome the experiment, many husbands find it a bit awkward at first. Allow us to encourage you men: if you stick with it the entire ninety seconds you're going to discover just how much you really enjoy it. (One couple misunderstood the experiment and tried to hug each other for ninety minutes each day. They admitted it was difficult at first, but now confess they really enjoy it. True story.)

The principle behind the hug is quite simple—if we act like we love and cherish our spouse, we will feel like we love and cherish our spouse. Often we have things the other way around. We wait until we feel affectionate before we act affectionate. Unfortunately that may mean waiting an entire lifetime.

Jacob loved and cherished Rachel. Seven years seemed like only seven days. Learn from his example and watch how ninety seconds can seem like . . . far less than ninety seconds.

MARRIAGE MINUTE TRUTH:

CONFIDENT PARENTS
PRODUCE CONFIDENT CHILDREN

. . . .

Primary Passage:
Children, obey your parents in everything,
for this pleases the Lord.
Colossians 3:20

. . . .

The National Adolescent Student Health Survey showed that 77 percent of eighth graders had tried alcohol. By tenth grade that figure climbs to 89 percent. The suicide rate for teenagers has tripled in the last twenty years. An astounding 34 percent of eighth and tenth graders have seriously considered taking their own lives. What can parents do in the face of these alarming and tragic figures? We'd like to offer ten suggestions to help your child obey Paul's words, "Children, obey your parents in everything, for this pleases the Lord." Consider these steps:

1. Pray for your children.
2. Pray about your own expectations.
3. Pray about your desire to love them unconditionally.
4. Tell them how God helped you with your own fears and concerns.
5. Be fair and consistent in discipline.
6. Be a consistent example.
7. Look for creative ways to express your love.
8. Take time to listen to their world.
9. Pray for opportunities to tell them about Christ.
10. Do your best and trust in the Lord for results.

MARRIAGE MINUTE TRUTH:

GOD EXPECTS US AS PARENTS TO BE OUR CHILDREN'S PRIMARY SOURCE OF SPIRITUAL KNOWLEDGE

. . . .

Primary Passage:
*When I was a boy in my father's house, still tender, and
an only child of my mother, he taught me and said, "Lay
hold of my words with all your heart; keep my
commands and you will live."*
Proverbs 4:3–4

. . . .

One unfortunate trend today is for some parents to raise children "on the side," much like ordering a dinner salad to supplement the main entree. God has given us as parents the clear and unmistakable duty to train our children in the fear and instruction of the Lord.

This will demand sacrifices of our time, career, and money. We can't microwave children. They take time. The stakes are high. We are talking about eternal beings with eternal hearts, minds, and souls. God does not accept the excuse "We made them; someone else can raise them." Nannies, day-care workers, relatives, and baby-sitters are not going to carry the same weight of responsibility on the day of Christ's return that we as parents will.

The good news is that we have tremendous potential as parents to teach our children wisdom and faith. God's love is our motivation, His Word is our guide, and His example as a loving Father is our hope.

MARRIAGE MINUTE TRUTH:

ANGER IS THE RESULT OF UNFULFILLED EXPECTATIONS

. . . .

Primary Passage:
*[Love] is not rude, it is not self-seeking, it is not
easily angered, it keeps no record of wrongs.*
1 Corinthians 13:5

. . . .

What makes you angry with your spouse? More often than not it's unmet expectations. Anger and unmet expectations go hand in hand. When we begin keeping a mental list of our partner's numerous failures in meeting our expectations, the road to disillusionment is wide open. It won't be long before we cross over into rage and bitterness. The marriage will eventually melt under the intense emotional heat of destructive anger and wrath.

What's the answer? To have no expectations? That isn't realistic or healthy. Instead, we need to speak to issues that consistently produce hurt and anger in our lives. Yet we must do so in an attitude of love. Biblical love is not rude, is not self-seeking, is not easily angered, and keeps no record of wrongs. Such love makes allowances for another person's failures and then forgives the person for Christ's sake. So expect less from your spouse and more from showing God's love. You won't be disappointed on either count.

MARRIAGE MINUTE TRUTH:

LOVE LEADS US TO BELIEVE
THE BEST ABOUT OUR SPOUSE

....

Primary Passage:
*Love does not delight in evil but rejoices with the
truth. It always protects, always trusts,
always hopes, always perseveres.*
1 Corinthians 13:6–7

....

*H*is name is mud."

Have you heard that expression? There's a fascinating story behind that short cliché. Shortly before the Civil War ended a group of conspirators who planned to assassinate Abraham Lincoln met with a medical doctor by the name of Samuel Mudd. Unaware of their murderous plans, he answered their questions about the roads leading out of Washington, D.C.

After John Wilkes Booth fired the shot that killed the sixteenth president of the United States, the government quickly arrested several key figures in the plot. One of those believed to be involved was Dr. Mudd. Despite his protest of innocence he was tried, convicted, and sent to a prison in Florida.

The only person in the country who truly believed in his innocence was his wife. She began a vigil outside the White House that lasted for weeks. Her perseverance eventually paid off. She gained an audience with President Johnson and convinced him to pardon her husband. Mudd's name was cleared by President Jimmy Carter. Love always protects, trusts, hopes, and perseveres. When everyone else may believe your spouse's name is mud, don't you.

MARRIAGE MINUTE TRUTH:

LOVE SHOULD BE THE LAST THING STANDING IN OUR LIVES

. . . .

Primary Passage:
*Love never fails. But where there are prophecies, they
will cease; where there are tongues, they will be stilled;
where there is knowledge, it will pass away.*
1 Corinthians 13:8

. . . .

When the great Chicago fire of 1871 swept through the city it annihilated everything in its path. More than 18,000 buildings were destroyed. One hundred thousand people were left homeless. A four square mile area of downtown Chicago was left in ashes. Saddest of all, at least one thousand people perished in the inferno.

A few days after the firestorm subsided an intriguing picture was published in the newspapers. In the midst of the four square mile area of devastation, one lone house stood untouched by the blaze. It had survived the nation's worst fire of the century.

Christ's love is much like that lone house. When the firestorm of family problems, financial setbacks, even disease and death has swept through your marriage, love will still stand. That indestructible love survived the whip of the Roman soldiers, the tauntings of the crowd, and the painful cross of Calvary, and that love emerged triumphant from the tomb on Easter morning.

No one can promise you that your lives will be spared flames and heat. But God does promise that when the smoke and ashes clear, His love will still be standing. And so will you.

MARRIAGE MINUTE TRUTH:
MARRIAGE IS FOR GROWN-UPS

. . . .

Primary Passage:
*When I was a child, I talked like a child, I thought
like a child, I reasoned like a child. When I became
a man, I put childish ways behind me.*
1 Corinthians 13:11

. . . .

*M*arriage counseling can be tense at times. Often one of the spouses will begin the session by conspicuously moving his or her chair slightly away from his or her mate.

"Pastor, tell him that I've had it with his basketball leagues," the wife will say.

"Tell her to quit nagging me," replies the husband.

The fact that they are sitting right next to each other and can hear each other quite clearly doesn't seem to matter. It's a principle we have seen over and over again. The greater the pain in a marriage, the more childish people's behavior. Perhaps it's the survival instinct learned as a small boy or girl that kicks in. When children are mad at someone, they just sit in a corner and pout. They refuse to speak to the person. They tell him or her to go away.

Grown-up marriages can't survive on childish behavior. We need to come to Christ and ask Him to fill us with His mature, grown-up love. It's only then we can make real progress in our marriage relationship. Make it your goal to put away childish things and love each other like the adults you are.

MARRIAGE MINUTE TRUTH:

TO BE FULLY LOVED WE HAVE TO RISK BEING FULLY KNOWN

. . . .

Primary Passage:
Now we see but a poor reflection as in a mirror; then we
shall see face to face. Now I know in part; then I shall
know fully, even as I am fully known.
1 Corinthians 13:12

. . . .

During the 1950s Clark Gable was considered the ultimate heartthrob by many adoring female fans. Once his wife, Carole Lombard, was asked what it was like to be married to the ultimate sex symbol. Her response was as eloquent as it was revealing, "Gable is no Gable," she replied.

Many husbands and wives fear being known for who they really are. They worry that if the other person really knew them for who they were, they would be rejected. So they keep up a false front.

But we can't love an image, only a real person. The Scriptures tell us that God knows everything about us yet He still loves and accepts us. When we reach heaven we will be fully known by others. Does that mean we will finally be rejected? No. We will experience a love far more complete than anything we've ever experienced on earth.

Why not get a head start on such love? Let your spouse get to know you as you really are. Let him or her reveal himself or herself to you. Then both of you respond to each other with unconditional love. It will be a little bit of heaven come to earth.

MARRIAGE MINUTE TRUTH:

LOVE IS THE ONLY ENDURING INHERITANCE WE CAN PASS ON TO OTHERS

Primary Passage:
And now these three remain: faith, hope and love.
But the greatest of these is love.
1 Corinthians 13:13

In the city of Chicago is Rose Hill Cemetery, where many of the most famous business names of the last century are buried. Walk among the sea of tombstones and you will find such famous names as John Sears, Montgomery Ward, and Marshall Fields.

Although each of these men left behind vast fortunes and successful business enterprises, all that's left of their personal influence is aging granite monuments.

A few miles away is a Bible college that trains young men and women to serve Christ in full-time ministry or missions work. Walking across the commons you find students laughing, cramming for a test, or perhaps bowed in prayer with a friend. The love of Christ radiates through the institution and it shows no signs, as of yet, of demise and decline. It is Moody Bible Institute, started by another great man of the nineteenth century in Chicago, Dwight L. Moody. It continues to make an eternal impact on the lives of others. Love, not money, is the legacy Moody left.

What will you and your spouse leave behind? Money? Businesses? Homes? The Scriptures tell us the only three things that will remain are faith, hope, and love. Invest in what lasts.

MARRIAGE MINUTE TRUTH:

CHRISTLIKE LOVE IS THE WILLINGNESS TO MAKE ANY SACRIFICE NECESSARY FOR THE SAKE OF OUR WIVES

. . . .

Primary Passage:
Husbands, love your wives, just as Christ loved the
church and gave himself up for her to make her holy . . .
Ephesians 5:25–26

. . . .

*S*urvivors of the Titanic tell tales of both ultimate heroism and extreme cowardice that fateful night. It seems when the order was finally given to abandon ship there was a chaotic scramble to gain seats on the few lifeboats available. The decision was made that women and children would receive first priority.

At that point many tearful good-byes were said on deck as loving husbands willingly gave up any hope of saving their own lives to see their loved ones rescued. Other men, realizing certain death was only minutes away, raced back to their staterooms and quickly donned dresses, silk stockings, and makeup. In the darkness and confusion of the night they then took seats on the lifeboats.

Paul makes it clear how husbands are to treat their wives. We are to give them our seats in the lifeboat, to love them more than ourselves. We are to love them "just as Christ loved the church and gave himself up for her." The Cross is the standard set for us as husbands. Do we have the courage for that kind of sacrifice?

MARRIAGE MINUTE TRUTH:

A HUSBAND IS TO PRESENT HIS WIFE WITHOUT STAIN OR WRINKLE

Primary Passage:
*. . . to make her holy, cleansing her by the washing with
water through the word, and to present her to himself as a
radiant church, without stain or wrinkle or any other
blemish, but holy and blameless.*
Ephesians 5:26–27

*T*hrough the years I have heard wives express regret and anger over the sexual pressures they felt from their husbands before they were married. Not wanting to upset or displease their fiancés, they gave in to the pressures and sexually compromised themselves before marriage.

Husbands are given a very specific job description to fulfill even before they are married. The Bible tells us we are to love our wives in such a way that we can present them before God "without stain or wrinkle or any other blemish, but holy and blameless."

Husband, if you failed in that task before you were married, today is the day to confess that to God, then ask your wife's forgiveness. The Scriptures promise us, "If we confess our sins, he is faithful and just and will forgive us our sins and purify us from all unrighteousness" (1 John 1:9). You need to claim that promise, receive God's pardon, and begin a new chapter in your married life. Pledge before God that from this day onward you will fulfill your job description by His grace.

MARRIAGE MINUTE TRUTH:

HUSBANDS SHOULD LOVE THEIR WIVES AS THEY DO THEIR OWN BODIES

. . . .

Primary Passage:
*In this same way, husbands ought to love their wives as
their own bodies. He who loves his wife loves himself.*
Ephesians 5:28

. . . .

*H*ave you noticed how the focus of most health clubs is to encourage maximum personal physical fitness? Club members spend hour after hour pushing themselves to their physical limit to achieve a better physique, develop an optimum heart rate, and shed unwanted pounds. Men are often willing to get up early, come in late, and give up weekends to maintain their strict exercise regimen. Why? Because they love their own bodies.

The apostle Paul says that husbands should be as committed to loving and caring for their wives as they are to tending their own physical fitness. We need to develop a regimen of listening to our wives' needs and then doing something about it. Are our wives feeling overwhelmed? Then we need to exercise encouragement. Are they tired? We need to exercise servanthood. Are they lonely? We need to exercise companionship.

We need to care about our wife's spiritual, emotional, and physical condition just as much as we care about our club membership (a great deal more, in fact). So do you want a marriage that's in great shape? Then do the ultimate exercise—sacrificial love.

MARRIAGE MINUTE TRUTH:

SUBMISSION IS VOLUNTARILY YIELDING IN LOVE

Primary Passage:
Wives, submit to your husbands as to the Lord.
Ephesians 5:22

*T*he well-known feminist Gloria Steinem once remarked, "A woman without a man is like a fish without a bicycle."

It's true that women don't need to be married or dating someone to experience fulfillment as a person. God created each of us to know true satisfaction in life through a saving relationship with Jesus Christ. Yet, He also created in each of us a desire to be in relationship with a member of the opposite sex. So when it comes to a marriage relationship, Steinem's remark falls far short of the truth. Our need for a companion is not a sign of weakness. It's the reflection of a God who said, "It is not good for the man to be alone" (Genesis 2:18).

No wife can experience true fulfillment without the caring attention and sacrificial love of her husband. Nor can a husband know true satisfaction in marriage without the caring and respectful love of his wife.

Which brings us to a discussion of submission. Submission may be defined as "voluntarily yielding in love." When a wife voluntarily shows respect and admiration for her husband, fulfilling one of his basic needs, she should hardly be considered a servile doormat. Rather she's a self-confident partner who loves her husband enough to give him what he truly needs—respect and admiration. In that light submission becomes strength, not stupidity.

MARRIAGE MINUTE TRUTH:

SPIRITUAL LEADERSHIP IS NOT SPIRITUAL DICTATORSHIP

. . . .

Primary Passage:
For the husband is the head of the wife as Christ is the head of the church, his body, of which he is the Savior. Now as the church submits to Christ, so also wives should submit to their husbands in everything.
Ephesians 5:23–24

. . . .

*W*e have witnessed male dictatorships in some homes, and it isn't pretty. We once knew a family where the father insisted his word was the law. He literally told his wife and children what they would think about politics, culture, and religion. He demanded complete subservience from his wife, unquestioned obedience from his children, and total deference from visitors.

The man scared us.

One daughter grew up to become an angry and bitter woman, eventually divorcing her first husband. His other daughter slipped into clinical depression and required hospitalization.

We have also witnessed godly male spiritual leadership in a home. Though the husband was a busy surgeon with a demanding practice, he generously gave of himself to his wife and children. He was the spiritual leader of his household, not the domestic ruler. His children prospered in their adult years. There's a distinct difference. Spiritual leadership, when properly understood and lovingly practiced, is as far from a dictatorship as biblical submission is from a state of slavery.

Marriage Minute Truth:

EACH MEMBER OF THE FAMILY IS A GIFT FROM GOD

. . . .

Primary Passage:
*Adam lay with his wife Eve, and she became pregnant
and gave birth to Cain. She said, "With the help of
the Lord I have brought forth a man."*
Genesis 4:1

. . . .

*Y*ou were a mistake."

That comment by a parent left a lifelong scar on the heart of a young man we counseled. He had spent his entire adult life tormented by the fact that his parents told him he was an "accident" and, therefore, unwanted. Regardless of the circumstances surrounding a child's conception, the Scriptures tell us we are given our children "with the help of the Lord."

From that perspective there is no such thing as a son or daughter who is a "mistake" or an "accident." Those words don't even exist in the vocabulary of God, who is never careless or in error.

If you find your marriage is hindered by old tapes from your childhood years that keep telling you that you weren't wanted, or loved, by your parents, you need a healthy dose of good theology.

You were born "with the help of the Lord." Rejoice in the fact God designed and created you and gave you a special place on this earth by design. Give your own children the gift of assurance that they are wanted and were given to you "with the help of the Lord." Although we can't change how our ancestors talked, we can change how we speak to our descendants—instilling value, dignity, and love.

MARRIAGE MINUTE TRUTH:

GOD DESERVES THE BEST OF OUR VERY BEST

Primary Passage:
Now Abel kept flocks, and Cain worked the soil. In the course of time Cain brought some of the fruits of the soil as an offering to the Lord. But Abel brought fat portions from some of the firstborn of his flock.
Genesis 4:2–4

*W*hen you sit down and write out your bills each month, who gets paid first? Is it the mortgage company? The utility company? Your car insurance agency?

When you plan your day or week, who or what gets written in first? Is it your business appointments? Your hair dresser? Your child's school concert? When you choose to volunteer your skills or time, who gets first shot at them? Your son's soccer team? The local high school parent's association? Your church? Or your favorite charity?

Treasure. Time. Talents. Every day we must make choices how to divide them among the many opportunities and demands we face. The Scriptures teach that God deserves the first portion of everything, whether it's our money, our hours, or our skills. It's called tithing, or giving a designated percentage to God.

Abel offered God the "fat portions" of the firstborn of his flock. When we are in right relationship with God, we delight in giving Him the best of the best. When we're out of right relationship, we offer Him the leftovers. Which does God get from you?

MARRIAGE MINUTE TRUTH:

THE ROOT OF ALL DESTRUCTIVE ANGER IS BEING OUT OF RIGHT RELATIONSHIP WITH GOD

. . . .

Primary Passage:
The Lord looked with favor on Abel and his offering, but
on Cain and his offering he did not look with favor.
So Cain was very angry, and his face was downcast.
Genesis 4:4–5

. . . .

What is the source of the hurtful, destructive anger that can sometimes plague our lives? Some people blame their upbringing. They claim they simply inherited their bad temper. Still others point to tough breaks in their lives. It was a series of hard knocks that produced their bitterness and rage. Although these answers may play a role in our anger problem, they don't go to the root of it. The Bible teaches that the core cause of destructive anger is being out of right relationship with God.

It's when our pride, our willful self, rebels against God in some area of our life that destructive anger results. In that sense anger always becomes the second sin we commit. Our first sin is our rebellion against God.

If you're struggling with bitterness, rage, or destructive anger today, stop and do a personal inventory. Where are you out of right relationship with God? Where has pride taken hold? What are you withholding from God? That's what you need to confess before God. That's where you will begin to discover freedom.

MARRIAGE MINUTE TRUTH:

SIN'S ULTIMATE DESIRE IS TO CONTROL OUR ENTIRE LIFE

. . . .

Primary Passage:
*Then the Lord said to Cain, "Why are you angry? Why is
your face downcast? If you do what is right, will you not be accepted?
But if you do not do what is right, sin is crouching at your door;
it desires to have you, but you must master it."*
Genesis 4:6–7

. . . .

When I (Bob) was in junior high I talked my parents into buying a dog. He was only a small puppy at the time; I could hold him easily in two hands. I promised my parents they would never have to take care of him and that this Labrador and German Shepherd puppy would never get any bigger than he was now.

From the very beginning the dog slept on the corner of my bed. It was something of an idyllic scene—a young boy with his puppy sleeping at his feet.

But over time things began to change. Day by day the dog grew. Although at first all he required was a small corner of the mattress, soon he demanded more and more of my bed. By the time he was full grown he weighed more than sixty-five pounds and occupied most of my bed. I was forced to lie on my side on the edge of the bed while he occupied 90 percent of the mattress—snoring peacefully, of course.

Sin is much like my dog. It starts out asking for only a small portion of our lives. God warned Cain that sin was crouching at his door, and it desired to have him.

When you give the sin of destructive anger even a small place in your life, it slowly, insidiously, begins to grow and demand more and more and more of you. Your only hope is to confess it, renounce it, and allow God to remove it from your life. Sin will never be content with just part of you. Deal with it today before you discover the dog snoring in your face. By then, it may be too late.

MARRIAGE MINUTE TRUTH:

THE DAY COMES WHEN ATTITUDE CROSSES THE LINE INTO ACTION

. . . .

Primary Passage:
Now Cain said to his brother Abel, "Let's go out to the field." And while they were in the field, Cain attacked his brother Abel and killed him.
Genesis 4:8

. . . .

*T*he story in the local newspaper left everyone in the community in a state of shock. The couple took care of their yard, showed respect for their neighbors, and were active in a local church. As far as anyone could tell they enjoyed a good marriage and a stable home. That's why no one could believe it when the morning newspaper carried the stunning news that the husband had been arrested for beating his wife to death with a baseball bat.

According to the article the couple had a loud argument that began in the kitchen and four hours later ended in the garage. After hours of intense arguing and rage, the husband reached for a baseball bat. When the paramedics arrived they found him holding his wife in his arms, sobbing and begging for her to please come back.

We fool ourselves when we don't admit that our attitudes will one day cross the line into actions. Have any angry or bitter attitudes developed in your marriage? Now is the time to confess them before God and get back into right relationship with God and with your spouse. Do so before your angry attitude crosses the line into action. Once that happens there may be no stepping back.

MARRIAGE MINUTE TRUTH:

OUR MODEL IS A SUFFERING SERVANT, NOT AN ANGRY TYRANT

Primary Passage:
*Jesus began to explain to his disciples that he must go to
Jerusalem and suffer many things at the hands of the
elders, chief priests and teachers of the law, and that he
must be killed and on the third day be raised to life.*
Matthew 16:21

In his famous series of children's books, *The Chronicles of Narnia*, C. S. Lewis symbolizes Christ as a powerful lion named Aslan. This strong, impressive leader went to mythical Narnia to set the inhabitants free because without him "It was always winter and never spring."

The climactic scene occurred when Aslan encountered the White Witch. Onlookers were stunned as Aslan allowed himself to be tied with ropes and his beautiful giant mane was sheared to the skin. Ultimately the witch pierced Aslan's heart with a knife on an ancient stone slab. Friends watched helplessly as he died.

The children's story points to the example of Jesus Christ. Though Lord of the universe, He voluntarily suffered at the hands of "the elders, chief priests and teachers of the law."

Husbands and wives, if you wish to follow Jesus Christ in your marriage, sacrificial obedience to God's will is the route you must walk. The story ends as Aslan broke the table of death in half and returned victoriously to life. And Scripture tells us that because of our great King, Jesus, the Resurrection will bear fruit in our own resurrection.

MARRIAGE MINUTE TRUTH:

UNFORTUNATELY ANGER, DISCORD, AND RAGE COME NATURALLY TO US

. . . .

Primary Passage:
*The acts of the sinful nature are obvious . . . hatred,
discord, jealousy, fits of rage, selfish ambition,
dissensions, factions and envy.*
Galatians 5:19–21

. . . .

*W*e have never met a parent who needed to teach his child how to be jealous or selfish or mean. "OK, Kristin, listen carefully. I want you to go over to your younger brother and push him over. If he cries just laugh at him." Or "Do as I say, Johnny. Mommy is going to put two granola bars on the table. You go over and shove both of them in your mouth to make sure your sister doesn't get one."

If we don't teach our youngsters such meanness and selfishness, where do they learn it? The Bible answers that question; such actions are "acts of the sinful nature." It's born in them. It's born in us.

The only way we can overcome our sinful human nature is to have a greater power at work in us. That power is the Holy Spirit who produces "love, joy, peace, patience, kindness . . ." (Galatians 5:22) and a host of other spiritual fruits. Anger and selfishness come naturally to us. Kindness and unselfishness come from a supernatural source. Ask God to fill both your lives with His Spirit today so that you can respond supernaturally to each other. You'll enjoy the taste of the sweet fruit.

THE FRUIT OF THE SPIRIT RESULTS FROM THE FILLING OF THE SPIRIT

Primary Passage:
But the fruit of the Spirit is love, joy, peace,
patience, kindness, goodness, faithfulness,
gentleness and self-control.
Galatians 5:22–23

*T*he story is told of the famous American tennis player, Arthur Ashe, who once faced a formidable competitor, Ilie Nastase, in a championship round. It was common practice for Nastase to try to rattle his opponents by taunting and insulting them across the net. On occasion he even used profanity.

After enduring hours of such degrading treatment Arthur Ashe walked off the tennis courts. "I'm close to losing control," he explained to the judge.

"But you'll forfeit the match," the official pleaded.

"I'd rather forfeit the game than my dignity," Ashe replied.

God would rather have us forfeit an argument than lose our self-control. When we are provoked the fruit of the Spirit changes our response. Rather than becoming defensive, angry, or aggressive, we demonstrate love, joy, peace, patience, kindness, and self-control. It's God living out His heart, mind, and emotions through our heart, mind, and emotions. The fruit of the Spirit results from the filling of the Spirit, something we can ask for each morning. Tennis, anyone?

MARRIAGE MINUTE TRUTH:

WE NEED TO SPEAK THE TRUTH IN LOVE AND LEAVE THE RESULTS TO GOD

Primary Passage:
*Instead, speaking the truth in love, we will in all things
grow up into him who is the Head, that is, Christ.*
Ephesians 4:15

*I*t's sometimes difficult to tell our spouses what's on our hearts. We get in the habit of hiding our true feelings from each other. We are afraid there will be negative consequences for the relationship if we tell our partner how he or she has hurt or disappointed us. So a distance opens up in our marriage, and it only grows bigger as time goes on.

There is only one remedy to the gradual drift that failing to speak the truth in love creates. You might have guessed it: We need to speak the truth in love. This doesn't imply that we blurt out every thought that comes to mind like a small child will sometimes do. Rather the Bible calls us to first be honest with ourselves. We need to acknowledge that hurt for what it is: a problem that requires loving confrontation and truth to be healed. The next step is to go to our spouse and in love and humility explain the effect his or her words or actions had on us. God will honor such a process. We need not fear such a confrontation. We can speak the truth and leave the results to God.

MARRIAGE MINUTE TRUTH:

WE SHOULD PURSUE THE GOAL OF A QUIET MIND

Primary Passage:
*Do not be anxious about anything, but in everything,
by prayer and petition, with thanksgiving, present your
requests to God. And the peace of God, which transcends
all understanding, will guard your hearts and
your minds in Christ Jesus.*
Philippians 4:6–7

*E*ach summer our family travels to Lake of the Woods in beautiful Ontario, Canada, for a weeklong fishing trip. The lake itself is almost forty by sixty miles wide and boasts almost three thousand separate islands. A lake that large can have a personality all its own. Some days it's blue and calm, shimmering like a giant glass counter in a jewelry store. Other days it's brown, choppy, and churning like the inside of a large washing machine.

What state of mind do the two of you live in? Is it a shimmering glass reflection of a deep calm? Or is it a muddy, churning tempest that never knows a moment's rest?

The Bible gives the secret of bringing calm to our troubled emotions. "Do not be anxious about anything, but in everything, by prayer and petition, with thanksgiving, present your requests to God. . . ." Pray. Tell Christ your needs. Give Him thanks. The result is a quiet mind that becomes a tranquil resort.

MARRIAGE MINUTE TRUTH:

THE CHURCH IS FIGHTING THE GREATEST BATTLE EVER FOUGHT

. . . .

Primary Passage:
*And I tell you that you are Peter, and on this rock
I will build my church, and the gates of Hades
will not overcome it.*
Matthew 16:18

. . . .

*G*eneral George Patton, the commanding officer whose Third Army liberated more than ten thousand European towns and villages during World War II, reportedly once told his troops, "I never want to get a message that we are holding our ground. Let the enemy hold their ground. We will be on the attack morning, noon, and night."

Like it or not, the church of Christ is engaged in a fierce battle. As followers of Jesus Christ so are we. It is the conflict between the kingdom of hell and the kingdom of God. The battleground is the hearts of men and women all over the world.

Are you on the offensive or defensive when it comes to this battle? Do you and your spouse spend time each day praying for your children and for the young people you love? Are you memorizing Scripture together to combat the spiritual assaults you experience on your job, in your home, even in church at times?

The good news is the outcome of this engagement has already been decided. When Jesus died He cried out, "It is finished." All of our sins have been canceled. The power of death has been destroyed. Our enemy, Satan, has been mortally wounded. Don't hold your ground. Go on the offensive in the power of Christ!

THE CHURCH IS EMPOWERED WITH THE GREATEST AUTHORITY EVER GIVEN

. . . .

Primary Passage:
I will give you the keys of the kingdom of heaven;
whatever you bind on earth will be bound in heaven, and
whatever you loose on earth will be loosed in heaven.
Matthew 16:19

. . . .

In the 1940s the railroad workers in America went on strike. The nation's economy faced virtual paralysis. President Harry S. Truman knew something had to be done immediately. He stood before the American people and announced he had just drafted every railroad worker in the United States into the military. Using his authority as commander in chief he immediately ordered them back to work. The strike ended that same day.

The church of Jesus Christ has been given ultimate spiritual authority. We have the only gospel by which people may enter heaven. Through the power of prayer we can exercise the authority of Christ to alter spiritual realities on earth and in heaven. Let me encourage you and your husband or wife to take full advantage of this spiritual authority you have in Christ. Pray for the salvation of your children, relatives, friends, and coworkers. Ask God to change the spiritual realities of your neighborhood and schools. Implore Him to send a great revival to our nation and world. As we align our will with God's will, we can use His authority to alter the spiritual landscape of our world.

MARRIAGE MINUTE TRUTH:

GOD IS SOVEREIGN EVEN OVER THE MOST UNPLEASANT SITUATIONS

. . . .

Primary Passage:
The Lord works out everything for his own ends—
even the wicked for a day of disaster.
Proverbs 16:4

. . . .

In all of our years in ministry there have been only a few Sunday mornings we really didn't want to get up and go to church. It has usually been on account of a difficult person, painful letters we've received the week before, or hurtful things that were said in a congregational meeting.

Each of these Sundays has been a test of our belief in the sovereignty of God. Can He bring good out of bad? Will He have the final word in even the most unpleasant situation?

That's where faith enters in.

When we get down on our knees and ask God to fill us with His love so that we can treat others with kindness who have been unkind to us—that's when our faith begins to grow. To forgive someone who doesn't ask for forgiveness is an act of faith. To believe someone is going to change who doesn't see the need to change is an act of faith.

A sovereign God can overrule any hard situation, any ugly circumstance, and any painful event and make it serve His purposes. Trusting your problem to God's sovereignty is a guaranteed formula for peace of mind.

MARRIAGE MINUTE TRUTH:

SUCCESS SHOULD BE MEASURED BY OUR OBEDIENCE TO GOD'S WILL

. . . .

Primary Passage:
Not everyone who says to me, "Lord, Lord," will enter
the kingdom of heaven, but only he who does the
will of my Father who is in heaven.
Matthew 7:21

. . . .

*T*he emcee was about to announce the awards at a senior farewell banquet in high school. This included reading the various citations class members had bestowed upon one another. It took several minutes for him to work his way through the list, "Best School Spirit," "Best Dresser," "Class Clown . . ."

Things went fine until he reached the final accolade. He looked down at the name and gulped hard. "And the person chosen 'Most Likely to Succeed' is . . . is . . ." There was his own name. Ever since that evening, now 25 years ago, he wonders if his life was a success or not.

What is success? Is it making megabucks in the stock market? Being elected to the legislature? Or graduating from Yale graduate school and going to work for an East Coast think tank?

The Bible says that God measures success in terms of our obedience to Him. Only those who do the will of God will enter the kingdom of heaven, and that will is trusting in Christ alone for our salvation. While we will not stand in the judgment of those who did not believe in Christ, the Bible says we will still stand before Jesus some day. At that time He will either reward us or not reward us according to our obedience or disobedience in following His will. Only then will the word "success" take on its true meaning.

MARRIAGE MINUTE TRUTH:

IMAGINED SLIGHTS ARE OFTEN JUST THAT—IMAGINED

Primary Passage:
*A quick-tempered man does foolish things,
and a crafty man is hated.*
Proverbs 14:17

A super sensitive person is difficult, if not impossible, to live with. Such a person can find slights, put-downs, and insults where none were ever intended. Often the person's response is quick and impulsive. He either demands an immediate apology or launches a stinging response to what he believes was a slight. If he isn't satisfied with his mate's response, he can inflict a variety of punishments: the silent treatment, walking out of the room, even driving off for an extended period of time.

What does God think of such behavior? Proverbs tells us that a quick-tempered person does foolish things. Crafty responses intended to manipulate the other person eventually produce ill will or even hatred in a relationship.

If you are a super sensitive person, how can you change? First, recognize your tendency to imagine or exaggerate insults. Things are rarely as bad as you imagine. Second, ask the Holy Spirit to bring balance and reason to your perceptions. He has promised to guide us into all truth if we ask. Third, take time to pray through your response when you feel you've been wronged. Prayer can restore your emotional equilibrium and keep you from acting out foolish responses to your spouse.

It is a glory to overlook some insults. For the super sensitive person, learning to do just that can mean a glorious new beginning to your marriage.

MARRIAGE MINUTE TRUTH:

DENIAL IS CHARACTERISTIC OF SOMEONE WITH AN ANGER PROBLEM

....

Primary Passage:
*Then the Lord said to Cain, "Where is your brother
Abel?" "I don't know," he replied. "Am I my brother's
keeper?" The Lord said, "What have you done? Listen!
Your brother's blood cries out to me from the ground."*
Genesis 4:9–10

....

*L*aw enforcement officials are increasingly turning to the use of video cameras to arrest and convict drunk drivers. One such video clip showed a driver loudly insisting he was sober. When asked to walk a straight line he took two or three steps forward, swerved way to the right, then fell over backward.

Denial is also a common response when a husband or wife is confronted with an anger problem. "Problem? What problem? You're the one with the problem." That was in essence Cain's response to God when he was asked the whereabouts of Abel. "I don't know," Cain shrugged his shoulders, "Am I my brother's keeper?"

Common statements of denial include: "OK, I get a little upset once in a while, but it's no big deal." "Yeah, we have a few words now and then, but doesn't everybody?" "So I hit her once or twice, but she had it coming."

No anger problem is ever healed by denial. We need to bring our behavior out of the darkness of self-deception and into the light of God's truth. That's where true change begins. All we have to lose is our excuses—and our chains.

MARRIAGE MINUTE TRUTH:

DESTRUCTIVE ANGER EVENTUALLY LEAVES US A RESTLESS WANDERER

. . . .

Primary Passage:
*Now you are under a curse and driven from the ground,
which opened its mouth to receive your brother's blood
from your hand. When you work the ground, it will no
longer yield its crops for you. You will be a restless
wanderer on the earth.*
Genesis 4:11–12

. . . .

*H*e eats in restaurants alone. He goes shopping alone. He spends many holidays by himself. Why? He's an angry person who never got better. He has lost his marriage, his children, and most of his friends. He spends most of his days now like Cain, a "restless wanderer on the earth."

The true cost of destructive anger is seldom evident right away. It takes time for the consequences to emerge. But once it does we pay a frightfully high price.

Destructive anger carries in it the seeds of its own judgment. When a father consistently berates and demeans his children, they may one day grow up and never come home again. When a wife continually shames, punishes, and attempts to control her husband, little by little he will withdraw from the relationship. Though he may stay married in person, his heart has left home.

God designed us to be peaceful individuals living in peaceful community with those around us, not restless wanderers cut off from vital relationships. The choice is ours.

MARRIAGE MINUTE TRUTH:

ARM YOUR CHILDREN TO BE ON GUARD AGAINST TWISTED DOCTRINE

Primary Passage:
The Spirit clearly says that in later times some
will abandon the faith and follow deceiving
spirits and things taught by demons.
1 Timothy 4:1

*M*ike was an honor roll student accepted by one of the leading universities in the nation. He wrote to tell us that he was leaving his studies to become an ordained minister. His letter described his dramatic conversion and a decision to give the rest of his life to the ministry.

At first we were thrilled with the news. Over time, however, we became more and more uneasy with our friend's newfound faith. He had joined a group we had never heard of before. We contacted his parents to see if our worst suspicions were true. They were—their son had joined a cult.

If you have children, how cult proof are they? Are the core values of your home faith, obedience, and service to Jesus Christ? Are you involved in their lives in a loving way? Are you teaching them the gospel and the Word of God?

Our children are living in a world of false doctrines taught by demons. Only the inerrant, infallible Word of God can arm them against such deception. Have you prepared them? It's your responsibility to give them the weapons they need to survive.

MARRIAGE MINUTE TRUTH:

OUR LIFESTYLE AND DOCTRINE AFFECT EACH OTHER IN A PROFOUND WAY

. . . .

Primary Passage:
*Watch your life and doctrine closely. Persevere in
them, because if you do, you will save both
yourself and your hearers.*
1 Timothy 4:16

. . . .

The day after one particularly humiliating defeat the legendary football coach Vince Lombardi started practice in an unusual way. "Gentlemen, this is a football," he said.

It's important to master the basics, particularly when it comes to sound doctrine and living. What areas should we be familiar with? The doctrine of the authority of Scripture, the doctrine of God, the doctrine of sin, the doctrine of Christ, the doctrine of the atonement, the doctrine of salvation, the doctrine of the church, and the doctrine of the return of Christ.

Why spend time on learning the basics of theology when you have clothes to wash, kids to feed, and grass to mow? Your doctrine and your life affect each other. If you don't have a correct understanding of God's Word, it will be difficult to know how to live a life pleasing to Him.

On the other hand, if you live carelessly, you will find it will begin to alter what you believe. Your mind will change your theology to justify your sinful actions. So watch both your life and your doctrine closely. This is no football game. The Super Bowl of life is played just once.

MARRIAGE MINUTE TRUTH:

BEWARE OF ANYONE PREACHING OR TEACHING A "NEW" TRUTH

. . . .

Primary Passage:
*I warn everyone who hears the words of the prophecy of
this book: If anyone adds anything to them, God will
add to him the plagues described in this book.*
Revelation 22:18

. . . .

*M*ost cult groups do not outwardly deny the Bible. Rather, they twist and distort its truth in subtle but significant ways. Or they add to what has already been written.

According to the experts, you need to be on guard against the following: new or specially revealed truth, novel interpretations of Scripture, nonbiblical sources of authority, a Jesus different from the one explained in the New Testament, a rejection of historic tenets of Christianity such as the existence of the Trinity, salvation by works, and false prophecy.[1]

Be on guard, because if it's a "new" spiritual truth, chances are it's a false spiritual truth. God has warned not to add or take away from what is written in His Word. Everything we need to know to experience salvation in Jesus Christ and receive eternal life is already written for us. Nothing new needs to be added.

Rather than searching for new or mysterious truths, fill your mind with the faith "once delivered" to all believers.

The truth of God's Word alone will one day deliver us safely on the shores of heaven.

1. Josh McDowell and Don Stewart, *Understanding the Cults* (San Bernardino, California: Here's Life, 1982), 20–29.

MARRIAGE MINUTE TRUTH:

OUR BEST ALLY IN DISCERNING TRUTH IS THE HOLY SPIRIT

Primary Passage:
*And I will ask the Father, and he will give you another
Counselor to be with you forever—the Spirit of truth.*
John 14:16−17

*A*n aging veteran who had been part of the invasion of Normandy during World War II told us a fascinating story. As a member of an elite airborne unit he parachuted behind enemy lines on the night of June 5, 1944.

Allied commanders had given each soldier a small metal clicker to use if they got lost or separated. As the paratroopers groped their way through the woods and fields they were to click twice and wait for a response. If they were greeted by the right signal from another clicker, they knew they had located an ally.

We have a trusted ally in our search for spiritual truth. He's the Holy Spirit. He's our Counselor and Helper. The Scriptures describe Him as the "paraclete" or "one who comes on alongside of us." Jesus sent His disciples out into a world of mystery religions, emperor cults, and a host of bizarre faiths. He promised that when He was gone He would give them a Comforter (the Holy Spirit) who would remind them of all truth.

Are the two of you letting your spiritual ally lead you daily into God's Word and truth?

MARRIAGE MINUTE TRUTH:

THERE IS ONE BAPTISM, BUT MANY FILLINGS OF THE SPIRIT

Primary Passage:
Do not get drunk on wine, which leads to debauchery.
Instead, be filled with the Spirit.
Ephesians 5:18

*Y*ears ago we read the small devotional classic, *My Heart, Christ's Home,* by Robert Munger. It helped us understand the work of the Holy Spirit in our lives.

The author likened our soul to a large home with many rooms. The living room was our social life, the den or library our thought life, and the bedroom our sex life. The question the booklet kept probing was "Have you allowed Christ into each room?"

When we trust in Christ as our Savior we are baptized with the Holy Spirit once and for all. From that moment on we possess all of the Holy Spirit we ever shall possess. But the question becomes "Does He have access into each room of our lives? Does He have all of us?" The filling of the Spirit means that we open every door, every room, every closet to His complete control.

Are there rooms in your marriage that you've kept locked and closed? Do you still control secret sins, hidden behaviors, and buried attitudes? Then you need to unlock those rooms and invite Christ in through honest confession and repentance.

Your marriage, Christ's home. It can become a reality.

MARRIAGE MINUTE TRUTH:

WE NEED TO GIVE OUR SENSE OF SHAME OVER TO CHRIST

. . . .

Primary Passage:
*Let us fix our eyes on Jesus, the author and perfecter of
our faith, who for the joy set before him endured the
cross, scorning its shame, and sat down at the right
hand of the throne of God.*
Hebrews 12:2

. . . .

The popular song "Tie a Yellow Ribbon 'Round the Old Oak Tree" is based on a true story. It seems that a young man from the country had made some bad decisions early in life. He was convicted of a felony and sent away to prison.

Just before he was to be paroled he wrote his parents and said, "I know I've brought you shame and embarrassment. I'll be taking a bus home once I'm out of prison. If you want me to stop and get off tie a single yellow ribbon around the old oak tree. If you don't, I'll just stay on the bus and go on."

The day came when the young man was released and boarded the bus for home. When he came to his home, he asked another passenger to look for him to see if he saw a yellow ribbon.

"No," came the reply. The boy's heart sank. "I see a hundred yellow ribbons," the passenger said. The bus stopped and the boy was reunited with his parents in a tearful reunion.

Does God forgive us when we fail? Is He willing to bear the shame of what we've done? The thousands of ribbons tied to the Cross of Christ bear the eloquent answer.

MARRIAGE MINUTE TRUTH:

GOD IS INTENSELY JEALOUS OF OUR LOVE FOR HIM

Primary Passage:
Or do you think Scripture says without reason that the spirit he caused to live in us envies intensely [for us]?
James 4:5

The young man's first date was a disaster. He was still in junior high and had a crush on a certain girl. He invited her to go with a group of friends to a fair. She, however, was interested in one of the other boys in the group. So while he shelled out all his money to buy her food and rides, she basically ignored him for another boy. He was left to watch in envy as she showered attention on someone else, even though she was his date.

Have you ever thought of how much God desires your first love and attention as a couple? The Scriptures say the Spirit envies intensely for our highest affection. God is grieved when we make our careers, vacations, or even our spouse or our children our first love. He is saddened as He watches us shower our time, attention, and money on someone or something other than Him.

If you can't honestly say that your first love as a couple is God and God alone, today is the day to repent of that. Come before God, admit your unfaithfulness to Him, and let Him bring you back into the love relationship He so desires.

MARRIAGE MINUTE TRUTH:

BEAUTY IS IN THE CHARACTER, NOT THE EYES, OF THE BEHOLDER

Primary Passage:
Charm is deceptive, and beauty is fleeting;
but a woman who fears the Lord is to be praised.
Proverbs 31:30

*O*ur culture worships beauty, youthful physique, and sex appeal. If you don't believe us, count the number of models over fifty years old used in television commercials (excluding the arthritis pain reliever ads). Or switch on *Monday Night Football* and count the number of wives or children portrayed. Chances are you won't find many there. Why? Because portraying the reality of the aging process and life's necessary commitments would pop the fantasy of good brews, good times, and good babes.

Far too many people choose their life's mate on the shaky premise that happiness and intimacy are the direct result of a muscular body or a shapely figure. Certainly physical beauty is one element of the mystery of love between a man and a woman. But it is meant only as a minor movement, not the basis for the entire symphony. As Proverbs aptly observes, "Charm is deceptive, and beauty is fleeting; but a woman who fears the Lord is to be praised." It is the lasting character traits of faith, devotion, and obedience to God that gives a wife the traits a husband can love for a lifetime. Is culture's list or God's list more important to you?

MARRIAGE MINUTE TRUTH:

FEELINGS CHANGE; COMMITMENTS DON'T

Primary Passage:
Love never fails.
1 Corinthians 13:8

A national magazine devoted its Valentine Day's issue to the subject of love. It reported on the results of a study done in a university research setting that revealed that the hormones that produce the warm sensation of being "in love" eventually lose their potency and wear out. Therefore higher and higher levels of the same hormone are required to produce the same feelings of exhilaration, dreaminess, and infatuation.

Their conclusion: It will take something other than high-voltage body chemistry to keep a couple together for a lifetime. The radioactive hormones that produce a "romantic high" just can't be sustained.

But where infatuation ends, real love begins. Let us encourage you to seek out an older couple you both know well who have a love relationship. Meet with them, ask them questions, and observe their behavior. You may not see the same dreamy-eyed emotions displayed that infatuation brings, but what you will observe is deep respect, a strong sense of attraction, and a deep satisfaction and joy just being together. Real love is just as exhilarating, if not more so, than adolescent hormone rushes. So be encouraged. Just because the infatuation stage may have ended, you haven't fallen out of love. Something far more precious, beautiful, and long lasting can take its place. It's called real love.

MARRIAGE MINUTE TRUTH:

GOD DID NOT DESIGN MARRIAGE FOR DIVORCE

. . . .

Primary Passage:
Some Pharisees came to him to test him. They asked,
"Is it lawful for a man to divorce his wife for
any and every reason?"
Matthew 19:3

. . . .

*T*he very notion of "no-fault divorce" is ridiculous. It is an oxymoron in the same category as "small St. Bernard," "fast turtle," and "friendly gunfire." No-fault divorce makes as much sense as no-fault adultery, no-fault theft, or no-fault slander. We can change the semantics as often as we wish, but divorce is still an unnatural, painful, and unmerciful wrong inflicted on another person, even if both of you agree to it.

What's wrong with divorce? It's the breaking of a solemn and sacred promise made to your spouse, others, and God. The people of ancient times, eager to find the fine print in their marriage vows, once asked Jesus, "Is it lawful for a man to divorce his wife for any and every reason?" His reply didn't deal with technicalities, but with the grand purpose and design of a union between a man and a woman. He explained that the creation of male and female was God's idea and asked why they did not understand that "'For this reason a man will leave his father and mother and be united to his wife, and the two will become one flesh.'? So they are no longer two, but one. Therefore what God has joined together, let man not separate" (Matthew 19:5–6). Could God's intention for your marriage be any more clear?

This entry and previous two adapted from Bob Moeller, *For Better, For Worse, For Keeps* (Portland: Multomah, 1993).

MARRIAGE MINUTE TRUTH:

HOW WE FINISH IS MORE
IMPORTANT THAN HOW WE BEGAN

Primary Passage:
*I have fought the good fight, I have finished the race, I
have kept the faith. Now there is in store for me the
crown of righteousness, which the Lord, the righteous
Judge, will award to me on that day—and not only to
me, but also to all who have longed for his appearing.*
2 Timothy 4:7–8

*W*hen Cheryl was in high school she had an avid interest in
running track. On one occasion she was leading the rest of the
pack as they neared the finish wire. Sensing she would need one
final burst to outdistance the others, she literally threw herself forward at the last moment and broke the wire. It was a bit of a rough
landing, but she was determined to finish and finish strong. That
she did.

The Scriptures tell us that how we finish is all important. The
beginning of your marriage may have been rocky, difficult, even
painful. You may have married on an impulse. Your in-laws may
have opposed the marriage. You may have even rebelled against
God in your values and lifestyle. But that's not the final lap of
your life together. The grace of God and the forgiveness of Christ
make it possible for you to get up if you have stumbled, get back
on track, and take off for the finish line.

And what does a strong finish look like? A couple more in love
with each other and God than when they began the race. Is that
your goal as a couple? Good. Ready, set, go.

MARRIAGE MINUTE TRUTH:

DESTRUCTIVE ANGER SHOULD BE DEMOLISHED, NOT MANAGED

. . . .

Primary Passage:
*For though we live in the world, we do not wage war as
the world does. The weapons we fight with are not the
weapons of the world. On the contrary, they have
divine power to demolish strongholds.*
2 Corinthians 10:3–4

. . . .

*A*nger management is a popular concept. It generally refers to developing coping skills to allow us to manage or control our angry impulses. Once we learn to manage our anger, so the theory goes, we are safe people.

Although there is value in learning methods of restraining and controlling our impulses, they simply don't go far enough in solving sinful anger. The answer is not to manage explosions of anger but to prevent them altogether. Put another way, anger management makes no more sense than lust management, theft management, or greed management. The Scriptures tell us we are to get rid of sin, not manage it.

How can we rid our lives of destructive anger? The answer is in demolishing strongholds. We confess and renounce our sin of anger, we use the authority of God's Word to take our angry thoughts captive, and finally we claim our position in Christ to remain free. Don't settle for anger management; go for the eradication of sinful anger itself.

MARRIAGE MINUTE TRUTH:

GOD'S SPIRIT HAS TO GO WITH YOU EVERYWHERE YOU GO

Primary Passage:
And do not grieve the Holy Spirit of God,
with whom you were sealed for the day of redemption.
Ephesians 4:30

*H*ave you ever eaten at a restaurant with someone who continually complained about the food? Not only can it become irritating, but it can also become downright embarrassing. "This is too cold," "This isn't what I ordered," or "Could I please see the manager about this?" If you could, you'd slip away unnoticed.

Have you ever considered that we may put the Holy Spirit in that same awkward position by our conduct or speech? He lives in our hearts moment to moment because of our saving relationship with Jesus Christ. That means He goes with us wherever we go, listens to all our conversations, and has to endure whatever foolish or angry things we might do or say.

The Bible says that we can grieve Him. His heart can be wounded or saddened by the grief we have caused someone else. Let's be mindful of His presence, even when we are angry with our husband or wife, and treat Him with the respect and love He deserves. He is our eternally faithful Counselor and Friend. So before a harsh or wounding statement leaves our mouths in anger we need to ask the question, "What will this do to my Friend?"

MARRIAGE MINUTE TRUTH:

BECAUSE GOD HAS FORGIVEN ALL OUR SINS WE MUST FORGIVE OTHERS

. . . .

Primary Passage:
*Be kind and compassionate to one another, forgiving
each other, just as in Christ God forgave you.*
Ephesians 4:32

. . . .

*G*reg Laurie, speaking for a gathering of men at a Promise Keeper's rally, painted a vivid picture of the meaning of God's forgiveness. He imagined a courtroom where we are the defendants and the prosecuting attorney is Satan himself. Minute after minute, hour after hour, he reads his list of indictments against you.

The devil, in summarizing his case against you, swaggers back and forth and says, "Your Honor, based on the weight of the accumulated evidence against the defendant I demand this person be convicted, sentenced, and punished. A just Judge must convict."

The Judge looks to the defense table where you are seated alongside your Advocate, Jesus Christ. "What say you?" asks the presiding Judge. "Is your client guilty or not guilty?"

Jesus stands up and in a strong voice proclaims, "Guilty, Your Honor, on all counts." Jesus then steps up to the Judge's bench, leans over it and says, "Your Honor, Dad, I don't deny the guilt of the defendant. But You also know that I paid the penalty for this person's crimes through My death on the cross. Because I have already received the condemnation and punishment, You must acquit."

"Case dismissed," comes the reply. All of heaven cheers.

MARRIAGE MINUTE TRUTH:

GOD'S MERCY IS A
MULTIFACETED JEWEL

Primary Passage:
*Jesus continued: "There was a man who had two
sons. The younger one said to his father,
'Father, give me my share of the estate.'
So he divided his property between them."*
Luke 15:11–12

*T*he time had finally come. I walked over to my father and said, "Dad, would you come downtown with me? I'm going to buy a diamond ring." My parents looked at each other in astonishment. They knew I didn't wear diamonds, so it could mean only one thing.

"You're serious about this?" my father asked.

"Sure am," I said. So on a cold and blustery January day we trudged downtown to a family friend who was a jeweler.

"I want a really nice diamond that doesn't cost much," I told him. He looked over his half-glasses at me, a hint of consternation in his face, then nodded without saying a word. He produced a diamond that glistened, sparkled, and flashed with iridescent beauty.

God's mercy is beautiful like that diamond. It has many bright and shimmering aspects to it. Yet they all belong to the same jewel of God's merciful character. The next several days we'll learn of the many facets of God's mercy from the parable of the Prodigal Son. It's truly an "engaging" story of God's love affair with us.

MARRIAGE MINUTE TRUTH:

GOD FIRST EXERCISES PERMISSIVE MERCY IN OUR LIVES

. . . .

Primary Passage:
*Not long after that, the younger son got together all he
had, set off for a distant country and there squandered
his wealth in wild living.*
Luke 15:13

. . . .

Al was born into a preacher's home. His dad, a godly man, suffered a heart attack and died when Al was only seventeen. Embittered by the loss of his father, he chose to live the next several decades of his life in open rebellion to God.

He joined a fraternity in college and regularly drank himself under the table during weekend binges. He then signed on with the Air Force and became a fighter pilot, using his off-duty time to party with fellow officers. When he married he deliberately chose a young woman who wasn't a believer. Every major decision in Al's life was made without reference to what God might think.

Why does God allow you and me to act that way? Why does He give us permission to break His heart? Why are we given the freedom, like the Prodigal Son, to go our own way? The answer lies in the doctrine of God's permissive mercy. God's redeeming work in our lives includes His granting us permission to make our own mistakes. He knows that this will produce consequences in our lives that inevitably move us one step closer to salvation. Tomorrow we learn consequential mercy.

MARRIAGE MINUTE TRUTH:

IN HIS MERCY GOD ALLOWS US TO EXPERIENCE THE CONSEQUENCES OF SIN

Primary Passage:
After he had spent everything, there was a severe famine in that whole country, and he began to be in need. So he went and hired himself out to a citizen of that country, who sent him to his fields to feed pigs. He longed to fill his stomach with the pods that the pigs were eating, but no one gave him anything.
Luke 15:14–16

In our younger days we served two country churches in a rural area. As many times as we witnessed the pigs eating in the mud, we were never once envious of their diet. Neither of us ever said, "Honey, stop the car. That looks too good to pass up."

Yet the young man in the story of the Prodigal Son was actually envious of the "pods" the pigs were eating. He had sunk so low he was jealous of swine swill. Believe it or not that was the mercy of God at work in his life. It was a dramatic example of "consequential mercy," the mercy that allows us to experience the full weight and consequences of our foolish decisions. God knows that unless He allows us to bear the brunt of the rebellious choices we make we may never understand our need for a Savior.

Consequential mercy is not God's temper tantrum. It is His wisdom and love pushing us ever closer to the day when we will finally cry out for Jesus. If we have to hit rock bottom to see our need for God, God will allow it, in His mercy. Next we will study convicting mercy.

MARRIAGE MINUTE TRUTH:

GOD IN HIS MERCY GRANTS US CONVICTION OVER OUR SINS

. . . .

Primary Passage:
When he came to his senses, he said, "How many of my
father's hired men have food to spare, and here I am
starving to death! I will set out and go back to my father
and say to him: Father, I have sinned against heaven and
against you. I am no longer worthy to be called your son;
make me like one of your hired men."
So he got up and went to his father.
Luke 15:17–20

. . . .

A radio advertisement in our city goes something like this:
"Hi, my name is Jack. I was a forty-two-year-old stock broker,
who watched his diet, ran five miles a week, and considered myself in excellent shape. Then I heard about Heart Exam Plus, a
painless, non-intrusive test to determine the health of my heart.
Am I ever glad I did. It showed me I had significant coronary
blockage."

The young man in the story of the Prodigal Son had never
thought that there was anything wrong with his heart—until he
found himself sitting in the field of pigs. It was then the Bible says
"he came to his senses." God took a spiritual x-ray of the young
man's heart and put it up for him to see. What he found was significant heart disease, arteries clogged with greed, lust, rebellion,
and pride. God granted him "convicting mercy," the mercy that
convinces us of the reality of sin and our desperate plight. Are you
willing to take a heart exam today?

MARRIAGE MINUTE TRUTH:

JUSTIFYING MERCY
RECONCILES US TO A HOLY GOD

. . . .

Primary Passage:
But while he was still a long way off, his father saw him
and was filled with compassion for him; he ran to his son,
threw his arms around him and kissed him. The son said to
him, "Father, I have sinned against heaven and against
you. I am no longer worthy to be called your son."
Luke 15:20–21

. . . .

*T*he late black evangelist Tom Skinner was once the leader of a notorious street gang, the Harlem Lords. There he learned to take broken beer bottles and twist them in the face of opponents.

His parents knew nothing of his activities. He was even on the honor roll in high school. One evening as he was planning the largest gang war in the history of the neighborhood he happened to turn on the radio. The speaker was a pastor explaining how we can be reconciled with God through faith in Jesus Christ alone for our salvation. That evening, the knife of conviction that pierced Tom Skinner's heart was not from the Crypts or the Bloods, but from the Holy Spirit.

Justifying mercy is what the Prodigal Son experienced from his father. His father, filled with compassion, embraced him and forgave all his sins that very moment. Have you two experienced that life-changing moment? Put your faith in Christ alone for your salvation. The Father is waiting to welcome you home.

MARRIAGE MINUTE TRUTH:

ONCE WE ARE BORN AGAIN
GOD GIVES US ASSURING MERCY

Primary Passage:
But the father said to his servants, "Quick! Bring the
best robe and put it on him. Put a ring on his finger and
sandals on his feet. Bring the fattened calf and kill it.
Let's have a feast and celebrate. For this son of mine was
dead and is alive again; he was lost and is found."
Luke 15:22–24

Flavio was only in elementary school when someone first brought him to our church. His mother moved him almost every month to a new address. He was a sweet kid who had been dealt a difficult hand in life. We lost track of Flavio when we moved out of state. The next time we saw his picture it was in a magazine. He was a grown man now, standing right next to General Colin Powell at a black-tie gala in Washington, D.C. Flavio was one of ten young people nationwide to receive the "Horatio Algier Award," an award given to those who have risen to remarkable heights and overcome their past circumstances.

Looking at Flavio standing in a tuxedo, we were reminded of the Prodigal Son. Despite the young man's difficult past of despair and rebellion, his father put a robe, sandals, and a ring on the boy—symbols meant to assure him he was again part of the family. That's what "assuring mercy" is all about. God grants us the assurance that we are born again and now part of His forever family. So grab your tuxedo or your evening gown—there's reason to celebrate.

MARRIAGE MINUTE TRUTH:

GLORIFYING MERCY IS THE FINAL ACT IN GOD'S DRAMA OF SALVATION

Primary Passage:
Listen, I tell you a mystery: We will not all sleep, but we will all be changed—in a flash, in the twinkling of an eye, at the last trumpet. For the trumpet will sound, the dead will be raised imperishable, and we will be changed.
1 Corinthians 15:51–52

*J*ust before our last baby was born the women of the church held a shower for my wife. The day before the shower I insisted she go out and buy something new for the event. She came home wearing a new dress, a new hairstyle from her favorite hair dresser, and a beautiful gold necklace that sparkled in the light. Add to that the glow of a mother about to be, and she was more beautiful than I remember her on our wedding day.

The Scriptures assure us that the "clothes" our spirits are currently wearing are someday going to be changed. This body of disease and aging is going to be replaced with an indestructible, glorified body that will be like Jesus Christ Himself.

That's what the Bible refers to as glorifying mercy. The final act of God's mercy in our lives will be to exchange our old and frail body with a new and eternal one. Salvation isn't completed in our lives until even our physical body has been redeemed from the ravages of sin. What a glow we shall all have on that wonderful day to come.

MARRIAGE MINUTE TRUTH:

JESUS IS EITHER A LIAR, A LUNATIC, OR THE LORD GOD HIMSELF

. . . .

Primary Passage:
*Jesus replied, "If I glorify myself, my glory means
nothing. My Father, whom you claim as your God, is the
one who glorifies me. Though you do not know him, I
know him. If I said I did not, I would be a liar like you,
but I do know him and keep his word. Your father
Abraham rejoiced at the thought of
seeing my day; he saw it and was glad."
John 8:54–56*

. . . .

*W*ho is Jesus to you and your spouse?

In *Mere Christianity*, the great Oxford scholar, C. S. Lewis, helps us understand why we must make a definite choice about the identity of Jesus, "A man who was merely a man and said the sort of things Jesus said would not be a great moral teacher. He would either be a lunatic—on a level with the man who says he is a poached egg—or else he would be the Devil of Hell. You must make the choice. Either this man was, and is, the Son of God: or else a madman or something worse."

Ernst Renan, a French atheist, once remarked, "Jesus is in every respect unique, and nothing can be compared with him." If you believe He is who He said He is, the eternal Son of God who knows the Father intimately, then you have discovered the most important truth in the entire universe. Exalt Him as Lord of your marriage and your home. Begin this day by thanking Him for revealing His true identity to both of you.

MARRIAGE MINUTE TRUTH:

JESUS IS WHO HE SAYS HE IS

. . . .

Primary Passage:
Therefore let all Israel be assured of this: God has made
this Jesus, whom you crucified, both Lord and Christ.
Acts 2:36

. . . .

*C*aptain Scott O'Grady is an Air Force pilot who was shot down over Bosnia. For seven days O'Grady was frustrated in his attempts to make radio contact with NATO forces he knew were looking for him. One fateful evening he took a chance and stepped out into a clearing on a hill. He pointed his hand-held radio toward the sky and whispered into it, "This is Basher Five Two. Do you copy?"

There was silence for a moment, then a garbled voice crackled over the radio, "What was the nickname of the squadron you served with in Korea?"

"Juvats!" said O'Grady. (Juvats is Latin for "the Bold.") Within five hours a massive task force plucked him out of a pasture and returned him to safety. Why did his simple broadcast produce such an enormous response? It revealed his true identity.

God has revealed to us the true identity of Jesus—He is both Lord and Christ. In this Easter season of the celebration of His death and resurrection, let us affirm with all our hearts, "Jesus is the Christ!"

MARRIAGE MINUTE TRUTH:

THE RESURRECTION OF CHRIST SETTLES HIS IDENTITY

. . . .

Primary Passage:
*Then he said to Thomas, "Put your finger here; see my
hands. Reach out your hand and put it into my side.
Stop doubting and believe." Thomas said to him,
"My Lord and my God!"*
John 20:27–28

. . . .

*W*e were in high school the year the rock opera, *Jesus Christ Superstar*, was released. The musical poses a number of novel theories about the life and identity of Jesus. The main chorus repeatedly asks the question, "Jesus Christ, Superstar, do you believe who they say you are?"

The question of the true identity of Christ could forever be an open question if it were not for one irrefutable, unprecedented, and unexplainable event—His resurrection from the dead.

Thomas, who actually spent three years walking, talking, and listening to Jesus, had given up all hope when Jesus was crucified. Three days later Jesus appeared to him and invited him to touch His scars. "My Lord and My God!" Thomas cried out.

The resurrection of Christ seals His identity. He is the Son of the Living God. His resurrection power can be unleashed in your marriage to bring back from the dead the love you once knew. He can transform your tensions, arguments, and loneliness into new love and intimacy through that same power. He is risen!

MARRIAGE MINUTE TRUTH:

JESUS WAS THE SANEST MAN WHO EVER LIVED

Primary Passage:
Then Jesus entered a house, and again a crowd gathered,
so that he and his disciples were not even able to eat.
When his family heard about this, they went to take
charge of him, for they said, "He is out of his mind."
Mark 3:20–21

*E*zra Pound was an American poet who some considered to be a genius. When World War II broke out, he volunteered to make propaganda broadcasts for the Fascist government in Italy. He often read rambling poems, made disjointed statements, and ranted and raved against the British and American governments. When the war was over, he was arrested for treason. His closest American friend, Ernest Hemingway, pleaded for a pardon for Pound, saying, "He is obviously crazy."

Claims that Jesus was deluded are nothing new. Even His own family appeared at the door one day to "take charge of him, for they said, 'He is out of his mind.'" Yet God vindicated His every word when He raised Christ from the dead on Easter Sunday.

Every word He ever uttered came from God Himself. That's why we can study His teachings, follow His example, and trust His character with utmost confidence. Jesus is the sanest man who ever lived. His resurrection is proof positive. So build your marriage on His words and wisdom. You'd be crazy not to.

ALL ATTEMPTS TO EXPLAIN AWAY THE RESURRECTION FAIL

. . . .

Primary Passage:
*He [Jesus] will be handed over to the Gentiles. They will
mock him, insult him, spit on him, flog him and
kill him. On the third day he will rise again.*
Luke 18:32–33

. . . .

*N*umerous people have questioned and even ridiculed the idea of the Resurrection. The author of *The Passover Plot* suggests that Jesus swooned or fainted on the cross. He was later revived by the cool, moist air of the tomb.

Despite such novel theories that attempt to explain away the resurrection of Christ, Josh McDowell points out several key historical facts that have never been refuted.[1] Let's examine two today:

(1) Jesus predicted His resurrection. Before His death Jesus told His disciples that "They will mock him, insult him, spit on him, flog him and kill him. On the third day he will rise again" (Luke 18:32–33).

(2) Jesus suffered actual death. Numerous doctors, researchers, and pathologists who have examined the account of Jesus' death have concluded He was definitely dead when He was taken down from the cross.

Tomorrow we'll examine more irrefutable facts that make disbelieving the Resurrection more of an act of faith than believing Christ is risen.

---

1. These points and those on April 13–14 are taken from Josh McDowell, *Evidence That Demands a Verdict*, vol. 1 (San Bernadino, Calif.: Campus Crusade, 1972).

MARRIAGE MINUTE TRUTH:

ATTEMPTS TO EXPLAIN AWAY THE RESURRECTION ARE FUTILE

. . . .

Primary Passage:
"Take a guard," Pilate answered.
"Go, make the tomb as secure as you know how."
Matthew 27:65

. . . .

We continue our study of irrefutable facts of the resurrection of Jesus Christ presented by the apologist Josh McDowell.

(3) Jesus was buried. No one has suggested, not even His enemies among the Jewish hierarchy, that Jesus was never buried. The leaders went to the ruling Roman governor Pontius Pilate and pleaded that the tomb be sealed and guarded (Matthew 27:62–66). No one would ask that an empty tomb be guarded.

(4) The tomb was empty—except for the grave clothes. If the tomb of Jesus wasn't empty on Easter morning, the ruling officials would have just had to produce the body for public viewing. That would have silenced everyone.

As you can see, all the attempts to discredit the Resurrection create more problems than they solve. Explanations that are more preposterous than the original assertion should be viewed with suspicion. We worship a living Christ. He is Lord of the universe and Lord of our marriages.

Two thousand years have not produced one credible proof that Jesus did not rise in glory on Easter morning. Neither will another two thousand years. As for me and my house, we will serve the Lord until His return.

MARRIAGE MINUTE TRUTH:

NO ONE IS WILLING TO DIE FOR WHAT HE KNOWS TO BE A LIE

. . . .

Primary Passage:
After he said this, he showed them his hands and side.
The disciples were overjoyed when they saw the Lord.
John 20:20

. . . .

*W*e conclude our study of the convincing proofs of the resurrection of Jesus Christ. Despite centuries of attacks, no critic has been able to adequately explain away the following arguments:

(5) Christ's enemies never refuted His resurrection. Although the early believers were persecuted for their faith, the facts of Jesus' resurrection were never publicly protested or refuted by His enemies (Acts 5:27–31).

(6) The disciples' lives were changed. Jesus' followers were demoralized, frightened, and confused after His death. Something significant changed this group of cowering fugitives into a group of fearless evangelists. What was it? The answer is simple—they saw the risen Jesus.

Our marriages can see a radical transformation too when we meet the risen Jesus. Our sins will be forgiven, our future in heaven guaranteed, and our daily life filled with his living Presence. The key is to place our entire faith in His finished work on the Cross. We can then become irrefutable, living arguments for the resurrection of Christ.

MARRIAGE MINUTE TRUTH:

GOD CANNOT REWARD WHAT IS CONTRARY TO HIS CHARACTER

Primary Passage:
*The Lord abhors dishonest scales,
but accurate weights are his delight.*
Proverbs 11:1

We were once offered free airline tickets if we would travel under assumed names. The person who offered them to us had only good intentions. He was trying to do us a favor. But as we discussed the plan we all decided it would require a deception to work. All of us were uncomfortable with that option.

Our daily behavior comes under the full view of God. Because He is a person of ultimate character and honesty, He finds unethical and deceptive behavior offensive, even when the apparent motives are well-meaning. We cannot prosper in the long run if our prosperity is built on dishonesty and deception. God cannot reward what is contrary to His character.

It's good to do a moral audit of our own integrity from time to time. When it comes to our income tax returns, are we completely honest in reporting income? Do we avoid exaggerating our expenses? When we receive too much change at the grocery store, do we return the money or chalk it up to the clerk's own error? Do we give our employer all the time we owe him, or do we shave hours off here and there? Proverbs reminds us, "The Lord abhors dishonest scales, but accurate weights are his delight." As we weigh our own actions in light of God's character, which way does the scale tip?

MARRIAGE MINUTE TRUTH:

JESUS SPOKE THE GREATEST WORDS EVER UTTERED

. . . .

Primary Passage:
Heaven and earth will pass away,
but my words will never pass away.
Luke 21:33

. . . .

*T*hat's one small step for a man, one giant leap for mankind."
Neil Armstrong, Apollo 11, July 20, 1969.

"I shall return." General Douglas MacArthur, the Philippines, 1942.

"Mr. Gorbachev, tear down this wall." President Ronald Reagan, West Berlin, 1987.

History is filled with memorable words from heroes, warriors, poets, and martyrs. But none compare to the words of Jesus Christ.

It's vital that we as husbands and wives learn and memorize the words of Christ. When you're tired and frustrated by the demands on your life, remember, "It is more blessed to give than to receive" (Acts 20:35). When you are facing a personal crisis recall, "Do not let your hearts be troubled. Trust in God, trust also in me" (John 14:1). Or when you just don't know which way to turn, trust this promise, "And I will ask the Father, and he will give you another Counselor to be with you forever" (John 14:16).

The words of Jesus—they are the gifts that keep on giving.

MARRIAGE MINUTE TRUTH:

KNOWING JESUS IS WORTH MORE THAN ALL OUR POSSESSIONS

Primary Passage:
*I consider everything a loss compared to the surpassing
greatness of knowing Christ Jesus my Lord.*
Philippians 3:8

A book entitled *Protestants in Russia* recounts the remarkable story of Czar Alexander II. He ruled a vast empire with millions under his command. One day a young noblewoman, his cousin from Austria, visited him. She was unimpressed with his power, wealth, and opulence. "You need Jesus Christ," she plainly told him.

Sometime later Napoleon invaded Russia and burned Moscow. The event shook Alexander II to the core of his being. He eventually defeated Napoleon, but died soon after. A closed casket funeral was held in his honor in St. Petersburg.

About that same time a man appeared in Siberia named Feodor. He spent his days caring for the sick and showing Christ's love. He was later considered a saint.

In the 1930s the communist government ordered all the caskets of the czars opened to search for possible state jewelry. When they came to Alexander's casket they made a profound discovery—it was empty. Many believe that Alexander arranged his own purported death to become Feodor of Siberia. When we meet Christ, we consider everything a loss compared to the surpassing greatness of knowing Jesus.

MARRIAGE MINUTE TRUTH:

JESUS ALONE MEETS THE CRITERIA OF TRUE DIVINITY

. . . .

Primary Passage:
Jesus answered, "I am the way and the truth and the life.
No one comes to the Father except through me."
John 14:6

. . . .

In the 1970s a new guru appeared on the religious scene in America. He claimed to be the master of perfect peace and tranquillity. His credibility suffered a major blow, however, when one of his relatives revealed he was suffering from a stress-related stomach disorder. Apparently he was not as "tranquil" or "peaceful" as he had claimed.

Josh McDowell lists eight expectations we could legitimately have of someone who claimed to be God. He would:

(1) Have an unusual entrance into the world; (2) Be without sin; (3) Be able to perform supernatural miracles; (4) Have an acute sense of difference; (5) Speak the greatest words ever spoken; (6) Have a lasting and universal influence; (7) Satisfy the spiritual hunger in man; and (8) Exercise power over death.[1]

Jesus of Nazareth meets all eight criteria.

If you're looking for true tranquillity, peace, and freedom from worry, the latest New Age teacher or imported guru from the East won't be able to offer it. Only Someone who is God can show you the way, the truth, and the life. Let Jesus point you and your spouse to God and eternal life and peace. The search for the Perfect Master is over.

1. Josh McDowell, *Evidence That Demands a Verdict*, vol. 1 (San Bernardino, Calif.: Campus Crusade for Christ, 1972), 107.

THE CHURCH IS FOUNDED ON THE GREATEST QUESTION EVER ASKED

. . . .

Primary Passage:
"But what about you?" he asked. "Who do you say I
am?" Simon Peter answered, "You are the Christ, the
Son of the living God."
Matthew 16:15–16

. . . .

In the 1960s Jimmy Hendrix was considered the greatest rock guitar player in America. The story is told that at one of his concerts an excited fan shouted, "Tell us the truth, Jimmy."

He stopped the music and in dead earnest asked the crowd, "What is truth?" For several minutes there was silence in the auditorium as he waited for someone to answer his question. No one ever did. The result was tragic. Not long afterward, Jimmy Hendrix was found dead of a heroin overdose. His brilliant guitar was silenced for all eternity.

Life turns on important questions. The eternal future of all of us rests on the question Jesus asked, "Who do people say I am?" The correct answer literally determines the difference between heaven and hell for every one of us. The correct answer was given by Peter, the disciple, "You are the Christ, the Son of the living God." Ultimately, Jesus gives the correct answer to every question you have about your children, your in-laws, your finances, your sex life, your career, and every other aspect of your life.

What is the truth? Jesus. It's just that simple.

MARRIAGE MINUTE TRUTH:

BREAKING FAITH WITH EACH OTHER IS BREAKING FAITH WITH GOD

. . . .

Primary Passage:
Have we not all one Father? Did not one God create us?
Why do we profane the covenant of our fathers by
breaking faith with one another?
Malachi 2:10

. . . .

*H*e let his children grow up just above the poverty line. As the result of abandoning his family both physically and financially, his former wife had to work two jobs until she reached the point of exhaustion. He did it all so he could marry a woman with money. He divorced his wife and left his entire family with the same nonchalant attitude some of us have when we change long-distance telephone companies to get a better rate per minute.

The Bible has a word for that behavior: profanity. The prophet Malachi says, "You have profaned the promises you made to God when you broke faith with your wife and children" (*see* Malachi 2:14–16). Admittedly these are strong words. We might be tempted to dismiss them as "Old Testament law" no longer in force. We are now under grace, not law, someone might argue. True. But Jesus reaffirmed God's view of marriage as a permanent covenant in Matthew 19:6, "Therefore what God has joined together, let man not separate."

Hopefully the temptation to divorce (for reasons other than adultery or desertion by an unbelieving mate) has never entered your marriage. But if such a thought should cross your mind, just remember profanity is not always found in four letter words. It also includes a seven letter word that starts with "D."

MARRIAGE MINUTE TRUTH:

WE LOSE THE BLESSING OF GOD WHEN WE BREAK FAITH WITH HIM

Primary Passage:
*Another thing you do: You flood the Lord's altar with
tears. You weep and wail because he no longer pays
attention to your offerings or accepts them with
pleasure from your hands.*
Malachi 2:13

*H*e was one of the most effective evangelists we had ever met. God had brought him to a place of national prominence. God was using him in a powerful way to draw sinners to Himself whenever he gave an evangelistic invitation.

Then he divorced his wife. His fall from effectiveness was not immediate, but gradual, like the diminishing light of a campfire dying out after dark. He finished his life a little known, and little used, individual in the work of God. The prophet Malachi warned that it's possible to lose the blessing of God because we have broken faith with the wife of our youth. God cannot, and simply does not, bless the breaking of promises.

We believe in the doctrine of grace. We believe that God forgives us when we confess and repent of our sins. He is the God of second chances. Our salvation is secure in Him at all times under all circumstances, but our usability in God's work can suffer significant loss. This happens when we break promises, especially our marriage vows. When Satan tempts us to break faith with the spouse of our youth we need to consider the cost of our usability to God. Let's end our lives still blazing white hot in faithfulness and obedience, not flickering out in the dying ashes of foolishness and sin.

MARRIAGE MINUTE TRUTH:

WE MUST TAKE EVERY ANGRY THOUGHT CAPTIVE TO CHRIST

(PART 1)

. . . .

Primary Passage:
We demolish arguments and every pretension that sets
itself up against the knowledge of God, and we take
captive every thought to make it obedient to Christ.
2 Corinthians 10:5

. . . .

*W*hen Bob was in elementary school he was elected to the school safety crossing patrol. This elite group of sixth graders was issued white belts, long metal poles with red stop flags on the end, and shiny silver badges. Bob loved his work.

The first day out he took up his position on a street corner and waited for the first group of children to reach the crosswalk. When they did, he stepped out into the street and let down his flag. To his utter astonishment the cars stopped. He even stopped a ten-ton garbage truck that morning. Was it his age? His size? His expression? No. It was his badge. He had been given authority that stronger forces were forced to recognize.

Therein lies the answer to our anger problem. We have the authority of God's Word to "take captive every thought to make it obedient to Christ." In other words, we can challenge every angry thought with the truth of God's Word and bring it to a screeching halt.

If you are believers, God has already handed you a badge and belt and pole. Use your authority in Christ and watch who stops.

MARRIAGE MINUTE TRUTH:

WE MUST TAKE EVERY ANGRY THOUGHT CAPTIVE TO CHRIST

(PART 2)

. . . .

Primary Passage:
*We demolish arguments and every pretension that sets
itself up against the knowledge of God, and we take
captive every thought to make it obedient to Christ.*
2 Corinthians 10:5

. . . .

I can't stand the way he just sits there and watches television. Why did I ever marry him in the first place?"

"If I never speak to her again it will be too soon."

Many destructively angry thoughts can go through our minds about our spouses in any given day. If we stop and dwell on them long enough, eventually our emotions will catch fire. Once they do, they burn with bitterness, malice, and hate. It's only a short step from sinful attitudes to sinful words and deeds. The answer is to take each angry thought captive to Christ. How?

Let's say the thought goes through your mind: *I really resent the way my wife talks to me. Just once I'd like to say something that would shut her up for good.* That thought isn't from God. It oozes with resentment and revenge. Take it captive by quoting Ephesians 4:31, "Get rid of all bitterness, rage and anger, brawling and slander, along with every form of malice." Once you do that, the hateful thought is rendered powerless. You've taken it captive. Try it today. It really works.

MARRIAGE MINUTE TRUTH:

JOB LOSS IS AN OPPORTUNITY TO LOVE YOUR SPOUSE THROUGH A CRISIS

Primary Passage:
*A friend loves at all times, and a
brother is born for adversity.*
Proverbs 17:17

A friend of ours was sitting at his desk when he received a memo. The chief executive was ordering large scale cutbacks in budget expenditures in his department. *My job goes next*, he thought. It didn't take long for our friend, Jim, to discover his instincts were right. Unfortunately, the same budget knife used to slash jobs also gouged a wound on his self-image.

The time may come in your marriage when one of you faces an unexpected job loss. For a husband in particular, this can be one of the worst crises of your entire life. If it is your spouse who has lost the job, knowing how to respond to your mate's self-esteem crisis is important for two reasons. First, it's an opportunity to encourage the person you love through one of life's most difficult experiences. Second, thoughtful and sensitive words can help restore dignity and, more important, hope.

The Bible teaches that a friend loves at all times and a brother is born for adversity. That friend or brother is you. It's a moment that you were born for as your spouse's closest confidante and encourager. Don't miss this opportunity to love your spouse through one of the most difficult periods of life.

MARRIAGE MINUTE TRUTH:

WE NEED TO STRESS OUR SPOUSE'S VALUE APART FROM HIS OR HER CAREER

Primary Passage:
A man of many companions may come to ruin, but there
is a friend who sticks closer than a brother.
Proverbs 18:24

I remember the day. October twenty-first. They called me in and told me they didn't need me anymore." Bill choked back emotion as he told his story to a group of men at a seminar. "Up until then I had lived for the company. I thought my life was over that very moment."

It's easy for us all to forget that our value as people and the ways in which we earn our livings are distinct from each other. God calls us to work in order to serve Him and provide for our needs and the needs of others. To put it succinctly, we should work to live, not live to work. In this volatile and changing economy very few positions are secure any longer. Statistics say it's quite likely that one or both of you may involuntarily lose your job in the course of your career. How you respond to each other in that moment of crisis may affect the rest of your married life.

The message we need to send to our spouses is this: Jobs may come and go, but their value to us as people will never end. We will believe in them come what may. That's what Proverbs is referring to when it describes a friend who sticks closer than a brother. Or to paraphrase it slightly, "There is a spouse who sticks closer to you than anyone else on earth—it's me."

MARRIAGE MINUTE TRUTH:

WE SHOULD LEARN TO
PLAY THROUGH OUR PAIN

. . . .

Primary Passage:
*I press on toward the goal to win the prize for which
God has called me heavenward in Christ Jesus.*
Philippians 3:14

. . . .

*Y*ears ago a church we served announced it was going to hold a birthday party for Cheryl. It was a thoughtful gesture, but she really didn't feel much like going to it. She sincerely loved the people, but she found it difficult to think of celebrating in the midst of a church crisis.

At the time several people did not agree with the church board over an issue involving the church's future. Feelings were running high on both sides. It seemed somewhat artificial for her to try to act happy at a party when she knew there would be people there who weren't speaking to each other.

Nonetheless she went and was glad she did. She chose to play through her pain.

Even if we are experiencing marital or family pain it's important to continue loving and serving each other, our children, and our friends. It's part of pressing on toward the high goal of Christ Jesus. It's setting aside feelings and circumstances to act on principle in a way that glorifies God. It's not always easy, but it's doing the right thing. And the right thing, in the long run, will always bring the right result.

MARRIAGE MINUTE TRUTH:

MATURITY IS ALLOWING WISDOM TO RULE OVER IMPULSES

Primary Passage:
*All of us who are mature should take such a view of
things. And if on some point you think differently,
that too God will make clear to you.*
Philippians 3:15

*Y*ears ago we knew an usher who reprimanded young children so severely that children were frightened of him. One of our boys even named him Robo Cop.

It was tempting to get angry at Robo Cop for his angry behavior. But what would that have solved? Instead we sensed the Holy Spirit was leading us in a different direction. After we talked the issue through with our children, they decided to bake him a cake.

We stood back and watched with great interest as our small children presented Robo Cop with his gift the next Sunday. His gruff, unyielding stare seemed to melt on the spot. We never saw him lose his temper with the small children again.

It's hard, sometimes very hard, to choose a mature response when our impulses are running high. But how will immature people ever grow up if they don't see what grown-up behavior looks like from us?

In what areas of our lives do we need to grow up? How can we begin to respond to each other in mature and loving ways? If Robo Cop can change, so can we.

MARRIAGE MINUTE TRUTH:

THE GRACE WE SHOW OTHERS CAN RADICALLY CHANGE THEIR LIVES

Primary Passage:
*But by the grace of God I am what I am, and his
grace to me was not without effect.*
1 Corinthians 15:10

*W*e once visited a family who had quit attending our church years before we arrived. It was a difficult night. For hours they rehearsed every hurt and slight they had ever experienced (or imagined they had experienced). Bitterness and anger seemed to ooze from the sofa pillows. Their hurts had become their identity.

A few months later the husband died of a sudden heart attack. The whole church body reached out to the widow with love and compassion. At the funeral we invited the widow to come back to the church. The invitation carried an element of risk. If she returned still carrying her bitterness, it could plant a root of such negative feelings in the congregation.

To make a long story short, grace did a miraculous work in her life. The love and acceptance she experienced from others seemed to melt away her bitterness and acrimony.

God doesn't treat us according to our sins but according to His mercy. His grace is extended to us when we don't deserve it. Can you show that same grace to others? To each other? It can create radical changes in the hearts of others. Think of what it has done in your own life—then give it away.

MARRIAGE MINUTE TRUTH:

WRATH IS TOO DANGEROUS FOR HUMANS TO USE ON EACH OTHER

. . . .

Primary Passage:
My dear brothers, take note of this: Everyone should be
quick to listen, slow to speak and slow to become angry,
for man's anger does not bring about the
righteous life that God desires.
James 1:19–20

. . . .

Destructive anger is an emotional rage response characterized by a desire to shame, punish, or gain control over people or circumstances. This definition helps us understand why James can say, "For man's anger does not bring about the righteous life that God desires." So what's the problem with man's anger? Here's a short list of the destructive things it can do in our marriages:

It leads us to do and say irrational things.

It opens the door to hatred and violence.

It leaves a deep wound in the hearts of our mates.

It sets up a painful cycle of shame among generations.

It creates fear and strangles love.

It becomes an addictive substitute for the power of the Holy Spirit working in our lives.

It robs God of His right to work true justice.

Man's anger or wrath is simply too radioactive for us to use. One biblical commentator notes that the New Testament never gives us the permission to turn our wrath on someone else. That prerogative belongs to God alone. Let's leave wrath where it belongs, with an all-knowing, all-just, and all-merciful God.

MARRIAGE MINUTE TRUTH:

CONFESSION IS THE FIRST STEP TO FREEDOM FROM ANGER

Primary Passage:
*Therefore, get rid of all moral filth and the
evil that is so prevalent.*
James 1:21

All throughout our region are remnants of the Underground Railroad that operated nearly 140 years ago. There are barns with secret cellars, houses with tunnels that lead to remote areas, and old farmhouses with false walls and ceilings. Runaway slaves, driven on by the desire of freedom, followed this celebrated road to the shores of the Great Lakes, and then over the border to Canada.

God has provided a road to freedom that each of us can travel to leave enslavement and bondage to our anger. It begins with a desire to "repent" or "get rid of all moral filth" in our lives. That's exactly how God views our destructive anger from a spiritual perspective. It's like a leaky sewer system in the basement of our soul. The problem needs to be cleaned out, not perfumed or hidden.

That involves confession of our sin to God, others, and ourselves. We have to quit pretending it isn't there and confess it before our Lord, our families, and those we've hurt. Confession is simply agreeing with God that we've done wrong.

Once we've agreed with God about the nature of our offenses, we ask His forgiveness. When we've done that, the matter is settled. We're pardoned. We're washed. We're free from the interruption in our fellowship with God that our sin caused.

God doesn't want us to "manage" our moral filth; He wants us to get rid of it. No plumber "supervises" sewage; he drains it away once and for all.

MARRIAGE MINUTE TRUTH:

WHEN YOU CAN'T CHANGE YOUR PAIN, YOU CAN CHANGE YOUR PERSPECTIVE

Primary Passage:
*Consider it pure joy, my brothers, whenever
you face trials of many kinds . . .*
James 1:2

We remember the day it rained in our kitchen. "Dad, come quick," our daughter yelled. "There's water pouring from the ceiling." Pipes from our upstairs bathtub had separated and were draining down into the cupboards. Men may be slow coming to the dinner table during a football game, but when the ceiling rains—we drop everything. Our hearing dramatically improves.

Although we are never commanded to pray for trials to come, we are told to pray about the trials that come to us. We are to ask God to give us wisdom. Sometimes what we need is wisdom to believe that He is at work in our lives through our painful circumstances. James tells us God is teaching dependence, humility, and perseverance.

The day will come, as it did in our lives, when the water quits dripping from the ceiling. What remains are the life-changing lessons we learned while we were getting wet. If you're like us, you'd prefer dry ceilings as well as a deep character, but God knows sometimes they just don't go together.

MARRIAGE MINUTE TRUTH:

WE HAVE ONLY TWO CHOICES IN LIFE: TO QUIT OR GO ON

. . . .

Primary Passage:
*. . . because you know that the testing of your
faith develops perseverance. Perseverance must finish
its work so that you may be mature and complete,
not lacking anything.*
James 1:3–4

. . . .

Joseph Stowell writes that near the end of the 1800s an ambitious plan was announced to dig a canal through Egypt that would join the Red Sea with the Mediterranean Sea. A French sculptor named Bartholdi had a vision to build a great monument at the end of the Suez Canal that would embody the ideals of liberty, freedom, and democracy. After ten years of intense efforts, his plan was rejected.

You may identify with some of Bartholdi's frustration and disappointment in your own life. You've saved for years for a better house, but you still can't afford one. You worked hard for a promotion, but it went to someone else. You have prayed for the salvation of someone you love, but that person still shows no interest in the things of God.

We really have only two options in such painful circumstances. One is to give up. Just quit. Risk ending up bitter and cynical. The other is to keep going. Keep praying. Keep believing. That's called perseverance. It deepens your character, quiets your pride, and frees your spirit.

Years after Bartholdi first proposed his monument, the French government chose his sculpture as a gift to send to America. It's called the Statue of Liberty—a monument to perseverance.

MARRIAGE MINUTE TRUTH:

GOD CAN STABILIZE OUR LIVES WITH HIS GENEROUS WISDOM

. . . .

Primary Passage:
If any of you lacks wisdom, he should ask God,
who gives generously to all without finding fault,
and it will be given to him.
James 1:5

. . . .

*T*homas Gray said, "Since sorrow never comes too late, and happiness too swiftly flies . . . where ignorance is bliss, 'tis folly to be wise." God's Word would argue with the poet's philosophy of life. It's not folly for us to be wise, particularly in facing an uncertain future. Then, more than ever, we need the stabilizing and calming effect of God's wisdom at work in our lives.

What issues are you facing as a couple? Are you uncertain about how long your job will last? Are you worried one of your children is seriously ill? Are you concerned that unresolved issues between you might just end the relationship? God invites you to ask Him for wisdom. Not just a bite-size portion, but a huge 747-size quantity of wisdom. It's yours if you ask. And when you ask you can be certain God won't be irritated with you. He's generous in His desire to give you wisdom. All He expects from us is that we listen when He speaks and not doubt Him. Why should He tell us anything if we won't believe Him?

MARRIAGE MINUTE TRUTH:

DOUBTS LEAVE US LOST IN A FOG OF CONFUSION IN OUR LIVES

. . . .

Primary Passage:
But when he asks, he must believe and not doubt,
because he who doubts is like a wave of the sea,
blown and tossed by the wind.
James 1:6

. . . .

In the early 1800s the British general Wellington attacked the French dictator, Napoleon Bonaparte, at a little known village in Belgium called Waterloo. The future of England literally hung in the balance as the pitched battle raged across the English Channel.

When it was over, the news was sent by signal lights, "Wellington defeated Napoleon at Waterloo." But fog rolled in across the English countryside. All that the anxious British citizens could make out was, "Wellington defeated . . ." That partial message created near hysteria in the English countryside.

Doubt is much like a fog that corrupts what God is saying to us. When we fail to trust Christ in our moment of crisis, we end up getting the wrong message. Frustration, worry, and even panic seize our soul.

Maybe you've prayed for an answer to a particular problem in your home or marriage. God answers. But then doubt and fear roll in. The solution is to doubt your doubts and trust your answers. God doesn't intend for any of us to live in a fog.

MARRIAGE MINUTE TRUTH:

DOUBT DESTABILIZES
OUR LIFE AND MARRIAGE

Primary Passage:
*That man should not think he will receive anything
from the Lord; he is a double-minded man,
unstable in all he does.*
James 1:7–8

My first serious attempt at sailing was in New England. My son and I signed up to take a small two-man sailing craft out for the afternoon on a beautiful lake in New Hampshire.

The trouble began even before we could climb on board. The wind would gust up and the main sail would come whipping around like a horizontal guillotine. Once we finally were on board, a contrary wind came up and sent us sailing straight ahead—right at several boats moored in the bay. We had to abandon ship to prevent ramming another vessel broadside.

James could have been describing us that day: "He is a double-minded man, unstable in all he does" (James 1:8).

Is your life or marriage characterized by indecisiveness, confusion, and instability? Do you have trouble making a decision then following through? Are you always in one crisis or another? Then perhaps doubt is the culprit in your lives. If so, confess before God that you have doubted His leading and direction. Ask Him to give you a second chance to listen, trust, and obey. It may be just the start to clear sailing.

MARRIAGE MINUTE TRUTH:

EVEN WHEN WE FEEL ALL ALONE WE ARE NOT ALONE

Primary Passage:
*They put gall in my food and gave me
vinegar for my thirst.*
Psalm 69:21

I vividly remember the day our high school debate team won the state championship. It was a moment that I worked more than five years to achieve. As a senior and captain of the team, this was the crowning moment of my long years of preparation. Unexpectedly the debate coach pulled me aside and said, "Bob, I've decided to have you sit out today. I think we have a better chance of winning with two other team members."

I was too stunned to reply. The other two team members did win all their rounds and we were awarded the state trophy. But for me it was a bittersweet triumph. Like David I felt, "They put gall in my food and gave me vinegar for my thirst." (Christ actually experienced this on the cross.)

Why does God allow such bitter moments in our lives? Why doesn't He protect us from those soul-crushing disappointments?

There's no simple answer to that question. Yet in those hours of deep disappointment we gain a fresh awareness of our need for God. I know I did. Not long after that painful experience I rededicated my life to Christ. Don't waste your pain. Let it drive you back to God.

MARRIAGE MINUTE TRUTH:

JUST BECAUSE WE EXPERIENCE FAILURE DOESN'T MEAN WE ARE FAILURES

Primary Passage:
During the days of Jesus' life on earth, he offered up prayers and petitions with loud cries and tears to the one who could save him from death, and he was heard because of his reverent submission. Although he was a son, he learned obedience from what he suffered.
Hebrews 5:7–8

Perhaps the most efficient means of ruining a person's character is to grant him an unbroken string of successes. It's a short journey from uninterrupted achievement and conquest to pride, arrogance, and insensitivity toward others.

If we are willing to stop and examine some of the benefits of failure in our lives, it can take on an entirely new meaning. The Bible says that Jesus, although the Son of God, yet "learned obedience from what he suffered."

Jesus was no failure, yet He lived with scorn, misunderstanding, and rejection. God was at work in the life of Jesus teaching Him perfect obedience. Augustine wrote, "God wants to give us something, but He cannot. Our hands are full and there is nowhere to put anything."

Failure has a way of emptying our hands so God can fill them with what He desires for us. Bring your failures to Christ today, whether in your finances, your career, or your relationships. Allow God to fill your hands with His presence and goodness.

WE ARE MOST VULNERABLE WHEN WE BELIEVE WE ARE INVINCIBLE

Primary Passage:
Pride goes before destruction,
a haughty spirit before a fall.
Proverbs 16:18

*P*rior to World War II the French government boasted that it had constructed an invincible line of defense against future attack. The Maginot Line, as it was called, was a series of concrete bunkers and reinforced gun emplacements that created a supposedly impenetrable barrier between France and Germany. Yet in May 1940, the German armies brought France to its knees in a mere forty days. How? They simply went around the so-called "invincible" line and attacked France through Belgium.

We are on dangerous ground if we believe we, or our marriage, are somehow invincible or beyond failure. Once pride and arrogance gain a foothold in our lives they can blind us to our weaknesses, infirmities, and vulnerability to temptation.

The only reliable defense against such dangers is a spirit of humility. Humility isn't the conviction that we are worthless, stupid, or weak. It's the recognition that life is temporary, no fame or achievement lasts forever, and we need God.

Humility is properly placed confidence. God is our all in all, isn't He?

MARRIAGE MINUTE TRUTH:

FAILURE CAN BECOME
THE MIDWIFE TO HUMILITY

Primary Passage:
When pride comes, then comes disgrace,
but with humility comes wisdom.
Proverbs 11:2

*M*ichael Jordan, billed the world's greatest athlete in the 1980s and 1990s, retired the first time from basketball to enter the world of professional baseball. What happened next was painful for everyone to watch.

He dropped fly balls, struck out numerous times, and even referred to the umpire as the "referee." He was sent to the minor leagues and batted .200 all season long. Perhaps he pursued the possibility of becoming a baseball star in part to fulfill a dream his recently deceased father had carried for him. Despite his nearly superhuman athletic ability and talents, his dismal performance on the baseball diamond earned him the title Error Jordan. Eventually Michael Jordan returned to basketball. He learned that even with noble motives, we all have limits to our abilities. Although the experience was no doubt painful, it afforded him new wisdom and humility to stay with what he did best.

If we allow failure to do its good work in our lives, we will take our embarrassments, setbacks, even fiascoes and let them teach us the value of modesty, caution, and preparation.

Humility comes before honor because it makes us aware of our need for others and God in order to succeed. So don't spend the rest of your life reliving your failures. Learn from them and go on in the confidence that God gives grace to the humble.

MARRIAGE MINUTE TRUTH:

FAILURE CAN EQUIP YOU TO COMFORT OTHERS

Primary Passage:
Praise be to the God and Father of our Lord Jesus
Christ, the Father of compassion and the God of all
comfort, who comforts us in all our troubles, so that we
can comfort those in any trouble with the comfort we
ourselves have received from God.
2 Corinthians 1:3–4

*W*e once experienced the pain and indignity of Bob's being laid off from a job. We went through all the typical emotions associated with that experience—grief, anger, and confusion. Yet because of the love and support of others, we made the transition successfully.

Not long after our own downsizing experience we met an individual who had just lost his job. We didn't try to offer him simple clichés or easy answers to his dilemma. Instead we simply offered him the assurance that we cared about him as a person and would pray for his situation. We could see a faint look of hope and gratitude awaken in his eyes as we shook hands and parted ways. We would not have known what to say to him just three years earlier. But failure had given us insight and empathy.

Failure can equip you to comfort others with the comfort you received from God. You can in turn use that same comfort to touch another life. It's a victorious cycle of love.

MARRIAGE MINUTE TRUTH:

PRAYER PREVENTS THE BOTTOM FROM DROPPING OUT OF SOMEONE'S LIFE

Primary Passage:
*He has delivered us from such a deadly peril, and he
will deliver us . . . as you help us by your prayers.*
2 Corinthians 1:10–11

*F*ormer President Richard Nixon was driven from office in disgrace by the Watergate scandal in 1974. Years later Nixon read in the newspaper that Robert MacFarlan, a former top aide to President Reagan, had attempted suicide in the aftermath of a political scandal. President Nixon immediately drove to the hospital where MacFarlan was recovering and spent more than an hour with the despondent aide in his room. Nixon told the man that he knew what it was like to be caught up in a public scandal and suffer humiliation. He encouraged MacFarlan to believe that all was not lost and life was still worth living.

Hopefully our own troubles and disappointments will spur us on to intervene in the life of others. The Bible tells us that the most effective encouragement we can offer is prayer. God delivers people from the dead, as He did in Paul's case (2 Corinthians 1:9), when we fervently pray for them. Ask God to bring someone to mind today who is close to giving up. Then, you and your spouse bring him or her before God in fervent prayer. If you've been through a similar situation, you know just how to pray.

Do it today. Someone's life may be hanging in the balance.

MARRIAGE MINUTE TRUTH:

CHARACTER AND HOPE
ARE THE FRUIT OF SUFFERING

. . . .

Primary Passage:
*Not only so, but we also rejoice in our sufferings, because
we know that suffering produces perseverance;
perseverance, character; and character, hope.*
Romans 5:3–4

. . . .

*B*ob grew up in a neighborhood where he was in the religious minority. He and his brother were harassed, ridiculed, even beaten up at times. On one occasion the neighborhood kids who lived behind him came across the back fence and tore apart a simple fort he and his brother had constructed. They then carried it back to their yard and set it on fire.

Growing up in that setting was often painful and difficult for him. But God did something more important *in* him than He allowed to be done *to* him. Bob learned to believe that God could be trusted even in dangerous circumstances. Those lessons served us well when we accepted a church in the inner city.

On one occasion we were forced to call the police as two drunken men attempted to beat down the door of the church. Another time Bob narrowly escaped harm when three drug addicts broke into the church office. God had taught him earlier in life that suffering can produce perseverance; perseverance, character; and character, hope. When we most needed those traits to survive, God in His mercy had already put them in place.

MARRIAGE MINUTE TRUTH:

WE CAN SOMETIMES SUCCEED BECAUSE OF OUR FAILURES

Primary Passage:
*So then, those who suffer according to God's will
should commit themselves to their faithful
Creator and continue to do good.*
1 Peter 4:19

*H*is mother died when he was just nine. As a young adult he entered into a business venture in which he lost everything. The woman he deeply loved refused to marry him. The woman he did marry suffered from serious bouts of mental illness. Two of their children died at an early age.

He ran numerous times for public office and lost virtually every election. Though he endured a lifetime of setbacks, heartaches, and defeats, he finally won an election. His name was Abraham Lincoln, the sixteenth president of the United States. His courage, grace, and nobility of character were shaped by his years of suffering and sorrows. Perhaps a fitting summary of his life might have been "He succeeded because of his failures."

You, too, can succeed because of your failures.

If you find yourself in the midst of suffering today, the Bible says to commit yourself to your faithful Creator and continue to do good. God is in control of your trials and difficulties. God is going to use you, and when He does, it will make a critical difference in the lives of people, perhaps even a nation.

MARRIAGE MINUTE TRUTH:

RECEIVING INSULTS CAN BE A SOURCE OF SPIRITUAL ENCOURAGEMENT

. . . .

Primary Passage:
If you are insulted because of the name of Christ, you are blessed, for the Spirit of glory and of God rests on you.
1 Peter 4:14

. . . .

John Wesley, the founder of Methodism, nearly perished as a young boy when his father's parsonage was set on fire by an angry parishioner. When he later became a famous outdoor preacher, he was frequently pelted with stones, raw vegetables, and even bricks. He once recorded in his journal how fortunate he felt to have only been assaulted one time that day.

The Scriptures teach us that if we are insulted because of the name of Christ we are blessed, because it is a sure sign God's Spirit rests on us.

We need to remember that the spiritual battles we encounter are proof that we belong to God. "Satan doesn't bother with those that are already his," a wise father used to tell his children.

It's true. The problems and adversities of life demonstrate that our lives are making a difference for Christ. The attempts to discourage us as a couple or household from following Jesus are clear evidence we're on the right track.

Do you need assurance that you belong to Jesus? Being insulted for Jesus' sake is a great indication you belong to God.

MARRIAGE MINUTE TRUTH:

IT IS SPIRITUALLY IMPOSSIBLE TO GET AWAY WITH SIN

Primary Passage:
*For a man's ways are in full view of the Lord,
and he examines all his paths.*
Proverbs 5:21

*O*ne of the most famous Russian novels of all time, *Crime and Punishment*, poses the question, "Is there such a thing as the perfect crime?" The central figure in the novel is so clever in committing a murder and covering his tracks that no one ever suspects him of the crime.

As the novel progresses his conscience begins to wear upon him. He knows that underneath his successful facade he deserves none of it. Driven by torment and guilt he chooses at last to publicly confess his crime. Then an even worse fate befalls him—no one believes him. He cannot gain absolution because no one accepts his guilt. The perfect crime has led to the perfect punishment.

The Bible teaches clearly that there is no such thing as the perfect sin. Those caught up in flirtation, fantasizing, using pornography, pursuing emotional involvement, or even physical intimacy with someone they aren't married to often believe they can get away with it. It will be their little secret. Remember, if no one on earth sees or knows what you do, God does. Take it as a matter of promise, His punishment will be as perfect as the deception itself.

MARRIAGE MINUTE TRUTH:

REPENTANCE IS FAR SWEETER THAN REVENGE

. . . .

Primary Passage:
*Do not take revenge, my friends, but leave room for
God's wrath, for it is written: "It is mine to avenge;
I will repay," says the Lord. On the contrary: "If
your enemy is hungry, feed him; if he is thirsty,
give him something to drink. In doing this,
you will heap burning coals on his head."*
Romans 12:19–20

. . . .

*W*e listened to a television interview one evening with the author of the book *Sweet Revenge*. Her premise was that there is something terribly satisfying about taking revenge on the people who have hurt us. She urged viewers to taste and see the sweetness of vindictiveness.

The Bible offers a very different view on getting even. A paraphrase of Romans 12:19–20 might read, "Revenge. Don't do it. Leave it to God. He's the only One who will get even when the time is right. For the time being do the very opposite of what your carnal instincts cry out for. If your worst enemy is in need, do everything in your power to care for him or her. In doing so you'll pierce the person's heart with conviction."

Showing kindness to those who have wronged us gives God's Spirit a chance to do a convicting work in their hearts. It causes them to look for a basket to dump burning coals into to carry on their heads (a symbol of deep repentance in the ancient Middle East). The best revenge is no revenge at all; it is genuine repentance.

MARRIAGE MINUTE TRUTH:

HUMILITY AND GOD'S WORD COMBINED CAN FREE YOUR ANGER

. . . .

Primary Passage:
Humbly accept the word planted in you,
which can save you.
James 1:21

. . . .

*S*everal years ago our family visited a zoo that had recently added an outdoor habitat for lions. The architect had constructed a clear Plexiglas wall that allowed visitors to come face-to-face with the lion king.

Our little children pressed their noses hard against the glass wall and giggled at the lion. He meandered over in their direction and then, without warning, stood up and hurled himself against the glass. The monstrous carnivore looked down at them and snarled. They screamed but stood their ground. The invisible Plexiglas wall prevented the lion from taking one step further.

When we are tempted with sinful anger, we can call on God to give us a wall of protection. It descends when we humble ourselves before God and turn the situation over to Him. When we take our angry thoughts captive to His Word, our enemy is prevented from taking another step toward us. He may snarl, even roar, but he cannot go a step further without God's permission. He is reduced to a helpless caged animal that can do nothing to harm us.

Humility and God's Word—your best protection against a roaring lion that seeks to devour you.

MARRIAGE MINUTE TRUTH:

EFFECTIVE PRAYER IS PRIVATE, CONCISE, AND SINCERE

Primary Passage:
*And when you pray, do not keep on babbling like
pagans, for they think they will be heard because of their
many words. Do not be like them, for your Father knows
what you need before you ask him.*
Matthew 6:7–8

*T*he great evangelist D. L. Moody once sat listening as a man prayed on, and on, and on. It was obvious the gentlemen was trying to impress everyone with his piety and eloquence. Finally Moody jumped to his feet and said, "Why don't we sing a hymn while this brother finishes his prayer?"

Jesus warns us in Matthew chapter six not to make a show of our prayers. Prayer is meant to be concise. Often a simple "God, help us" is all that is needed. The wonderful thing is He knows our needs even before we ask.

We need to spend time in prayer with our spouses every day. Together we should spend considerable time in praising Him, confessing our sins, thanking Him for His goodness, and asking Him for our needs. God wants to hear all about it. But He wants our prayers to be characterized by simplicity and humility, trusting that He already knows our needs. He's waiting to hear from you right now.

MARRIAGE MINUTE TRUTH:

IF WE PRAY THE WAY JESUS PRAYED, WE'LL GET THE ANSWERS JESUS GOT

Primary Passage:
This, then, is how you should pray . . .
Matthew 6:9

*T*eaching our children the skill of casting for fish has been fun, though a little dangerous at times. On one occasion one of them released his thumb on the reel just a little early. The steel lure shot backward like a cruise missile out of control. It just missed several of us and ended up dangling from a tree.

Jesus taught His disciples an even more useful skill—the skill of prayer. He was trying to teach them more than mere words to repeat. He was trying to instill in them the right heart attitude of prayer. If they could learn to pray as He did, they could expect to receive the same answers He did.

Can you think of some aspect of your life, or marriage, or family that needs the kind of answers Jesus got when He prayed? In the next few days we are going to study the Lord's Prayer and learn to pray the way Jesus prayed. You and your spouse can learn a skill that can shake the very foundations of heaven and earth. Are you ready? "This, then, is how you should pray."

MARRIAGE MINUTE TRUTH:

HONORING GOD SHOULD BE OUR FIRST PRIORITY IN LIFE

Primary Passage:
Our Father in heaven, hallowed be your name . . .
Matthew 6:9

*B*illy Graham is one of the twentieth century's most remarkable figures. He has preached to literally hundreds of millions of people, and his ministry has taken him into virtually every nation on earth.

What has been the secret of his amazing success? One writer speculates it is his eyes. They generate a charisma people can't resist, he suggests.

The more likely explanation of why God has used Billy Graham is found in the prayer Jesus taught His disciples to pray. It's found in Matthew chapter six. It begins with, "Our Father in heaven, hallowed be your name." There's Billy Graham's secret. He chose to honor Jesus Christ first and foremost in his life. His one and only goal has been to "hallow" or "honor" the Heavenly Father.

Is that the first priority of your marriage? Is bringing glory to God the reason you get up each morning, go to work, wash dishes, pay bills, raise kids, and serve in the church? If so, you can expect God to honor your life just as He has Billy Graham's, though perhaps in different ways. Why not start each morning with the simple prayer, "Our Father in heaven, hallowed be your name . . ." God honors those who honor Him.

MARRIAGE MINUTE TRUTH:

WE EXPERIENCE SOMETHING OF HEAVEN WHEN WE DO GOD'S WILL

Primary Passage:
*. . . your kingdom come, your will be done
on earth as it is in heaven.*
Matthew 6:10

*J*oni Eareckson Tada is confined to a wheelchair. She tells the story of sitting in front of a mirror in a public restroom when an Asian woman in a beautiful silk dress came over to her.

"How have you been able to accept your suffering?" the woman asked. The Cambodian woman went on to explain that she had lost her entire family to the Khmer Rouge and Pol Pot reign of terror in the 1970s. Only she had survived the Killing Fields.

"I can't explain why this has happened to me," replied Joni. "I only know that Jesus is the answer to the questions I can't answer." Such unplanned, dramatic spiritual encounters are not unusual for Joni Eareckson Tada. Perhaps more than any believer in our society today, God has given her a forum to touch physically broken and disillusioned lives.

Would you as a couple like God to use you to touch other hurting lives? Would you enjoy being His instruments to encourage people who are close to giving up? Then begin by sincerely and earnestly praying, "May Your will be done on earth as it is in heaven." God takes such prayer seriously. He will bring people into your lives that need Him. They too can then discover that heaven intersects earth when we pray.

MARRIAGE MINUTE TRUTH:

GOD DELIGHTS IN
GIVING US WHAT WE NEED

Primary Passage:
Give us today our daily bread.
Matthew 6:11

*G*eorge Mueller was a German believer who opened his heart to the thousands of orphans and homeless children in nineteenth-century England. His life and work are most noted for His faith in God's provision. On one particular morning the cook walked up to George Mueller and said, "We have nothing to feed the children. Should we send them back to their rooms?"

"No," insisted Mueller. "Have them sit down with bowls and spoons in front of them. We are going to have breakfast." Mueller prayed with thanks for the food they were about to eat, despite the fact all the bowls on the table were empty. Before his prayer was finished there was a knock at the door. A frustrated milkman stood on the front stoop. "I've broken my cart," he explained. "I can't get the milk to town. Do you have any use for it?"

We all face needs every day. There are groceries to buy, utilities to pay, cars to keep serviced. Beyond that there are clothes to buy, doctors to visit, and college to pay for. God knows all our needs. Yet He still asks us to bring them before Him and ask for His daily provision. Is it because He's forgetful and needs a gentle reminder? No. He wants us to remember each and every day that He's the source of all we have. He delights in giving us our daily bread. Even when our cupboards are empty He's ready to serve us breakfast.

MARRIAGE MINUTE TRUTH:

FORGIVING OTHERS SETS US FREE

. . . .

Primary Passage:
Forgive us our debts, as we also have forgiven our debtors.
Matthew 6:12

. . . .

Christian Reader magazine tells the fascinating story of a young Army Air Corp corporal named Jacob DeShazer. On April 18, 1942, he and eighty other young airmen took off from the flight deck of the U.S.S. Hornet. Their ultrasecret objective was nothing less than Japan itself. Jimmy Doolittle was in command.

The raid was successful, yet all of the sixteen crews were forced to bail out over China or Russia. DeShazer was later captured. For the next three-and-a-half years he was subjected to torture, filthy conditions, and threatened execution. During this ordeal he discovered his need for Jesus Christ. He also discovered that Jesus taught he should forgive his enemies. By faith, DeShazer chose to do just that. When the war was over he returned to Japan to preach the gospel and start churches.

You may have people in your life you find difficult to forgive. They may have hurt you deeply. Jesus tells you to release them from the moral debt they owe you. God will deal with their unrepentant sin, but if you are to be free, you must forgive. As Jacob DeShazer learned, when you forgive another person someone goes free—you.

MARRIAGE MINUTE TRUTH:

WE SHOULD PRAY TO AVOID TEMPTATION BEFORE IT ARRIVES

Primary Passage:
And lead us not into temptation . . .
Matthew 6:13a

*Y*ears ago an FBI undercover operation was aimed at rooting out corruption at the highest levels of government—in this case the United States Senate. Undercover agents, posing as wealthy oil sheiks, set up meetings with various senators and attempted to bribe them.

In one memorable secretly recorded video clip, they offered a senator a substantial sum in return for his influence. Once the senator realized what they were suggesting, he got up and stormed out of the meeting. There, on videotape, was a living example of a man unwilling to enter into temptation.

Jesus taught us to pray to do the same—avoid even entering into temptation. In your marriage you face temptations every day: to harbor resentment, to be critical of your spouse, or to be attracted to someone other than your spouse. The time and place to begin dealing with those temptations is not when you are neck deep into the allurement. No, the time to begin dealing with temptation is before it ever arrives. It's like putting your car in the garage before it rains or setting aside money for your taxes before April fifteenth. Together, in prayer, the two of you can help arm each other to win the battle before it's ever fought. That's a smart strategy.

MARRIAGE MINUTE TRUTH:

PRAYER IS OUR MOST POTENT WEAPON AGAINST THE DEVIL

Primary Passage:
But deliver us from the evil one . . .
Matthew 6:13b

*T*he devil laughs at our work but trembles when we pray," wrote S. D. Gordon, one of the great Christian devotional writers of the last century. When we pray as a couple we are entering into the throne room of God Almighty. And when we ask Him to deliver us from the snares and plans of the devil, He answers with power and might.

Is Satan disrupting the harmony between the two of you? Then you need to pray—together—for God to throw him out of your relationship. Is our enemy causing you to miss your time together in God's Word? You need to pray—together—for God to prevent those untimely interruptions and crises. Is one of your teenagers heading out on a rebellion trip? You need to pray—together—that the powers that would bind your son or daughter would be bound themselves.

Jesus Himself prayed to find refuge and deliverance from the assaults of the Evil One. We have been given the marvelous privilege of using prayer to protect our marriage and home. The same God who delivered Jesus from the Evil One will deliver us. It's His promise.

MARRIAGE MINUTE TRUTH:

FORGIVENESS IS FOR OUR BENEFIT, NOT JUST THAT OF THE ONE WHO SINNED

Primary Passage:
For if you forgive men when they sin against you,
your heavenly Father will also forgive you. But
if you do not forgive men their sins, your
Father will not forgive your sins.
Matthew 6:14–15

*L*eadership Journal tells the story of two brothers in Belgium in the 1300s who both wanted the throne for themselves. Raynald had his brother Crassus arrested and imprisoned to prevent him from seizing the kingship of the medieval kingdom.

Raynald constructed a prison with open doors and windows. There was just one catch. His brother would have to lose a significant amount of weight to go free. Every day Raynald sent a sumptuous meal (fit for a king, no doubt) to his brother's prison cell. Crassus, unable to control his appetites, gorged himself and remained a prisoner.

Unforgiveness is a tempting, alluring banquet table of what appears to be sweet delights—malice, gossip, rage, revenge, and hatred. But the price of unforgiveness is high—we remain a prisoner of our own making. That's why Jesus urges us to forgive when people sin against us. It's for our sake, not just theirs. The doors and windows are open. Will you forgive and go free?

MARRIAGE MINUTE TRUTH:

THERE IS ALWAYS A WAY OUT OF OUR ANGER

. . . .

Primary Passage:
*But when you are tempted, he will also provide a way
out so that you can stand up under it.*
1 Corinthians 10:13

. . . .

*I*t was Christmas Eve day. Our family had gotten up bright and early to pack for the long trip home to celebrate with friends and relatives.

We first noticed that something was wrong when we stepped out the front door. Running across the entire length of our windshield was a long, ugly, twisted crack. Someone during the night had taken a screwdriver and hammer and smashed the glass.

Why? What had we done to anyone to deserve this? And where could we find a garage open? We were tempted to anger at that moment, real anger. Someone had violated our car and our holiday.

Yet that morning someone seemed to whisper, "There is an alternative to upset and anger. Just trust God with this situation. Take the trip with the broken windshield. It will turn out just fine."

For some reason we listened. We loaded the car, drove the four hundred miles without incident, and enjoyed the holidays. When we returned, we were delighted to learn the insurance company would pay all the damages. There is always an alternative to bitter anger—always. The question is, "Will we take it?"

MARRIAGE MINUTE TRUTH:

WE CANNOT BE TRUSTED WITH DESTRUCTIVE ANGER

. . . .

Primary Passage:
In your anger do not sin.
Ephesians 4:26a

. . . .

*Y*ears ago people could purchase fireworks in practically any state. Firecrackers, M-80s, Cherry Bombs, a wide assortment of explosives were available.

Since those days most state legislatures have outlawed all but the most impotent fireworks. Tiny sparklers, little tanks that buzz across the driveway, and innocuous candles that give innocuous puffs of smoke are all that's left. Why? Legislators recognized that high explosives in the hands of the common person didn't make sense.

Scripture teaches us the same thing about the dangers of anger. In highly concentrated doses it becomes a lethal weapon in the hands of people. That's why God specifically warns us, "In your anger, do not sin."

How can we be certain that in our anger we do not sin? We need to unwrap our angry emotions and look for gunpowder. The book of Ephesians offers a list of criteria to keep anger from crossing over into sin: we don't let the sun go down on our anger; the devil is not given a foothold; it involves no unwholesome talk; it builds others up; it does not grieve the Holy Spirit; it is free of rage, slander, or brawling; and, even if it is accompanied by intense emotion, it is ultimately guided by a sense of kindness and compassion toward the person we are angry with.

If your anger is free of flammable explosives then it's probably right to be angry. If not, stand back, and get away. You're in danger and so is everyone around you.

MARRIAGE MINUTE TRUTH:

THERE IS NO EXCUSE GOD OR OTHERS WILL ACCEPT FOR ADULTERY

Primary Passage:
*Men do not despise a thief if he steals to satisfy his
hunger when he is starving. Yet if he is caught, he must
pay sevenfold, though it costs him all the wealth of his
house. But a man who commits adultery lacks judgment;
whoever does so destroys himself.*
Proverbs 6:30–32

*I*t made national news when the mayor of a community in the eastern United States was arrested for bank robbery. Seized with remorse, he called the bank and tried to return the money. It was too late. He was arrested and charged with a federal crime. Community leaders could only shake their heads and ask, "How could a mayor commit such a stupid crime?" The same question could be asked of spouses who commit adultery. The Scriptures say they lack judgment, a polite way of saying, "Given how much you already have, how could you do something so stupid?"

Why is an affair so foolish? We steal something we already possess. If we're married we have access to sexual satisfaction and gratification. It isn't like the thief who steals bread because he's starving to death. Another reason adultery doesn't make sense is the exorbitant price we pay. It costs us all we have to get something we can't possibly keep.

Thinking mayors don't rob banks. Thinking spouses don't rob partners. It's that simple.

MARRIAGE MINUTE TRUTH:

PRIDE CAN ENTER
OUR HEARTS UNDETECTED

Primary Passage:
*The Lord detests all the proud of heart. Be sure
of this: They will not go unpunished.*
Proverbs 16:5

A water softener salesman once paid a visit to our home and asked if he could draw a small vial of water from our tap. After he had done so, he added a chemical that caused all the hidden minerals to suddenly appear. It came as quite a shock. Instead of drinking the pure water we assumed had been coming from our tap, it looked more like we were sipping on the leftovers of a chemistry experiment.

Pride can be well hidden in our lives as well. As a couple, examine your lives for trace elements of pride. These questions might be helpful: Do you believe that the home you own, the cars you drive, and the careers you enjoy are the result of your own efforts, skills, and intelligence? Could you get along just fine for days at a time without talking to God or spending time in His Word? Do you find yourself faultfinding with others, particularly your spouse or children?

If so, pride may have entered your heart undetected. Now is the time to confess that pride before God and let Him empty your life of it. If you ask God to show you where pride exists, you may be certain that He'll answer you. The sooner the better.

MARRIAGE MINUTE TRUTH:

IT IS DANGEROUS TO
DEVELOP A TOLERANCE FOR SIN

. . . .

Primary Passage:
*He did what was right in the eyes of the Lord, just as his
father Amaziah had done. The high places, however, were
not removed; the people continued to offer sacrifices
and burn incense there.*
2 Kings 15:3–4

. . . .

*O*ver the years we have detected a subtle trend at work among Christian families. Years ago most families either did not go to movies at all or would allow their children to view nothing more than G-rated films or videos, PG in some cases. Over time bracket creep set in, and soon PG films, and PG-13 in some cases, became the acceptable norm. Now it's common to hear families discussing the latest R-rated video they rented.

We are both opponents of legalism when it comes to the Christian life. It's all too easy to invent man-made standards of righteousness that always leave us looking good. Yet we are profoundly concerned that the moral decline taking place in our culture is being mirrored in the church. Because the church is usually two or three steps behind the secular trends, we rest in a certain smugness that we're holding the line, even though our "morality" is based more on being a little better than cultural norms than it is on God's unchanging Word.

In the days of Israel, godly and good kings reigned. Yet each seemed to have developed a tolerance for certain sins. Have we grown accustomed to certain sins? Sin is still sin whether we're comfortable with it or not. God gives only one option when it comes to sin—get rid of it.

MARRIAGE MINUTE TRUTH:

WE WERE CREATED
FOR MARRIAGE NOT DIVORCE

Primary Passage:
*They asked, "Is it lawful for a man to divorce his wife
for any and every reason?" "Haven't you read," he
replied, "that at the beginning the Creator
'made them male and female.'"*
Matthew 19:3–4

*R*uth Bell Graham, the wife of Billy Graham, was asked if she had ever considered divorcing her husband. She thought for a moment, then with a wry grin answered, "Divorce? No. Murder? Yes."

Her humorous response underscored an important biblical truth: God created us for marriage, not divorce. Jesus was challenged in His day by nit-picking spiritual leaders in search of loopholes to lifelong marriage vows. Rather than discuss the technicalities, He stepped back and drew a picture as bold and panoramic as Creation itself. "Haven't you read," he replied, "that at the beginning the Creator made them male and female?"

Marriage is an act of creation. It's the skillful, imaginative, and loving artistry of God given as a gift to men and women.

Your marriage has the fingerprints of the Creator God upon it. Treasure and defend it for the magnificent work of art it truly is. The word divorce shouldn't even be in your vocabulary (even when you're joking).

MARRIAGE MINUTE TRUTH:

EVERY MARRIAGE NEEDS THE REFRESHMENT OF RE-CREATION

. . . .

Primary Passage:
I will refresh the weary and satisfy the faint.
Jeremiah 31:25

. . . .

*D*uring World War II Bob's father was a pilot in Italy. After several dangerous and exhausting missions, he was given an unexpected gift. He was given a three-day leave on the beautiful Isle of Capri in the Mediterranean Sea.

All of us need refreshment and breaks from the daily demands of our lives. No one can continue a constant cadence of work, taking care of kids, managing a budget, responding to minor or major crises, and keeping a marriage going without risking exhaustion.

The scriptural remedy is refreshment, or what we could call re-creation. How can we find re-creation in our marriage? Follow Willard Harley's advice to schedule five to fifteen hours a week to be alone with each other. Listen to music after the children have gone to bed, get a baby-sitter one night a week for a date night, or take a thirty-minute walk through your neighborhood each evening.

God wants to refresh the two of you. So spend time in unhurried prayer and Bible study together at least three times a week. Rest in His presence. It will re-create your life and marriage.

MARRIAGE MINUTE TRUTH:

A GODLY HOME HAS A LIFETIME INFLUENCE

. . . .

Primary Passage:
*Train a child in the way he should go
and when he is old he will not turn from it.*
Proverbs 22:6

. . . .

*C*heryl grew up in a pastor's home. She has enduring memories of the Sunday school contests that took place between various churches in her denomination. Large rallies would take place on a district level to select the outstanding Sunday school superintendent in that area.

Competition would become so fierce for the coveted award that on one occasion a shoving match broke out on the school playground between rival Sunday schools. It's hard to imagine that level of interest and commitment to Sunday school today, and shoving matches were certainly not what Sunday school teachers encouraged even then, yet it may be time for us as parents to re-evaluate the goals we are setting before our children.

Have soccer or other athletic pursuits for our children replaced church attendance and involvement in youth activities? Is it more important to us that our children achieve academically than that they excel in knowing the Word of God? Are we more concerned that our kids have the latest designer wear than that they learn what it means to clothed with the righteousness of Christ?

God used Cheryl's home and upbringing to call her to full-time Christian service by the time she was eleven years old. God can use you to influence your children toward serving Christ for a lifetime, if that is your priority as well. Train them in the way they should go, and the Word of God promises that your influence will not be lost decades from now.

MARRIAGE MINUTE TRUTH:

THE BLOOD OF CHRIST IS THE ANSWER TO OUR GUILT

. . . .

Primary Passage:
*If we claim to be without sin, we deceive ourselves
and the truth is not in us. If we confess our sins, he is
faithful and just and will forgive us our sins and
purify us from all unrighteousness.*
1 John 1:8–9

. . . .

*P*astor, I have something very difficult to say. My fiancé and I are pregnant. We never intended this to happen. We are both so ashamed. Will you still marry us?"

The moment we hear such a confession we know that this couple is facing more pain, confusion, and despair than most of us can imagine in a lifetime. It is not only pregnant couples who find themselves struggling with damaging emotions and paralyzing guilt. Those who have progressed to a point just short of full sexual intercourse also carry the heavy burdens of sexual sin.

What hope do we offer to a couple in such pain? It's the blood of Christ. What our regret, self-hatred, or tearful penance can never accomplish, the marvelous life-giving blood of Christ can do with perfection. If we are willing to confess our sin before God and put our faith in Christ's finished work on the Cross, we can be washed, cleaned, and set free. The old hymn assures us, "There is a fountain filled with blood, drawn from Immanuel's veins, and sinners plunged beneath that flood, lose all their guilty stains." Dip into it today and discover true freedom from your guilt.

MARRIAGE MINUTE TRUTH:

RESPECT IS THE GLUE OF EVERY MEANINGFUL RELATIONSHIP

. . . .

Primary Passage:
*Husbands, in the same way be considerate as you live
with your wives, and treat them with respect as the
weaker partner and as heirs with you of the gracious gift
of life, so that nothing will hinder your prayers.*
1 Peter 3:7
And the wife must respect her husband.
Ephesians 5:33

. . . .

*J*ames Dobson claims that respect is the glue of all human relationships. Without it, love will wither and die. That's why the Scriptures are so clear when it comes to husbands and wives. Both are commanded to respect the other.

Peter tells husbands to be considerate of their wives and treat them with respect for several reasons. One reason is the greater physical strength most husbands possess. It would be cowardly and unmanly to use physical stature to intimidate a woman. Another is the common gift of salvation a husband and wife enjoy. Finally, God won't listen to our prayers if we're mistreating our wives.

Why should wives show respect to their husbands? It's how men feel loved. When a wife respects and admires her husband, she brings out the very best in that man. It is the highest compliment a wife can pay her husband. Respect is a two-way street. Learn to travel on it for a lifetime.

MARRIAGE MINUTE TRUTH:

RESPECT IS A WILLINGNESS TO HONOR AND VALUE ANOTHER PERSON

. . . .

Primary Passage:
Show proper respect to everyone: Love the brotherhood
of believers, fear God, honor the king.
1 Peter 2:17

. . . .

*T*he first American casualty in the Vietnam War occurred in the 1950s. Before the war ended many more had perished. Respect is always the first casualty in a prolonged conflict between a husband and wife. It can die the first day one spouse or the other refuses to honor and value his or her mate. It may be as subtle as refusing to show common courtesy when the couple is out together in public. It may be as blatant as adultery.

Disrespect has no place in a healthy marriage. The two of you need to face the issue, wherever or whenever it surfaces, and repent of it. Not tomorrow, not the next day, right now.

How can you deal with disrespect when it arises in your marriage? First, grant each other permission to express the feelings of being treated with disrespect when it occurs. Next, don't argue with your spouse's feelings. If the person has felt disrespected, acknowledge it. Finally, apologize and take steps to restore the "line of respect" that every healthy marriage maintains. Rodney Dangerfield has made a living insisting, "I get no respect." Why not build a marriage by insisting that both of you do, each and every day?

MARRIAGE MINUTE TRUTH:

WE MUST ALLOW NO EVIL TO DWELL IN OUR HOMES

. . . .

Primary Passage:
*If you devote your heart to him and stretch out your
hands to him, if you put away the sin that is in
your hand and allow no evil to dwell in your tent,
then you will lift up your face without shame;
you will stand firm and without fear.*
Job 11:13–15

. . . .

*S*haron was tired of Adam's temper tantrums. She was fed up with his tirades against the children over simple infractions. Most of all she was exhausted by playing the role of the accommodating victim in the marriage. Her answer? She went out and found a boyfriend, then ordered her husband out of the house.

Some in our society would cheer for Sharon. They would say she at last found the "strength" to end her abusive relationship and discovered the love she so richly deserves.

God would say Sharon made the wrong choice. Although she was absolutely correct in drawing a line with Adam's abusive behavior, her decision to end the marriage by committing adultery was wrong. It will only add further pain and confusion to her life.

The writer of Job tells us that we are "to allow no evil to dwell in [our] tent." Abusive behavior is an evil that must be confronted. If you need help doing that, seek out a pastor or Christian counselor. But don't fight evil with evil by using adultery as a weapon. It's a lose-lose situation for everyone.

MARRIAGE MINUTE TRUTH:

PASSIVE CHRISTIANITY IS NOT BIBLICAL CHRISTIANITY

. . . .

Primary Passage:
*Love must be sincere. Hate what is evil; cling to what
is good. Be devoted to one another in brotherly love.
Honor one another above yourselves.*
Romans 12:9–10

. . . .

*L*et's not talk about this; let's talk about something else." That simple sentence is one of the most devastating and damaging remarks that can be uttered in a marriage. The refusal to discuss difficult and painful issues virtually guarantees the marriage will slip into a passive, catatonic state, and love itself will enter into an emotional coma.

We are not advocates of arguing, bickering, and fighting. That too can drain the love and intimacy out of a relationship. We are advocates of facing issues head on, however. We have found the only way out of a problem is through it, to paraphrase Ralph Waldo Emerson.

The New Testament regularly gives believers active commands such as "Hate what is evil; cling to what is good. Be devoted. . . ." This isn't armchair advice. It demands that we get up out of our passive postures and take the risk of become active problem solvers.

When's the best time to begin solving your issues? You guessed it. Right now.

MARRIAGE MINUTE TRUTH:

ROMANCE IS AVAILABLE TO EVERY COUPLE

Primary Passage:
*Like an apple tree among the trees of the forest is
my lover among the young men. I delight to sit
in his shade, and his fruit is sweet to my taste.*
Song of Songs 2:3

One summer afternoon we were introduced to a romance novelist for a popular secular publishing house. It's her job to create myths and fantasies that will allow her female audience to escape into a world of romance, infatuation, and sexual exhilaration.

It's a sad reality that so many women have to use an "escape" of extended fantasy to experience the feelings of romance. We'd like to suggest that married couples can experience romance without the need for fiction writers of tawdry plots. The essential ingredients are surprise, mystery, privacy, imagination, and receptivity.

For example, could you surprise your spouse some morning by leaving a series of enigmatic notes around the house? Each mysterious clue would lead to another. Each would be for your spouse's eyes only. The final clue would leave a phone number that the person would call to receive a message intended only for him or her.

Silly? Perhaps. But didn't you experience just a slight tingle of romance as you read it? Solomon's wife said she delighted "to sit in the shade" of her lover. Romance is not so much a formula as it is an attitude of the heart. Why not write your own novel? You only need to sell one copy for it to be a best-seller.

MARRIAGE MINUTE TRUTH:

TO BE MARRIED TO THE RIGHT PERSON YOU MUST BE THE RIGHT PERSON

Primary Passage:
Love is patient, love is kind. It does not envy,
it does not boast, it is not proud.
1 Corinthians 13:4

"How can I know if I'm married to the right person?" the caller asked the radio host. "And what if I did marry the wrong person? Doesn't that mean I can get out of my marriage because I wasn't in God's will?" You could hear in his voice a desperate search for an excuse, any excuse, to justify leaving his wife.

We waited to hear if the host would ask him the right question, "Are you the right person to be married to?" You see, we all have little, if any, control over the behavior, character, and thinking of our spouse. But we do possess enormous control over our own lives.

A happy and fulfilling marriage doesn't start with changing our spouse's behavior. It begins when we start to model the love God calls us to: "Love is patient, love is kind, it does not envy, it does not boast, it is not proud." It's amazing what patience, kindness, and humility can do to transform a marriage.

When we begin to model the traits we desire to see in our spouse, it slowly but surely begins to call out those same virtues in the other person. Would you like to be married to the right person? You now know who to begin with.

MARRIAGE MINUTE TRUTH:

OUR MARRIAGE IS GOD'S PROPERTY, NOT OUR OWN

Primary Passage:
Has not the Lord made them one?
In flesh and spirit they are his.
Malachi 2:15a

The states of New York and New Jersey engaged in a lawsuit to decide who owns most of Ellis Island, the historic point of entry for millions of immigrants in New York harbor. When the island was first developed, it was no larger than four acres and was deeded to New York. The surrounding bay area was given to New Jersey. Over the years, as soil was carried out by barge, the island expanded to twenty-four acres. Both states claimed that the additional property belonged to them, and they spent millions of dollars fighting it out.

Property disputes can be nasty and costly. When it comes to our marriages the matter of who owns the relationship is settled by Scripture: God does. Malachi, the Hebrew prophet, speaking of marriage and divorce, says, "Has not the Lord made them one? In flesh and spirit they are his." We deceive ourselves when we believe marriage vows can be dissolved at will. That's assuming a level of ownership that God never grants. He created our marriage. He performed the miracle of taking two people and making them one. He witnessed our vows and solemnized them. Who are we to seize property we have no claim to? Our marriage certificates should say at the bottom: "Property of the Most High God."

MARRIAGE MINUTE TRUTH:

DIVORCE IS AN ACT OF SPIRITUAL VIOLENCE

. . . .

Primary Passage:
"I hate divorce," says the Lord God of Israel, "and I hate
a man's covering himself with violence as well as with his
garment," says the Lord Almighty.
Malachi 2:16

. . . .

*T*he helicopter recorded the entire incident on videotape. A vehicle loaded with illegal aliens was attempting to outrun the police. A high speed chase ensued. When the truck was finally forced off the road, officers quickly surrounded it. The police yanked open the doors and pulled out the occupants (who showed little or no resistance to arrest). Then inexplicably the police began to beat the occupants with their night sticks. Charges were later filed against the officers for unnecessary use of force.

If we were able to watch divorce proceedings from God's point of view, we would often see spiritual violence being carried out in the courtroom. In so many cases, for no apparent valid reason, one partner chooses to attack the marriage covenant and beat it mercilessly. Often the other spouse, the victim of such spiritual violence, has no recourse other than to hire an attorney and fight back to protect him- or herself from being completely destroyed.

What does God think of such a scene? "I hate divorce," He says in straightforward language. "I also hate violence," He adds. Is there a connection between the two? Watching the video of the beating death of a marriage should answer the question.

MARRIAGE MINUTE TRUTH:

BE CAREFUL OF SPLIT SCHEDULES AND MULTIPLE JOBS

. . . .

Primary Passage:
Because so many people were coming and going that
they did not even have a chance to eat, he said to them,
"Come with me by yourselves to a quiet
place and get some rest."
Mark 6:31

. . . .

*J*im worked two jobs. During the day he was a repairman; at night he was a security guard. Meanwhile Janet took care of the kids all day and then worked the night shift as a dispatcher at the police station. They kept up this relentless schedule for several years until the predictable finally happened—their marriage crashed and burned.

They should have seen it coming. For years they had run red lights, living a lifestyle of exhaustion, fatigue, routine, boredom, and stress. Add to all this the fact they never saw each other because of their split schedules. They made one unwise decision after another.

More and more couples are living this type of marginless lifestyle. Although the two of you may be able to make it work for a year, two years, or even longer, the day will come when it all collapses. Everything you've worked so hard to acquire will be lost to both of you.

Jesus has a better plan for your marriage than complete exhaustion and collapse. He was the one who said to His disciples, "Come with me by yourselves to a quiet place and get some rest."

MARRIAGE MINUTE TRUTH:

JESUS IS OUR ULTIMATE REST

. . . .

Primary Passage:
Come to me, all you who are weary and
burdened, and I will give you rest.
Matthew 11:28

. . . .

*I*t had been a long and grueling twenty-four hours. Our high school youth group had marched with full backpacks through the scorching heat and barren wasteland of the Great Sand Dunes National Monument near Alamosa, Colorado. Three students had collapsed from dehydration and had to be evacuated to safety.

The last few miles of the march were the worst. Students hobbled along with socks turned red from their bleeding blisters. Others used makeshift walking sticks to steady themselves. As the group straggled into the base camp we looked like the remnants of a routed army—tired, wounded, and discouraged.

We climbed onto the waiting bus and collapsed in exhaustion. An hour later we sat up and rubbed our eyes in astonishment. Right in front of us was a huge municipal swimming pool filled with ice green sparkling water. Within minutes we were splashing, laughing, and drinking in the refreshment of this wonderful oasis of renewal.

Has your marriage been a desert experience lately? Jesus said, "Come to me, all you who are weary and burdened, and I will give you rest."

MARRIAGE MINUTE TRUTH:

HIS STRENGTH IS PERFECT
WHEN OUR STRENGTH IS GONE

Primary Passage:
He gives strength to the weary and increases
the power of the weak.
Isaiah 40:29

The Rose Bowl Parade is one of America's most enduring New Year's Day traditions. Things were going well in the parade one year when suddenly the entire entourage came to a screeching halt. Walkie-talkies crackled with anger and exasperation. Why had the parade stopped? The answer was as embarrassing as it was unexpected. The Amoco Float, sponsored by one of the world's largest producers of petroleum, had run out of gas.

Even the most fuel-rich marriages can run out of gas. It happens when we don't pay attention to our physical, spiritual, and emotional gauges. If we don't get enough sleep, fatigue little by little begins to make us impatient with each other. If we don't keep short accounts with each other, sarcasm soon enters our conversations. If we don't take the time to pray together daily, it's only a matter of time until our joy evaporates.

How can a couple refill their tanks when they find they're running on empty? It begins by reconnecting with God. We need to confess our busyness, unforgiveness, and prayerlessness. We need to invite Him to once again make His strength perfect in our weakness.

That type of spiritual honesty gets the parade moving again.

MARRIAGE MINUTE TRUTH:

YOU MUST CHOOSE WHO YOU AND YOUR HOUSE WILL SERVE

Primary Passage:
But as for me and my household,
we will serve the Lord.
Joshua 24:15

The Kennedy family has been known for serving politics. The Hearst family gained its reputation for serving journalism. The Trump family has become famous for serving legalized gambling.

What about your family? Who would people say your family serves? One way to answer that question is to do an audit of your checkbook, calendar, and friends. Where is your money going? What events get first priority in your discretionary time? What does your choice of friends tell about your values?

Joshua looked the nation of Israel square in the eye and asked, "Whom are you going to serve?" He knew that the land was filled with false gods and idols. He knew it was one short step between living among corrupt deities and actually worshiping them. Their only defense would be a strong, decisive choice to serve God and Him alone.

Today is our anniversary. The day we were married our wedding announcements read, "But as for me and my household, we will serve the Lord." Let us encourage you today to make your family be known for serving Christ first and foremost. It is the one choice in life we can promise that you will never live to regret.

MARRIAGE MINUTE TRUTH:

LISTENING IS SHOWING
LOVE TO ANOTHER PERSON

Primary Passage:
He who answers before listening—
that is his folly and his shame.
Proverbs 18:13

*M*en and women have trouble understanding each other. That's no news to any of us who have been married for more than twenty-four hours. Men usually tell their problems in a search for answers and solutions. Women often discuss their problems in an attempt to establish sympathy and understanding.

Unfortunately we don't often understand the subtleties of this difference. So husbands think they're being helpful when they offer solutions to help "fix" their wives' problems. "The baby woke you up crying at 3:00 A.M. again last night? Have you tried feeding her a lactose-free formula?"

Women, on the other hand, think they have done their husbands a great favor when they offer sympathy, "Your boss blamed you for the dip in sales? Why don't you just lie down here and I'll give you a back rub."

Everyone means well. But what's really needed is the ability to listen to each other. Listening to your husband means helping him analyze his issues, sort out his options, and make good choices. Listening to your wife means accepting her feelings, helping her label her emotions, and offering her the support and nurture she needs to weather the storm.

Are you listening?

MARRIAGE MINUTE TRUTH:

SHARED VALUES WILL HELP
YOU WEATHER STORMS TOGETHER

Primary Passage:
Where you go I will go, and where you stay I will stay.
Your people will be my people and your God my God.
Ruth 1:16

A tornado tore through our inner-city neighborhood the first summer we lived there. It demolished billboards and turned sedans into convertibles as fallen signs took the roofs off cars. Despite the fact that numerous homes were destroyed in outlying suburbs, our turn-of-the-century neighborhood sustained only minor damage.

It wasn't a difference in wind velocity. The same tornado that tore through several other communities touched down in ours. The meteorologists concluded the essential difference was in the quality of construction. Our older neighborhood had been built with heavy, reinforced foundations and ceilings. The newer neighborhoods had been constructed with light, prefabricated materials. One community stood firm while the other collapsed like a house of cards.

Shared values in a marriage are like reinforced foundations and ceilings. They can allow us to weather incredible adversity and storms yet emerge intact. Build faith, monogamy, trust, forgiveness, and love into your values base. They won't protect you from a storm, but they'll prevent your basement from being filled with the upstairs when the strong winds blow.

MARRIAGE MINUTE TRUTH:

PRAYING TOGETHER ALLOWS YOU TO SHARE YOUR HEARTS WITH EACH OTHER

Primary Passage:
*But the angel said to him: "Do not be afraid, Zechariah;
your prayer has been heard. Your wife Elizabeth will bear
you a son, and you are to give him the name John."*
Luke 1:13

The deepest point in the Pacific Ocean is known as the Marianas Trench. It is a place of mystery, wonder, and awe. Yet very few of us will ever visit or experience this remote region.

The same is true of prayer. A life of prayer with your spouse can allow you to plumb the depths of your relationship far beyond what most people ever experience. You can enter into a world of spiritual reality and power that very few venture into or explore.

Zechariah and Elizabeth must have had a remarkable life of prayer. Though they were past the childbearing years, the angel told Zechariah, "Your prayer has been heard. Your wife Elizabeth will bear you a son."

If it has been a long time since you've experienced a moment in which the heavenly Father seems incredibly near to you, seek God together in prayer. Plumb the depths of your souls together before Him. Pour out your hearts and needs before His throne. It will bring a depth to your relationship that will open a new world to you.

MARRIAGE MINUTE TRUTH:

THE HEART OF A FATHER NEEDS TO STAY TURNED TO HIS CHILDREN

. . . .

Primary Passage:
He will turn the hearts of the fathers to their children,
and the hearts of the children to their fathers; or else I
will come and strike the land with a curse.
Malachi 4:6

. . . .

*A*t first it looked like just another phone message left on Bob's desk. "Your son called," the secretary had jotted down. "He wants to know when you're coming home."

As a busy pastor Bob sometimes received numerous notes on any given day. But this day he took a second look at the message. It hit him hard. "Yes, when are you going home?" the Holy Spirit seemed to ask him.

He leaned back in his chair and thought of the many days and nights he had given to the church. There had been more than one occasion when he had gotten home just before midnight.

"He's your son. He needs you. He needs you just as much as anyone else does in your congregation," the inner voice seemed to say. God wasn't asking him to abandon his duties and responsibilities to our congregation. Instead, the Holy Spirit was reminding him that our five children have only one father on earth. His heart needs to stay turned toward them in a special way.

Bob kept that note in his desk for a long time. Fathers, if you're not there already, when are you going home?

MARRIAGE MINUTE TRUTH:

AN ABSENT FATHER CANNOT BRING UP HIS CHILDREN IN THE FEAR OF GOD

Primary Passage:
*Fathers, do not exasperate your children; instead, bring
them up in the training and instruction of the Lord.*
Ephesians 6:4

*U*nfortunately our society seems to reward father absence. The highly competitive workplace often promotes the man who puts in unending hours at the office. The media frequently exalts the young, single, virile male whose only attachments in life are to adventure, conquest, and self-indulgence. The sports world consistently glorifies the athlete who gives his all to the team, even if he's away from his family for weeks at a time.

If our assessment seems a bit harsh or overstated, ask yourselves, "When was the last time we saw a nationally televised event to hand out awards to the nation's best fathers?" We never see men receiving gold Oscars for sitting up all night with a sick child, going camping with their teenage sons, or teaching their first-grade daughter how to ride a bicycle.

Men, will you become countercultural and pass up the allurement of promotions, awards, and trophies to win the ultimate prize—watching your children grow up in the fear and training of the Lord? It's a high calling with no excused absences.

MARRIAGE MINUTE TRUTH:

FATHERS TEACHING THEIR CHILDREN IS A LIFE AND DEATH MATTER

Primary Passage:
These commandments that I give you today are to be upon your hearts. Impress them on your children. Talk about them when you sit at home and when you walk along the road, when you lie down and when you get up.
Deuteronomy 6:6–7

Our church once hosted a community gang awareness seminar. The police officer speaking at the event held up a T-shirt that said "RIP Lucky."

"This T-shirt was retrieved from the grave site of a seventeen-year-old boy in our local cemetery," he explained. "It's standard gang ritual to come to the grave of one of their fallen members on the one-year anniversary of their death. They leave a T-shirt just like this one to honor their memory."

It was hard not to miss the irony of the moment. Here was a seventeen-year-old boy gunned down in the springtime of his life, and he had been given the street name "Lucky." There's a deeper irony here, also. Gangs often function as pseudo-families for lonely young people, as visitation of the grave demonstrates. The officer explained that it is virtually impossible for gangs to recruit a young man whose parents are heavily involved in his life.

The Scriptures teach that we are to spend significant time with our children. We are to teach them the commandments and statutes of the Lord. There is simply no substitute for involved fathers impressing spiritual truth on the hearts of their kids.

Will your children end up fortunate or lucky? It's up to you.

MARRIAGE MINUTE TRUTH:

ACCEPT YOUR SPOUSE
JUST AS HE OR SHE IS

Primary Passage:
*Accept one another, then, just as Christ accepted
you, in order to bring praise to God.*
Romans 15:7

It was one of the most remarkable medical recoveries we had ever witnessed.

A young man, no older than twenty-five, had contracted a rare virus that had destroyed the lining of his heart. After days of anxious waiting came the good news—a donor heart had been found. The complex operation took hours to perform. The wait was on to see whether his body would accept or reject his new heart. Three weeks after the surgery the young man sat smiling in a pew on a Sunday morning. He was told he could expect to live a normal lifespan.

What a difference a new heart can make. How fatal rejection can become. The same is true of our marriages. Rejection causes so much heartache in marriages. One spouse rejects the other because of annoying behaviors, appearance, lack of education, weight, family background, or something else.

Yet God's Word tells us we are to accept one another as Christ has accepted us. If any of these signs of rejection are present, then perhaps your marriage has heart problems. It may even be time for a transplant. Tomorrow we look at the definite signs of a rejecting heart.

MARRIAGE MINUTE TRUTH:

THERE ARE SEVERAL SIGNS OF A REJECTING HEART IN MARRIAGE

. . . .

Primary Passage:
Therefore let us stop passing judgment on one another.
Instead, make up your mind not to put any stumbling
block or obstacle in your brother's way.
Romans 14:13

. . . .

*T*he two sat and glared at each other. She was angry at him for his lack of ambition in life. He was fed up with her critical attitude toward him. They had both come to the conclusion that their marriage was over.

The real problem, however, was not his small paycheck or her biting tongue. An even deeper problem was at work—both had failed to accept each other. Signs of a rejecting heart include trying to change your spouse, living with perpetual regret over marrying the other person, and acting with a spirit of criticism and sarcasm that permeates the relationship.

Many couples get hung up on the idea that acceptance equals tolerating every irritable or hurtful behavior. It does not. Biblical acceptance is a willingness to receive, value, and honor another person with unconditional love while reserving the right to reject certain behaviors. Let's deal with the real problem—acceptance. It's time to reject rejection once and for all.

MARRIAGE MINUTE TRUTH:

WE NEED TO VALUE OUR SPOUSES FOR THE GIFTS THEY ARE

. . . .

Primary Passage:
*Again, the kingdom of heaven is like a merchant looking
for fine pearls. When he found one of great value, he went
away and sold everything he had and bought it.*
Matthew 13:45–46

. . . .

*T*he love affair between Joy Davidson and C. S. Lewis is one of the remarkable romance stories of this century. The two met when Joy, who was an American, began reading to her sons the books that C. S. Lewis, a scholar at Oxford, had written for children.

Eventually Joy Davidson asked C. S. Lewis if he would marry her to make her eligible for British citizenship. Lewis agreed, and after a civil ceremony the two went their separate ways. Davidson discovered she had cancer, and, in the process, she and C. S. Lewis also fell in love. They were married in a Christian ceremony in her hospital room. For the remainder of their brief marriage they experienced a depth of love and commitment neither believed possible.

Lewis grieved her loss for the remainder of his life. He had come so close to missing the pearl of great price God had placed in his life. God has given you a mate of rare value and beauty. Do you value that person for the treasure he or she is? Have you come to appreciate your mate as the priceless gift of God in your life?

It's still not too late.

MARRIAGE MINUTE TRUTH:

GOD IS A WITNESS TO OUR MARRIAGE COVENANT

. . . .

Primary Passage:
You ask, "Why?" It is because the Lord is acting as the witness between you and the wife of your youth, because you have broken faith with her, though she is your partner, the wife of your marriage covenant.
Malachi 2:14

. . . .

We were once called to testify in an attempted murder trial. A recently released convict had met a neighbor of ours in a local bar. The two got drunk, then drove home to our neighbor's house. A brawl broke out, resulting in the convict attacking both the husband and wife. We happened to be dropping off a baby-sitter across the street when we heard screaming and called the police. The testimony of several witnesses, including us, helped send the man back to prison for seven more years.

It was no joyful experience to serve as a witness against another man. God is forced to take up that painful role when we break faith with the spouse of our youth and divorce him or her for un-biblical reasons. We put God in the unfortunate circumstance of testifying against us that we are guilty of fraud and betrayal. Why fraud? Because we promised something we didn't deliver. Why betrayal? Because our mate put complete trust in us and we abused that trust for our own personal selfishness.

In our society divorce is treated lightly. Scripture sees things differently. With God as our witness let's keep our vows.

Marriage Minute Truth:

IT IS IMPOSSIBLE TO EMERGE FROM ADULTERY UNSCATHED

Primary Passage:
*Can a man scoop fire into his lap without his clothes
being burned? Can a man walk on hot coals without his
feet being scorched? So is he who sleeps with another
man's wife; no one who touches her will go unpunished.*
Proverbs 6:27–29

*T*he musical *Camelot* ends with the destruction of the kingdom as forces loyal to King Arthur engage troops loyal to Lancelot, the king's most trusted friend. The cause of their mutual demise is Guinevere, the wife of King Arthur who has become Lancelot's lover. Although the story tends to romanticize the illicit love relationship, it is honest enough to depict where the whole sordid and tragic affairs ends—in the death of a marriage, the king, and the grand ideal once known as Camelot.

The Scripture teaches that it is simply impossible to be involved in adultery and emerge unscathed. For a season no one may know of our indiscretion or unfaithfulness. But as surely as there is a God in heaven, we cannot get away with it. One way or another the fire we scoop into our laps will leave its burns and scars on our soul.

Let's promise each other that the final scene of Camelot will not become the final act of our marriage. Let's commit ourselves again and again to remaining true to our vows. The joy of our life together will become the stuff legends of integrity are made of.

MARRIAGE MINUTE TRUTH:

SOUND DOCTRINE IS CRITICAL TO SOUND LIVING

Primary Passage:
*For the time will come when men will not put up with
sound doctrine. Instead, to suit their own desires, they
will gather around them a great number of teachers to say
what their itching ears want to hear.*
2 Timothy 4:3

*S*everal years ago when Bob was in college he had the unfortunate experience of spending the entire night at Chicago's O'Hare International Airport. When he woke up, standing over him was a smiling young man in an orange robe with his head shaved. "Would you like to find a life of peace and tranquillity?" he said in a polite voice.

Still somewhat groggy, Bob reached into his carry-on bag and produced a Bible. "I already have found the peace and tranquillity you describe in Jesus Christ," he said. "I will read your literature if you will read mine." He offered the man the Bible. The man took a step backward, handed Bob a magazine, then disappeared.

A false teacher had led that young man to believe a lie. If he doesn't hear the sound doctrine of the gospel of Christ, he will perish and spend an eternity in hell.

The stakes are high when it comes to doctrinal truth. Stay immersed in the Word of God. Don't be misled by new and novel doctrines. Guard your life and doctrine closely.

MARRIAGE MINUTE TRUTH:

KNOW WHAT YOU BELIEVE; BELIEVE WHAT YOU KNOW

. . . .

Primary Passage:
But in your hearts set apart Christ as Lord. Always be
prepared to give an answer to everyone who asks you to
give the reason for the hope that you have.
1 Peter 3:15

. . . .

*M*ost of us will be confronted by a cult member sooner or later. Whether it will be a member of the Jehovah Witnesses going door to door, young men dressed in white shirts and black ties doing two years of missionary work for the Mormons, or even "Moonies" selling flowers at freeway entrances, the cults will find us.

Are we prepared to give an answer for the hope we have in us? Or will we fervently pray the cult members skip our house?

Confidence comes from learning the simple plan of salvation so that we can explain it even to cult members. What is that plan? All of us are sinners separated from God (Romans 3:23). God loved us despite our sin and sent Christ to die on the cross to reconcile us to God (Romans 5:8). Salvation is a free gift we receive by placing our faith in what Christ alone has done (Romans 6:23). When we trust in the finished work of Christ alone for our salvation, we receive eternal life (Romans 10:9–10).

Are you prepared to give a reason for the hope within you? Know what you believe, then believe what you know. The doorbell could ring at any moment.

MARRIAGE MINUTE TRUTH:

PROVIDING FOR OUR FAMILY'S NEEDS IS A WITNESS TO OUR FAITH IN CHRIST

Primary Passage:
*If anyone does not provide for his relatives, and especially
for his immediate family, he has denied the faith and is
worse than an unbeliever.*
1 Timothy 5:8

*P*aul warns us that when we fail to provide for our family's needs because of laziness or lack of concern, it is a denial of our faith. Those are strong words. He gets even stronger in his warning. Such irresponsibility puts us in a category "worse than an unbeliever."

Yet, if we take that same passage and apply it in a positive sense, it can be a great encouragement to us. Let's reword it this way: "If anyone does provide for his relatives, and especially for his immediate family, he has affirmed the faith and is a powerful example of what a true believer is." Whether we work inside or outside the home to provide for our family's basic needs, we can take comfort in knowing God will use it as a witness that says, "We love and value the people God has put in our care. No sacrifice on our part is too great to provide for their basic needs. God has provided for my needs, and it's my privilege to be used by Him to provide for my relatives and immediate family." There are a variety of ways we can witness to others. Dedicating our work to serving our family's needs is one very effective means of claiming Christ as our Lord.

MARRIAGE MINUTE TRUTH:

WORSHIPING GOD AND GOD ALONE WILL BLESS OUR MARRIAGE

. . . .

Primary Passage:
And God spoke all these words: "I am the Lord your
God, who brought you up out of Egypt, out of the land
of slavery. You shall have no other gods before me."
Exodus 20:1–3

. . . .

On our wedding day we arrived at the honeymoon hotel exactly the same time as another set of newlyweds. They were still dressed in their wedding gown and tuxedo as we rode up the elevator together. We were both starting our married lives on the same day, in the same city, even at the same hotel. That alone should have given us much to talk about. Instead we never said a word to each other. The reason? The other couple was so drunk they were hardly aware we were even there. It's hard to exchange names and addresses when someone is semiconscious.

We've often wondered what happened to that couple. Did they have the resources of a personal relationship with Jesus Christ to keep them through the rough times ahead?

The Ten Commandments found in Exodus 20 contain principles vital to building a solid foundation for a satisfying life and marriage. We shall see how each applies to the task of building a solid marriage. God's first prescription is for us to have no other gods in our life. We had made that commitment the day we climbed into the elevator to start our life together. Did the other couple? Or have they discovered that truth by now? We can only hope so.

MARRIAGE MINUTE TRUTH:

WE PASS ON EITHER A LEGACY OF SIN OR BLESSING TO THE NEXT GENERATION

. . . .

Primary Passage:
*You shall not make for yourself an idol in the form of
anything in heaven above or on the earth beneath or in
the waters below. You shall not bow down to them or
worship them; for I, the Lord your God, am a jealous
God, punishing the children for the sin of the fathers to
the third and fourth generation of those who hate me, but
showing love to a thousand generations of those who love
me and keep my commandments.*
Exodus 20:4–6

. . . .

*N*ow in its third generation, one of the more prominent political families in the United States continues to be plagued by allegations of sexual misconduct and misbehavior. Numerous biographies have pointed back to the grandfather, the patriarch of the family, as the one who passed on to his sons the legacy of marital unfaithfulness. The generations since then have been plagued by scandal, divorce, and even premature death.

God's Word reminds us that we are going to leave our children, and our grandchildren, a legacy of either sin or blessing. If we worship other idols in our lives, whether they be money, sex, or power, our jealous God will punish to the third and fourth generations. Yet if we love God and His commandments, His Word says He will show His love to a thousand generations. None of us can change our ancestors, but all of us can influence our descendants.

MARRIAGE MINUTE TRUTH:

GUARDING THE NAME OF GOD WILL BLESS YOUR MARRIAGE

. . . .

Primary Passage:
You shall not misuse the name of the Lord your
God, for the Lord will not hold anyone
guiltless who misuses his name.
Exodus 20:7

. . . .

*N*ow that I'm an elder in the church I'm expecting you girls to change your behavior," warned the father. "I have a reputation to guard." His daughters couldn't help but see the irony. The fighting between their mother and father, who both professed to be Christians, had for years shattered the girls' security and broken their hearts. Sunday was often the worst day of fighting in their house. Neither parent was known for cursing or swearing. Yet, by their hateful behavior and arguments, both had misused the name of God. Professing to be believers, but treating each other as mortal enemies, they left the girls confused, angry, and ultimately rebellious.

If God is to bless our homes and marriages we need to guard His name. That goes far beyond avoiding swear words that involve the name of our Lord and of His Son. It also requires that we live a life of love, integrity, gentleness, and grace that honors the name of Jesus, particularly in front of our children.

They are the first to know when we misuse the name of God. They instinctively know when we are living as Christ-ones. Live carefully. People you love are watching.

MARRIAGE MINUTE TRUTH:

A DAY OF REST IS ESSENTIAL TO THE HEALTH OF YOUR MARRIAGE

Primary Passage:
*Remember the Sabbath day by keeping it holy. Six days
you shall labor and do all your work, but the seventh day
is a Sabbath to the Lord your God.*
Exodus 20:8

*I*f you were to ask us what is the number one thief of marital joy and intimacy in our modern culture, our answer might surprise you. It isn't the media with its often demeaning view of marriage. It isn't the New Age movement with its narcissistic philosophies. Nor is it even the wreckage caused by the sexual revolution. It is busyness. We are all simply too busy for our own good. As Richard Swenson, author of the best-selling book *Margins*, point outs, we have lost the margin of time and physical energy needed to enjoy life. Dual careers, heavy indebtedness, and a frantic cultural pace have left many couples with little or no time for rest and refreshment.

God never intended us to be that busy. To guarantee margin in our lives He set aside one day a week exclusively for rest and re-creation. Unfortunately we are tempted to spend that day catching up on shopping, putting in extra work at the office, and taking exhausting trips. God has a better plan. He wants us to set aside at least one day a week to spend together with each other and Him. The only agenda items should be the worship of God and genuine relaxation. Don't let busyness steal your margin—it's far too valuable.

MARRIAGE MINUTE TRUTH:

HONORING OUR PARENTS CREATES A BETTER FUTURE

. . . .

Primary Passage:
*Honor your father and your mother, so that you may live
long in the land the Lord your God is giving you.*
Exodus 20:12

. . . .

*W*e have a policy in our marriage of not criticizing each other's parents. There's a good reason behind the rule: it not only increases harmony in our home, but it also creates a better future for us. The logic behind honoring each other's parents goes like this. We both are the product of the people who conceived us and/or raised us. When we continually criticize each other's parents, we are essentially criticizing the person they produced (the person we are married to). But when we build up our spouse's parents, we are strengthening our own relationship and creating a better future for us.

Should we avoid the obvious problems that our in-laws can cause us? Of course not. They have to be addressed in a healthy manner for our marriages to remain healthy. Even while we work through those issues we can still honor our father and mother. We suggest telling how a particular parent's behavior makes us feel without demeaning that person's character. We make observations, not accusations. We agree that we each will represent the other's interests to his or her own parents if there is a problem. We have found that as we honor each other's parents we honor each other. That creates a better future for everyone.

MARRIAGE MINUTE TRUTH:

CONTEMPT CAN KILL A MARRIAGE

Primary Passage:
You shall not murder.
Exodus 20:13

Despite the tragic stories of domestic violence we see on television or read in the newspapers, the majority of homes are not threatened by actual physical assault. So what relevance does the commandment, "You shall not commit murder" have to marriage? It's possible to break the commandment while never lifting a finger in actual violence.

Listen to the words of Jesus:

You have heard that it was said to the people long ago, "Do not murder, and anyone who murders will be subject to judgment." But I tell you that anyone who is angry with his brother will be subject to judgment. Again, anyone who says to his brother, "Raca," is answerable to the Sanhedrin. But anyone who says, "You fool!" will be in danger of the fire of hell. (Matthew 5:21–22)

Jesus warned us that contempt can have the same devastating impact as murder. When contempt enters our thoughts, vocabulary, or actions in marriage, it can leave mortal wounds. Contempt can kill the love and intimacy necessary to sustain a marriage. We should eliminate from our marriage relationship any words and attitudes that carry even a trace of contempt and disdain. Otherwise we risk being an accessory to a crime—the death of intimacy and love. That's a tragedy in the first degree.

MARRIAGE MINUTE TRUTH:

WE ARE NOT TO ROB
EACH OTHER IN MARRIAGE

Primary Passage:
You shall not steal.
Exodus 20:15

*T*he Bible tells us we are not to steal from one another. Although the Scriptures refer primarily to taking physical property that does not belong to us, it is possible to commit theft in marriage in other ways. When we fail to give our spouses the time and attention they deserve in order to advance in our careers, we have stolen something from them.

When we tear down our mates by either demeaning their personality traits or diminishing their self-worth, we have again stolen something from them. We promised them the day we married that we would "love, honor, and cherish" them. Unkind and insensitive behavior robs them of that promise.

When we give another person the love and affection that is reserved exclusively for our spouse (whether a parent, a friend, or another lover), we again commit theft. It can be as simple as giving our family of origin first preference in our loyalty and devotion. If our spouse does not come first in our lives we have robbed him or her of something he or she legitimately ought to possess.

One of the profound secrets of marriage is respecting our mate's property, whether emotional, spiritual, or physical. Guarding what legitimately belongs to our spouse is not only wise; it is essential if our marriages are to prosper.

MARRIAGE MINUTE TRUTH:

HONESTY AND TRUTH TELLING
ARE FOUNDATIONAL TO MARRIAGE

Primary Passage:
You shall not give false testimony against your neighbor.
Exodus 20:16

A daily advice columnist once featured letters from her readers on the subject of honesty in marriage. One woman stated bluntly that one of her children was conceived by another man, but she never intends to tell her husband. Another boasted that she had carried on an affair for several years and has no regrets. She never intends to tell her husband either.

Even if we're not keeping secrets that dark and deceptive from each other, are there times when we give a type of "false testimony" to our spouses? Do we tell them only half the truth or leave out details we'd rather they not know? Do we exaggerate problems or hide mistakes? The Scriptures tell us we are not to lie to one another but to engage in honesty and truthfulness. We can never know true intimacy with our spouses if we do not allow them to know us for who we are. As risky as truth telling can be, it's the only route to true acceptance and intimacy. All else falls into the category of false impressions and illusions. In our hearts we know that if our spouses are in love with us, they are in love with the illusion we have created, not who we truly are.

Is there an area of your marriage where you need to be more honest and open with each other? It's time to quit playing "I've Got a Secret" and allow truth to set us free.

MARRIAGE MINUTE TRUTH:

ENVY DOES TO CONTENTMENT WHAT SALT WATER DOES TO THIRST

. . . .

Primary Passage:
*You shall not covet your neighbor's house. You shall
not covet your neighbor's wife, or his manservant
or maidservant, his ox or donkey, or anything
that belongs to your neighbor.*
Exodus 20:17

. . . .

The great British preacher W. E. Sangster pointed out we are jealous only of those people we perceive to be on our level. We usually don't envy people many times wealthier than we are. Nor are we jealous of the person much poorer than ourselves. True jealously gets started when we look at someone who makes roughly what we do (or just a little more), has the same amount of education (or just a little more), or has succeeded just about as much as we have (or perhaps a little bit more).

To know true contentment in a marriage we have to resist the temptation to covet someone else's house, car, or spouse. How can we guard our hearts against envy or covetousness? First, remind each other of God's sovereignty. If God had wanted us to own a newer car or bigger house, He would have given it to us. Second, remind each other of the costs you don't see in owning someone else's possessions. Ask anyone who has owned a pool and they'll likely tell you they've nearly drowned in the maintenance. The only thing we should covet is contentment. That we ought to pursue with a holy jealousy.

MARRIAGE MINUTE TRUTH:

TAKE RADICAL STEPS, WHEN NECESSARY, TO AVOID SEXUAL SIN

Primary Passage:
You have heard that it was said, "Do not commit adultery." But I tell you that anyone who looks at a woman lustfully has already committed adultery with her in his heart. If your right eye causes you to sin, gouge it out and throw it away.
Matthew 5:27–29

*L*ust is a deceptive experience. Because it can feel warm and powerful, it can pose as love or affection. Because it can be experienced from a distance, it presents itself as a safe indulgence. Because it's difficult for anyone to read our minds, it promises anonymity and protection. These are all lies from the Father of Lies. Lust is neither love nor affection; it is selfishness and greed. Nor is it a harmless amusement. It always draws us closer to behavior and conduct that threatens our very soul. Nor is it anonymous. Discerning individuals can read the telltale signs of lust in our eyes, words, and actions.

Jesus said that active lust is the spiritual equivalent of active adultery. It is a radical sin with radical implications for our marriages. The only known remedy for lust is to completely renounce it in favor of seeking a pure heart. Renouncing lust may involve radical steps. We may need to cancel cable television, get off the Internet, or ask that we be transferred to another department if our desire for a coworker is growing. Lust cannot be managed. It must be destroyed. Radical sins demand radical responses.

MARRIAGE MINUTE TRUTH:

DIVORCE CAN SET IN MOTION UNFORESEEN CYCLES OF SIN

. . . .

Primary Passage:
*But I tell you that anyone who divorces his wife, except
for marital unfaithfulness, causes her to become an
adulteress, and anyone who marries the divorced
woman commits adultery.*
Matthew 5:32

. . . .

*I*t's difficult to preach about divorce in our modern setting. With many churchgoers choosing divorce as the remedy to their marital problems, pastors are bound to step on someone's toes as soon as they mention the topic, much less read the relevant Scriptures.

For example, Jesus said in the Sermon on the Mount that divorce was permitted only in cases of marital infidelity. All other instances constitute adultery (assuming the divorced partners remarry someone else). Paul seems to add desertion by an unbelieving mate as one more ground for divorce (1 Corinthians 7:12–15), but he too upholds a high standard for marriage.

One reason Scripture condemns divorce is that it sets in motion unforeseen cycles of sin. When one mate divorces the other for non-biblical reasons, it's likely that the ex-mate will sooner or later marry again. Once that happens, Jesus says, adultery occurs. Now four people are involved in sin where once it was just two. It's not popular to depict easy divorce and remarriage as adultery. But Jesus, the architect of marriage, warns it is just that.

MARRIAGE MINUTE TRUTH:

IT IS A GIFT TO BE SIMPLE IN MARRIAGE

Primary Passage:
Simply let your "Yes" be "Yes," and your "No," "No";
anything beyond this comes from the evil one.
Matthew 5:37

The devotional writer E. Stanley Jones tells of a sign he saw posted in a research laboratory. It said, "The solution to this problem, when discovered, will be simple."

Simplicity could become a powerful friend to many marriages today. Rather than trying to explain away or justify our wrongful actions, we could learn to simply say, "I am sorry. I was wrong. Please forgive me."

Rather than arguing over who should get up and check the doors at night, we could practice the simplicity of servanthood and get up and do it ourselves.

Rather than going through the costly and complicating experience of divorce, we could simply learn to keep our promises. If we keep our vows, they will keep us. It's that simple.

It's a basic law of the spiritual universe that holiness simplifies and sin complicates. Jesus said the best approach to life is to simply let our "yes" be "yes," and our "no" be "no."

All other add-ons, footnotes, explanations, and rationalizations come from the Evil One. It is a gift to be simple. Give that gift to each other and watch how uncluttered life can become.

MARRIAGE MINUTE TRUTH:
SOME SUCCESSES ARE TOO COSTLY

Primary Passage:
Choose my instruction instead of silver, knowledge rather
than choice gold, for wisdom is more precious than rubies,
and nothing you desire can compare with her.
Proverbs 8:10–11

$\mathcal{G}$eoffrey was wildly successful in his career as a stockbroker. He made money and climbed the corporate ladder with astonishing speed. The problem is that he had to barter away his role as an involved father and husband to do it. Over time he became a stranger to his family.

What if our pursuit of success has taken us away from each other? Is there a way back to right priorities and an intimate relationship? Yes, but it begins with our need to reorder our priorities in life. We need to first admit that our drive to succeed at all costs is fueled by pride, insecurity, and a basic selfishness. We need to quit viewing our family members as commodities and begin regarding them as precious gifts given to us by God. We need to also recognize that spiritual wealth far outlasts material prosperity.

Most important, we must recognize the true market value of biblical instruction, knowledge, and wisdom. The husband or wife who invests in these precious commodities will reap dividends unheard of on Wall Street. These commodities will give new meaning to the term "securities" in our marriage.

MARRIAGE MINUTE TRUTH:

WE SHOULD BE GRATEFUL FOR THE PORTION GOD HAS GIVEN US IN LIFE

. . . .

Primary Passage:
*Lord, you have assigned me my portion and my cup; you
have made my lot secure. The boundary lines have fallen
for me in pleasant places; surely I have a delightful
inheritance. I will praise the Lord, who counsels me;
even at night my heart instructs me. I have set the
Lord always before me. Because he is at my
right hand, I will not be shaken.*
Psalm 16:5–8

. . . .

Gossip columns are fueled not so much by an insatiable desire for information as they are by envy. It's because people are secretly envious of the famous, the beautiful, and the wealthy that reading about their foibles, shortcomings, and sins is so much fun for so many.

Yet if we really knew the inner pain and struggles of the glamorous and famous, we wouldn't want their lives. More likely than not we would thank God for the life we now enjoy.

Scripture encourages us to believe that there is wisdom and God's direction behind our portion and lot in life. The psalmist described the boundary lines of our home, marriage, and family as a "delightful inheritance." God has shaped our lives and fortunes and families to give us something better than wealth or notoriety. He gives us Himself.

Forget gossip columns. The story of our own lives is far more fascinating. It's a manuscript written by God Himself.

MARRIAGE MINUTE TRUTH:

IF WE STUMBLE, WE SHOULD FALL FORWARD

. . . .

Primary Passage:
*It was good for me to be afflicted so that I might learn
your decrees. The law from your mouth is more precious
to me than thousands of pieces of silver and gold.*
Psalm 119:71–72

. . . .

The scientist who discovered penicillin did so by accident. He had left several Petri dishes out on his table overnight, and when he returned the next morning, he found green mold growing in one of them. Standard procedure was to discard the contaminated dishes and start over. Instead he kept them and studied the development of the bacteria. In 1929 he stunned the world with the discovery of the first antibiotic, penicillin. His simple experiments set in motion a medical innovation that eventually saved millions of lives.

Failures and mistakes are facts of life. The early years of marriage can be particularly hazardous. We can make financial choices that prove ruinous. We can enter marriage with unrealistic expectations that set us up for disappointment. Or we can fail to appreciate our spouses' unique makeup and expend enormous amounts of energy trying to remake them.

God's Word assures us that our failures can be redemptive if we learn from them. "It was good for me to be afflicted so that I might learn your decrees," the psalmist wrote. Failure can be a marvelous teacher if we are humble enough to learn its lessons. As one devotional writer put it, "When we stumble we need to fall forward."

MARRIAGE MINUTE TRUTH:

PRAYER BRINGS CLEANSING AND FORGIVENESS INTO OUR LIVES

Primary Passage:
*I will cleanse them from all the sin they have
committed against me and will forgive all
their sins of rebellion against me.*
Jeremiah 33:8

*W*e once had a new kitchen floor installed. It required that we move all the appliances out of the room, including our large refrigerator. When we pulled it away from the wall, we both gasped—we found things underneath it we wish we had not seen. In a variety of sickening and disgusting colors, old food spills and stains had been baked onto the floor by the heat from the bottom of the refrigerator. Getting them off would require getting down on our hands and knees and scrubbing them away.

When we invite God to search our hearts, the Holy Spirit may show us things we may not want to see: unforgiven sins, past bitterness, and even hardened hearts. Thank God that through prayer we can confess these stains and spots and find complete cleansing and forgiveness. The blood of Christ can rinse away even the worst stains in our relationship. As these stains are removed, our hearts are free to love one another on a deeper level. Joy, intimacy, and trust begin to flow between the two of us once more. The end result is a beautiful thing to behold—two people truly bonded to one another.

MARRIAGE MINUTE TRUTH:

EVERY MARRIAGE IS
ON A JOURNEY OF FAITH

Primary Passage:
*By faith Abraham, when called to go to a place he would
later receive as his inheritance, obeyed and went, even
though he did not know where he was going.*
Hebrews 11:8

What do the following people have in common? (1) An elderly husband and wife who are facing the difficult choice of staying in a home too big for them to maintain or selling the house that has been so much a part of their lives for so long; (2) A newly married couple that discovers one spouse is facing a life-threatening illness; and (3) A middle-aged couple in which the husband just lost his job and their financial future is now shaky.

As different as each of these couples are, they all have one common characteristic—they are on journeys of faith. Each journey is one none of them would have chosen for themselves given all its difficulties. It's filled with unanswered questions, dangerous crossings, and anxious moments. But like Abraham of old, their journeys will not be traveled alone. God is leading them through, although the destinations may not be apparent.

Every marriage is on a journey of faith. God is leading all of us to a destination of His own choosing. Like Abraham we may not know exactly where we are headed. But we are convinced by faith that God has an inheritance waiting for us. Our job is to trust and walk on.

MARRIAGE MINUTE TRUTH:

OUR JOURNEY OF FAITH WON'T END UNTIL GOD DECIDES IT SHOULD

. . . .

Primary Passage:
*Now faith is being sure of what we hope for and
certain of what we do not see. This is what the
ancients were commended for.*
Hebrews 11:1–2

. . . .

*S*ome experiences would be much more bearable if we knew when they were going to end. When will this illness end so I can feel like myself again? When will our financial pressures let up so that we can sleep again at night? When will our son or daughter come back to the Lord?

God rarely answers such questions in a direct manner. The ways of God are often completely beyond our knowing.

It is still possible to find rest in what we know, however. One certainty is that our difficult circumstances will end only when God has accomplished all He wishes to accomplish in our lives. Another certainty is that God is allowing our difficulties to develop our life of faith. A final certainty is that God will not bring our trials to a conclusion until He has taught those around us the lessons He may wish to convey through our suffering.

God doesn't tell us when hard times will end. He only promises us that when we reach the end of the difficult journey, He will be standing there waiting to welcome us home.

MARRIAGE MINUTE TRUTH:

SUBSTITUTING OUR PLAN B FOR GOD'S PLAN A IS A GREAT MISTAKE

Primary Passage:
Now Sarai, Abram's wife, had borne him no children.
But she had an Egyptian maidservant named Hagar;
so she said to Abram, "The Lord has kept me from
having children. Go, sleep with my maidservant;
perhaps I can build a family through her."
Abram agreed to what Sarai said.
Genesis 16:1–2

*P*erhaps the worst mistake we can make in our lives is to take matters into our own hands. When we substitute our plans for God's plans, sorrow and regret are inevitable. Abram and Sarai had decided God wasn't going to give them children, even though He had specifically promised He would do so. So they took matters into our own hands, and Abram slept with Hagar instead. The disastrous results of hatred and enmity continue to this day.

So often we come to the conclusion that God has failed because He hasn't acted according to our timetable. Those who have had the patience to walk with God for a lifetime tell a different story. They insist God's timing is perfect and His plans for our lives are flawless.

When we are tempted to substitute our plans for God's plans we need to ask ourselves an important question: "Is it possible for God to fail?" If it is, then we should immediately go ahead with our schemes. If not, then we should stop and wait on God for His leading. Forget "Plan B." It's short for Plan Bogus.

MARRIAGE MINUTE TRUTH:

LOSING FAITH IN GOD IS THE GREATEST DANGER WE FACE

. . . .

Primary Passage:
*As he was about to enter Egypt, [Abram] said to his wife
Sarai, "I know what a beautiful woman you are.
When the Egyptians see you, they will say, 'This is
his wife.' Then they will kill me but let you live.
Say you are my sister."*
Genesis 12:11–13

. . . .

*W*e often do irrational things when we lose faith in God. In an effort to maintain control of our situation we tell lies, manipulate others, and do foolish things. Abram did all those things. It began when he was forced to travel to Egypt to avoid starving to death. When he arrived he temporarily lost faith in God. He reasoned that Egypt's despotic ruler would find his wife, Sarai, beautiful and Abram an inconvenience. So to keep himself alive he told Sarai to lie about her true identity. It was a foolish decision that nearly got everyone killed.

The journey of faith can be terrifying if we don't believe that God can protect us and keep us. We know that any number of enemies and dangers lurk out there ready to harm us. But what Abram had to learn, and what we need to realize as a couple, is that no situation we face is beyond God's control. He can be trusted to deal with our intimidating and even terrifying circumstances. "Even though I walk through the valley of the shadow of death, I will fear no evil, for you are with me...."

Let's stay rational and obedient. God is in control.

MARRIAGE MINUTE TRUTH:

WE ARE NO FOOLS TO GIVE UP WHAT WE CANNOT KEEP TO GAIN WHAT WE CANNOT LOSE

. . . .

Primary Passage:
*By faith Abraham, when God tested him, offered Isaac
as a sacrifice. He who had received the promises was
about to sacrifice his one and only son, even though
God had said to him, "It is through Isaac that
your offspring will be reckoned."*
Hebrews 11:17–18

. . . .

*T*he words of the missionary martyr, Jim Eliot, continue to challenge Christians of every generation, "He is no fool to give up what he cannot keep to gain what he cannot lose." Abraham had to learn this lesson when God told him to offer his only son Isaac as a sacrifice. If Isaac died, all the promises of future offspring would perish with him. But Abraham had learned by now to trust God. He obediently led his only son to the mountain of sacrifice. Just as Abraham raised his knife, God intervened and gave him back Isaac. Abraham left Mount Moriah not only with his son, but with the knowledge that everything he possessed belonged to God.

We must never take back for ourselves what rightfully belongs to God. The journey of faith is continually giving to God what we cannot keep to gain what we cannot lose. It is turning over to God our loved ones, our money, our health, our reputations, our careers, our plans, and our dreams for His safekeeping. Abraham discovered that nothing in life is truly ours until it is truly God's. What do we need to turn over to God this day?

MARRIAGE MINUTE TRUTH:

GOD LOVES THE WORLD ONE PERSON AT A TIME

Primary Passage:
*For God so loved the world that he gave his one and
only Son, that whoever believes in him shall
not perish but have eternal life.*
John 3:16

A widely circulated story tells about an elaborate practical joke hatched by a group of college students. They supposedly enrolled, registered, and even graduated a person who never existed. The student never appeared in person, never said "hello" to a professor, and never bought a textbook, yet he passed one course after another until he was awarded a diploma. The students wanted to prove to the university that they were little more than numbers lost in an educational system that had become anonymous and depersonalized.

Sometimes we are tempted to believe we are little more than numbers in this massively impersonal world of six billion people. We receive little recognition for our accomplishments, only a handful of people remember our birthdays, and when we retire a dozen people take us out to lunch and say good-bye. But to God we are much more than numbers. We are valuable and unique people with valuable and unique souls. When Jesus died for the sins of the world, He carried in His body the sins of untold millions of people. Yet He died for us as individuals. Take heart; God knows our name, not our number.

MARRIAGE MINUTE TRUTH:

OBEDIENCE INVITES GOD'S PROTECTION OVER OUR FAMILIES

. . . .

Primary Passage:
And Noah did all that the Lord commanded him.
Noah was six hundred years old when the floodwaters
came on the earth. And Noah and his sons and his
wife and his sons' wives entered the ark to escape
the waters of the flood.
Genesis 7:5–7

. . . .

We were traveling in the West one summer when we encountered a large orange highway truck parked perpendicular to the road. A highway employee walked up to our window and said, "I wouldn't try and go over that hill if I were you."

"Why not?" we asked.

"There's a river fifty feet across where there used to be a highway." His down-home grin convinced us he was telling the truth. Recent heavy rains on the prairie had caused severe flash floods. With his permission we drove to the top of the knoll and took a look for ourselves. Beneath lay a ferocious, frothing, snakelike river. Our entire family breathed a sigh of relief that the man had kept us from driving over the hill.

God saved Noah and his family from a flood too. He rescued them not because they built an ark but because they were obedient to Him. Obedience to God and His Word can protect us from a host of dangers: divorce, bankruptcy, and division in our family. Although rain may still fall into our lives, God will preserve the obedient from drowning.

MARRIAGE MINUTE TRUTH:

WE ARE ON EARTH TO MAKE A NAME FOR GOD, NOT OURSELVES

Primary Passage:
*They said, "Come, let us build ourselves a city, with a
tower that reaches to the heavens, so that we may make
a name for ourselves and not be scattered over the
face of the whole earth."*
Genesis 11:4

We need to ask ourselves a serious and important question: Are we on this earth to make a name for ourselves or for God? That simple question can lead either to our ruin or to our blessing.

The people of the ancient city of Babel hatched a plan to build a tower they vainly imagined would reach heaven itself. Its express purpose was to exalt human pride "so that we may make a name for ourselves." God's response to the presumptuous building project was to shut it down by confusing their languages and scattering the various peoples across the entire earth. God will not bless a city or home where pride and arrogance are the foundation.

How do we make a name for God in our marriage and family? His desire instead is that we build our homes on the foundational character traits of humility, submission, and obedience to Christ Himself. Instead of allowing us to scatter, He will unite us in true love and fellowship. Instead of confusing our language, He will give us the ability to communicate openly and effectively.

God grants building permits to such godly contractors.

❦❦❦❦

MARRIAGE MINUTE TRUTH:

WHEN WE PITCH OUR TENTS NEAR WICKEDNESS, WE ARE SOON LIVING IN WICKEDNESS

. . . .

Primary Passage:
Abram lived in the land of Canaan, while Lot lived among the cities of the plain and pitched his tents near Sodom. Now the men of Sodom were wicked and were sinning greatly against the Lord.
Genesis 13:12–13

. . . .

The story of Lot and his family found in Genesis is a biography of moral compromise and its tragic results. When Lot first moved into the region of Sodom, the Bible says he pitched his tents "near" the city. Despite the wicked reputation of the area, Lot convinced himself he could live on the border of sin and disobedience but still maintain his integrity. The next time we read of Lot something interesting has happened. An alliance of kings has attacked the city. We read, "They also carried off Abram's nephew Lot and his possessions, since he was living in Sodom" (14:12). Did you catch that? Over time Lot had moved from living near the city to living in the city.

We must be on guard as a couple not to pitch our tents near wickedness, that is, to live on the edge of moral compromise. Flirting with such sins as pornography, materialism, or the occult is extremely dangerous. They all have the power to draw us into their borders. When it comes to sin we must commit ourselves not to even enter the county, much less the city limits.

❦❦❦❦

MARRIAGE MINUTE TRUTH:

IT OUGHT TO HURT WHEN WE LOSE SOMEONE SPECIAL; IT'S A SIGN THE PERSON WAS INDEED SPECIAL TO US

. . . .

Primary Passage:
Sarah lived to be a hundred and twenty-seven years
old. She died at Kiriath Arba (that is, Hebron)
in the land of Canaan, and Abraham went
to mourn for Sarah and to weep over her.
Genesis 23:1

. . . .

*O*ver the course of our years in the local church, we have conducted many funerals. The saddest ones we've been to have not been where many tears were shed and people's grief was nearly inconsolable. No, the saddest funerals we've seen are where no one cried and no one seemed to care that the person was gone.

Great grief often signifies a great love. The more it hurts for us to say good-bye to someone, the stronger the evidence that we truly loved him. Abraham deeply loved his wife Sarah. When she died he was never really the same again. He went to great lengths to buy a burial plot that would be forever theirs to share.

None of us likes to think of the day when we shall lose our mate. But you need not fear that day either. As sorrowful and grief choked as it will be, it will also mean that the two of you had something very special. Only those who have loved greatly can mourn greatly. So rejoice in the marriage God has given you today, for, like Abraham, one of you will discover that marriage does not last forever.

MARRIAGE MINUTE TRUTH:

MANIPULATIVE BEHAVIOR CAN BECOME A CURSE ON A MARRIAGE

. . . .

Primary Passage:
Jacob said to Rebekah his mother, "But my brother Esau
is a hairy man, and I'm a man with smooth skin. What
if my father touches me? I would appear to be tricking
him and would bring down a curse on myself rather
than a blessing." His mother said to him, "My
son, let the curse fall on me."
Genesis 27:11–13

. . . .

*O*ne daughter drank heavily. Another did cocaine. A son was frequently in trouble with the law. As we watched the sad drama of this dysfunctional family played out in a midwestern city, we couldn't help but notice the role a manipulative mother had played in the undoing of their lives.

Rather than raise them with clear boundaries based on unconditional love and acceptance, she used manipulation and guilt to carve them into the image she desired. The result? Rebellion, resistance, and ultimately heart-breaking behavior.

Rebekah learned that lesson too late in life. Rather than trusting God to work out which son would inherit her husband Isaac's blessing, she opted for an elaborate ruse. Jacob, her younger son, pretended to be Esau, her older son, to steal his blessing. The result was a family torn apart by hatred and jealousy. If we are tempted to use manipulation in our homes, remember Rebekah. She lost everyone and everything because of it. Trusting God to work things out is so much wiser.

MARRIAGE MINUTE TRUTH:

GOD CAN BE FOUND IN THE MOST UNLIKELY PLACES

Primary Passage:
When Jacob awoke from his sleep, he thought, "Surely the Lord is in this place, and I was not aware of it." He was afraid and said, "How awesome is this place! This is none other than the house of God; this is the gate of heaven."
Genesis 28:16–17

One of the more enduring devotional works of all time, *Practicing the Presence of God*, was written by a simple monk during the Middle Ages. His main assignment at the monastery was to wash dishes. There, scrubbing pots and pans in a drafty and dark kitchen, he sang aloud and celebrated the presence of God. From his own experience of finding God in the pantry and over the sink came his classic devotional work.

Jacob too discovered that God could be found in the most unlikely places. Running from his brother Esau, he stopped to sleep for the night in an open field. There in a dream God suddenly showed him the very stairway of heaven with angels ascending and descending. Jacob named the location Bethel, meaning "the house of God." God can be found in the most unlikely places in our lives too: at the kitchen sink, rolling on the family room carpet with our children, or kneeling in prayer by our bed as a couple. God is not imprisoned in stained glass architecture or centuries-old cathedrals. He's found in the daily and ordinary places of life. Our homes can be a Bethel as well—the very house of God.

Marriage Minute Truth:

WE MUST TURN AND FACE OUR PAST MISTAKES

Primary Passage:

Jacob looked up and there was Esau, coming with his four hundred men; so he divided the children among Leah, Rachel and the two maidservants. He put the maidservants and their children in front, Leah and her children next, and Rachel and Joseph in the rear. He himself went on ahead and bowed down to the ground seven times as he approached his brother.

Genesis 33:1–3

*J*acob's answer to problems in life was always to flee. He ran away from his brother Esau after defrauding him of his blessing. He ran from his father-in-law Laban after taking his two daughters from him. Now, at last, he had come to the place in his life where he had nowhere to run. Esau was pursuing him with four hundred men. With so many livestock and children in tow, Jacob had no chance of outrunning him. His only option was to turn around and go face-to-face with his brother, which he did.

It's no use to try to run from our past mistakes. There is nowhere on earth we can hide. The day comes when it all catches up with us. The right choice is to do what Jacob did. He turned and faced his problems. Whatever sins or mistakes we carry with us need to be confronted. Whatever broken relationships exist we need to make an effort to mend. Whatever wrongdoing still haunts us needs to be addressed, the sooner the better. True freedom is found not in running from what we fear, but in running to it.

MARRIAGE MINUTE TRUTH:

REVERING THE HOLINESS OF GOD IS HEALTHY FOR A MARRIAGE

Primary Passage:
*When the Lord saw that he had gone over to look, God
called to him from within the bush, "Moses! Moses!"
And Moses said, "Here I am." "Do not come any
closer," God said. "Take off your sandals, for the place
where you are standing is holy ground."*
Exodus 3:4–5

In 1970 a tremendous revival broke out at a small southern campus. It was our privilege to later study at that campus and observe the site of this memorable visit of God. There was a sense in which we knew we were standing on holy ground.

Moses had a similar experience when he was confronted by a burning bush in the desert of Midian. Despite the hot flames and crackling heat, the bush was not consumed. Curious, Moses approached the scene and was confronted by nothing less than the voice of God Himself. Moses immediately took off his sandals as he was commanded to do, which was a sign of ultimate respect and submission in that ancient culture.

Healthy marriages need more than good communication, mutual respect, and common values to succeed. They also need a proper reverence or fear for the holiness of God. God's absolute moral, ethical, and spiritual purity provides an incentive for us to lead upright and pure lives. It serves to keep us living within the moral boundaries that are best for us. Figuratively speaking, we need to take off our shoes in His presence each day. The bush is still burning.

MARRIAGE MINUTE TRUTH:

THE BLOOD OF CHRIST
NEEDS TO COVER OUR HOME

. . . .

Primary Passage:
*The blood will be a sign for you on the houses where you
are; and when I see the blood, I will pass over you. No
destructive plague will touch you when I strike Egypt.*
Exodus 12:13

. . . .

*O*ur family has watched Cecil B. DeMille's film classic, *The Ten
Commandments*, on several occasions. Despite its epic budget,
elaborate sets, and cast of thousands, it still comes short of captur-
ing the truly incredible events of that first Passover in Egypt.
There, in the span of just one day, more than a million people
were set free by a powerful act of God. The angel of death visited
every home in the land and killed every firstborn child—except
for those homes where the blood of a lamb had been sprinkled
on the doorpost. When the angel saw the shed blood he "passed
over" the home and spared the life of the firstborn.

The entire Passover event was a foreshadowing of the future
sacrifice of the true Lamb of God, Jesus Christ. Because of His
shed blood on the cross, God now "passes over" our sins and
spares us the penalty of the second death. As a family our hope is
in the blood of Christ made as sacrifice to cover our sins. Although you won't find red-stained wood on our doorpost, it's our
daily prayer that the shed blood of Christ will cover our home
and family. Like the ancient Israelites, we are forever grateful a
Lamb's blood has given us life when we deserve death.

MARRIAGE MINUTE TRUTH:

CELEBRATE THE CHOICE YOU'VE MADE IN A HUSBAND OR WIFE

Primary Passage:
Many women do noble things, but you surpass them all.
Proverbs 31:29

*T*he night I proposed to Cheryl I did actually get down on my knees and say, "Will you marry me?" I remember her beautiful brown eyes looking into mine as she simply nodded her head yes.

"You will?" I asked with some astonishment. She politely nodded her head a second time. That night we called the most important people in our lives to ask them to celebrate the moment with us. We were so excited that we lost track of time and ended up calling some people much too late. They offered us groggy congratulations and politely suggested we call them tomorrow for further comment.

Why is it that three, five, or twenty years into so many marriages a sense of celebration slips away? I still consider it a miracle I found such a wonderful wife. Like the writer of Proverbs, I celebrate the mate God gave me: "Many women do noble things, but you surpass them all."

Don't quit celebrating the spouse God has given you. When you stop and think about it, it's truly amazing he ever asked you to marry him or she ever said, "Yes," isn't it?

MARRIAGE MINUTE TRUTH:

REMEMBER WHO IT IS THAT MARRIED THE TWO OF YOU

Primary Passage:
Therefore what God has joined together,
let man not separate.
Matthew 19:6

*O*ne of the first weddings Bob performed after seminary was held in someone's home. In an apparent effort to cut expenses there were no hired musicians or soloists. The bride simply stood at the top of the stairs near the bathroom and yelled down, "Start the record!" Someone walked over and put the needle on the stereo album, and the wedding march was underway.

Though Bob has officiated at some unusual weddings in some unusual venues (He once performed a wedding under a white trellis in an unused section of the church graveyard), he has never actually married anyone. Not one couple. According to Jesus it is God who "joins together." The pastor simply serves as His representative; it is God who actually takes two people and makes them one.

We like to encourage couples to take out their wedding albums each year and recall the people who shared that special day with them. Then we ask them to imagine Jesus standing in the middle of the wedding entourage, smiling and celebrating the joyous event with them. He was present that day just as He was present at the wedding in Cana of Galilee. He is the author of marriage. Whenever we need a fresh appreciation of the eternal value of our marriage, we simply remember who married us. Not the pastor, not the priest, but Jesus Himself.

MARRIAGE MINUTE TRUTH:

ALWAYS TREAT YOUR SPOUSE
AS A PERSON OF VALUE

. . . .

Primary Passage:
Your wife will be like a fruitful vine within your house;
your sons will be like olive shoots around your table.
Thus is the man blessed who fears the Lord.
Psalm 128:3–4

. . . .

A speaker at a Promise Keepers rally challenged the husbands present in a way we had never heard men challenged before. To paraphrase his comments, "Husbands, consider how your wife prospered in the home of her father growing up. Why don't you make it your aim to see that she prospers twice as much in your house as she did in her father's house?"

For a wife to prosper she needs to be treated as a person of great value. Just as a proud father delights in his beautiful little daughter, a proud husband needs to delight in the beautiful and valuable woman God has entrusted to him.

How can we treat our wives as people of true value to us? We need to listen with empathy. We need to respect their judgments. We need to speak well of their character to others. We need to give them first priority in our time and attention. We need to encourage and call out their gifts. We need to honor them in front of our children.

Husbands, let's make it our aim to see that our wives prosper more in our care and love than they ever did before they came to live with us. Let's give them twice the love they knew growing up. Even their father will thank you for that.

MARRIAGE MINUTE TRUTH:

PRACTICE THE ONE AND ONLY RULE

. . . .

Primary Passage:
So guard yourself in your spirit, and do not break faith.
Malachi 2:16

. . . .

*H*ollywood has never been known as a place of great virtue. Yet Paul Newman, married to the same woman for nearly fifty years, was once asked if he found other leading ladies tempting. "Why would I settle for hamburger at work when I can enjoy steak at home?" was his famous reply. He had discovered the power, joy, and attraction of the one and only rule.

The one and only rule for spouses is quite simple to remember. It goes like this: you are my one and only. We'll repeat it again for impact: You are my one and only. It is the exclusivity of our love for our spouse that gives our marriage unique power and satisfaction. We enjoy a relationship with each other no one else on earth has the right to invade. We have secrets, dreams, and memories that are known only to us. We offer a level of respect for and knowledge of each other that no one else can approach.

The one and only rule cannot accommodate small compromises or exceptions. It must be all or nothing. Is there anyone in our lives today who poses a threat to our exclusive relationship? We must abandon that person and break off that relationship immediately. We must guard our spirit and not break faith. It's our one and only chance for a truly fulfilling marriage.

MARRIAGE MINUTE TRUTH:

GOD MAY BE WAITING FOR YOU TO ASK HIM FOR WHAT YOU NEED

. . . .

Primary Passage:
You do not have, because you do not ask God.
James 4:2b

. . . .

*E*ach year billions of dollars in scholarship money for college educations goes unclaimed. It's sad to think that many students who want a college education will not receive one because they failed to access the funds that were already available.

A similar tragedy occurs in many marriages. Even though both spouses have deep and heartfelt needs, they fail to access the answers even though the resources are available. James puts it this way, "You do not have, because you do not ask God." God would give us His forgiveness, wisdom, peace, guidance, and acceptance if only we would ask Him for it. All He is waiting for is for us to ask. Our prayerlessness deprives us of the things we need so badly.

Fortunately, the solution to a prayerless marriage is accessible and available. It's time to come before God as a couple in humility and trust and to lay our needs before Him. We must come in a spirit of faith that God does answer prayer. This doesn't mean He'll grant us our every whim or wish. He is not a celestial Santa Claus. But He will provide for every legitimate and heartfelt need that is consistent with His will and His Word.

Imagine, the only thing standing between your needs and God's provision might be your failure to ask. That can be remedied this very moment, can't it? Let's pray.

MARRIAGE MINUTE TRUTH:

CONFESSION AND MERCY
CAN SET YOUR HEART FREE

Primary Passage:
He who conceals his sins does not prosper, but whoever
confesses and renounces them finds mercy.
Proverbs 28:13

*W*e once heard a former professional football player tell the story of how God set his heart free after years of inner struggle and turmoil. After he asked God to show him the problem in his marriage, the Lord pointed him back to their engagement period. During that time he had been involved with other women. His wife never knew that. After hiding the secret all these years, he believed God was leading him to confess that wrongdoing to her. Though he had faced three-hundred-pound linemen from some of the NFL's most talented teams, he had never felt such fear in his life.

Yet he couldn't live with the inner pain and distance between him and his wife any longer. The two were away on a short vacation when he sat down with his wife and told his secret. There were tears of pain and disbelief and, of course, even anger. Yet God gave him the grace to humble himself and gave her the grace to forgive him. The freedom and joy of their renewed love and marriage is evident today in both their faces.

Hiding our sins from each other won't bring prosperity to our relationship. But when we confess and renounce them, the floodgates of mercy can be opened. We are awash in freedom and peace.

MARRIAGE MINUTE TRUTH:

FORGIVENESS IS TO MARRIAGE WHAT OXYGEN IS TO BREATHING

Primary Passage:
*Bear with each other and forgive whatever grievances
you may have against one another. Forgive
as the Lord forgave you.*
Colossians 3:13

Dave Barry, the humor columnist, tells the story of how his brother Sam accidentally left his wife stranded in an unfamiliar city. They were on a trip to see old friends and Sam's wife was driving. Sam continued to insist that his wife, Pat, was lost.

"So Pat decided, okay, if Sam was so good at directions, then HE could drive the stupid car. She got out, slammed the front door, and opened the back door to get in the back with their two-year-old son, Daniel. And then she decided, hey, why should she ride in the back, like a child? So she slammed the back door. But before she could open the front door, Sam, assuming she was in the car, drove off."

The two were later reunited at the police station.

Unresolved anger and conflict can leave us stranded in some strange and unhappy places. We need to forgive the grievances we have against each other rather than acting on them. We are to forgive as the Lord has forgiven us. As Dave Barry explains, "I hope Pat and Sam's experience serves as a lesson to you spouses about the importance of not letting your anger fester . . . [and] on long car trips one of you should ride in the trunk."[1]

1. "Conflict Management," by Dave Barry, from the book, *Dave Barry Is from Mars and Venus* (New York: Crown, 1997).

MARRIAGE MINUTE TRUTH:

SHARED TIMES OF SILENCE
ALLOW GOD TO SPEAK VOLUMES

. . . .

Primary Passage:
Be still, and know that I am God.
Psalm 46:10

. . . .

*T*he late Mother Teresa of Calcutta once said,

All we need is to find God and He cannot be found in noise, and restlessness. God is the friend of silence. Silently the firmament proclaims the glory of God and all nature sings His praises. In the silence of our hearts He will speak to us, if we stop talking and give Him a chance, if we listen, if we are quiet. The psalmist sings:

"Be still, and know that I am God." He will speak.

How often have the two of you enjoyed the sweet experience of complete silence? If you live in a busy city, have two or three televisions, a fax, a beeper, a phone, and children (or any combination of the above), the chances of enjoying regular periods of silence are almost nil. Serenity and stillness remain an "undiscovered country," as Shakespeare put it.

The lack of silence, however, takes a great toll on our lives. It robs us of the chance to hear what God might be trying to say to our weary, overtaxed, and underrested souls. Why not plan into your lives at least five or ten minutes of silence each day? Sit by each other, hold hands, come before God in absolute quiet. Unplug everything that can make noise, and turn off everything that could distract. Be still and discover again that God is the friend of silence—and that silence is a friend of your relationship.

MARRIAGE MINUTE TRUTH:

REJOICING PRODUCES GENTLENESS IN YOUR MARRIAGE

Primary Passage:
Rejoice in the Lord always. I will say it again: Rejoice!
Let your gentleness be evident to all.
Philippians 4:4–5

A church youth group canoe trip was stranded in the beautiful woods and lakes region of the Boundary Waters Canoe area in Minnesota. A combination of bad weather and high waves had left the group thirty-five miles from their destination with just one day to get back home. Food and other provisions were running low. The leader of the group called the kids together and said, "Look, tomorrow we will be forced to canoe from sunrise to midnight. It will be one of the most difficult, strenuous days of your life. The only way we will all get through it is if we all choose to rejoice. No matter how painful or tired you are, we just can't afford any complaining."

The kids accepted the youth leader's challenge. The next day they used every adversity as an opportunity to offer praise and rejoicing. There were no arguments, no shouting, and no complaining the entire day. Despite long portages and backbreaking paddling, a spirit of gentleness prevailed in the group.

Why not get together with your spouse and promise each other that for one day you will rejoice in all things? There will be no complaining, no arguing, no self-pity, just thanks to God in each situation. Our guess is that anger, anxiety, and tension will all take a tremendous paddling.

MARRIAGE MINUTE TRUTH:

WHEN GOD IS IN CONTROL WE CAN RESPOND WITH GENTLENESS

. . . .

Primary Passage:
*I will extol the Lord at all times; his praise will always be
on my lips. My soul will boast in the Lord; let the
afflicted hear and rejoice. Glorify the Lord with me;
let us exalt his name together.*
Psalm 34:1–3

. . . .

*J*im Cymbala, pastor of the Brooklyn Tabernacle in New York City, looked up with a mixture of shock and disbelief. Right in the midst of their time of worship and praise a young man had walked up the center aisle with pistol in hand. It happened so fast no usher could apprehend him before he reached the platform. With the gun pointed right at him, Pastor Cymbala had no time to react either. As the crowd continued singing, the young man reached the pulpit yet at that very moment Pastor Cymbala felt the peace of God surround him even as he prepared to die.

But rather than pulling the trigger, the man put the gun down on the pulpit and began to cry. He had come not to shoot the pastor but to surrender his weapon to him.

Praise and worship can accomplish amazing things. As we are faced with the perils and dangers of living, we can live free of panic, intimidation, and fear. If we're to conquer the burdens and worries that plague our marriages, we must build praise and worship into our relationships. We need to extol the name of God together. Only then can we experience peace at point blank range.

MARRIAGE MINUTE TRUTH:

GENTLENESS IS A MIGHTY ACT OF FAITH

. . . .

Primary Passage:
Let your gentleness be evident to all. The Lord is near.
Philippians 4:5

. . . .

$\mathcal{G}$ordon McClean, a worker with Metro Youth for Christ in the Chicago area, tells the story in *Cities of Lonesome Fear* of a young man he met in a juvenile detention center with the street name Sweet Pea.

Sweet Pea arrived home one evening to find his mother's boyfriend attacking her. Enraged, Sweet Pea went after the man and killed him. While in the juvenile detention center awaiting trial, he came to a saving faith in Jesus Christ. Soon he was attending Bible studies and following Christ in a radical fashion.

One day a new boy arrived on the cell block. He accidentally ran afoul of some of the gang members at lunch. That evening the gang members took a vote and decided to give the new boy a beating. Sweet Pea objected. Upset, the group offered to give Sweet Pea the beating instead. He agreed and was beaten severely by the young men. Yet his example of gentleness created a sense of the presence of God in that jail. Eventually several of the boys came to Christ, including the young man he had saved from a beating.

Let's allow God's gentleness to rule in our homes and marriages. It's a mighty act of faith to respond in gentleness to adversity. It allows others to be drawn to God. Who knows what prisoners may go free as a result?

MARRIAGE MINUTE TRUTH:

GOD'S NEARNESS LEADS US TO PRAY

Primary Passage:
*The Lord is near. Do not be anxious about anything, but
in everything, by prayer and petition, with thanksgiving,
present your requests to God.*
Philippians 4:5b–6

*D*uring the Gulf War of the early 1990s, we served a church that included several families with children in the armed services. What made this church unique is that several members of the congregation were first generation immigrants from Baghdad, Iraq. They had numerous cousins, nephews, and uncles who had been conscripted into Saddam Hussein's Iraqi army.

We had families of soldiers in two opposing armies in the same congregation. As war broke out we sensed the need to pray. We invited everyone with loved ones involved in the conflict to remain after services one Sunday for an extended time of prayer. What a day of prayer it turned out to be. The presence of God descended on us in a powerful fashion. As we collectively poured our hearts out before God, it seemed as if He was walking up and down the aisles ministering among us. Praise God, all loved ones from both armies returned home safely.

When we face anxious and fearful situations in our marriages, we can experience the nearness of God. As we pour our hearts before Him in prayer, petition, and thanksgiving, we realize just how close and available He is to us. His nearness gives us the courage to face any and every situation. God has a plan to give us peace that no army can invade. It's called prayer.

MARRIAGE MINUTE TRUTH:

PEACE IS GOD'S DOWN PAYMENT ON ANSWERED PRAYER

Primary Passage:
Do not be anxious about anything, but in everything,
by prayer and petition, with thanksgiving, present
your requests to God.
Philippians 4:6

*S*everal years ago one of our children had to undergo a biopsy to examine a swollen lymph node. The doctor felt he needed to remove it just to be certain it was not cancerous. The days leading up to the surgery were some of the most anxious of our entire lives. Yet, during the entire ordeal, God gave us the grace to surrender the problem to Him. As we sat in the surgical waiting room the day of the surgery, the woman sitting next to us, a total stranger, began telling of her faith in Christ. We were comforted to know that God had sent one of His people to sit with us during the long wait.

What we remember most about that experience is the peace God gave us in advance of the surgery. It was as if it was a down payment on an answer to prayer. We knew our child was going to be all right even before the surgeon emerged in his scrubs to give us the good news.

Answers to prayer do not always come immediately. Problems are not always solved exactly according to our timetable. But when we bring our issues to God in prayer, regardless of when He chooses to answer, He is able to give us the peace necessary to wait. Once the peace of God has spoken, nothing further needs to be said.

MARRIAGE MINUTE TRUTH:

GOD VALUES
DIFFERENCE IN A MARRIAGE

. . . .

Primary Passage:
After this I looked and there before me was a great
multitude that no one could count, from every nation,
tribe, people and language, standing before the throne
and in front of the Lamb.
Revelation 7:9

. . . .

*W*hat if each of us were exactly like our partner? We'd be able to agree on everything, right? We'd never again argue about money, rearing kids, or the color of wallpaper. We would create a tension-free zone running from the front of our driveway to the back of our fence, right? Wrong. Unfortunately, if we were exactly alike in every respect we would double the weaknesses in our marriage and cut in two the strengths we enjoy. Not a good idea.

Scripture teaches that God values differences in people. The vision of heaven the apostle John was shown displayed a stunning variety and diversity of nations, tribes, peoples, and languages standing before the throne of God.

We are as different as we are in marriage because God designed it that way. He created us with diverse gifts, temperaments, strengths, and talents. We should not despise our differences; we should celebrate them. They are the product of a creative God who delights in variety. Let's view our differences not as a problem but as a foretaste of heaven to come.

MARRIAGE MINUTE TRUTH:

SALVATION IS THE TRUE BASIS OF UNITY IN MARRIAGE

Primary Passage:
*And they cried out in a loud voice: "Salvation belongs to
our God, who sits on the throne, and to the Lamb."*
Revelation 7:10

*T*hrough the years we've watched couples try to build unity into their marriage in a variety of ways. Some have tried buying investment property together. Others have taken ballroom dancing lessons. Still others tried an exotic vacation to Ireland where they rode horses through the bogs. Although each couple no doubt enjoyed the adventures together, we doubt that true unity developed in their marriage as a result. Why? Because it takes something more than learning to gracefully dance together to the Blue Danube to take two souls and make them one for a lifetime.

So what can bring a couple together for a lifetime? An unexpected place to find an answer to this dilemma is in the book of Revelation. In chapter seven we find a scene in heaven in which a multitude of people, diverse in their race, language, and national origin, all have one thing in common—salvation. Each person there has experienced the saving power of Jesus Christ in their lives. As a result they now enjoy true, transcendent, and eternal unity. We can experience the same thing in our marriages today as we celebrate the one thing that can give us a lifetime of authentic oneness—our salvation in Jesus Christ. Our experience of the new birth in Jesus Christ should be the basis of our unity. Although we won't waltz through life, we won't need ballroom dancing to know true oneness.

MARRIAGE MINUTE TRUTH:

OUR WORSHIP OF GOD SHOULD BE THE FOCUS OF OUR MARRIAGE

Primary Passage:
*All the angels were standing around the throne
and around the elders and the four living creatures.
They fell down on their faces before the
throne and worshiped God.*
Revelation 7:11

We once knew a family that enjoyed a remarkable degree of unity and harmony in their home. The children were polite and well behaved. Their house was usually clean, and the husband and wife seemed to genuinely love each other. Oh, one other thing. They had ten children.

Our friends were often sought out by frazzled, fatigued, and discouraged couples who would ask them, "What's your secret? How do you do it? Our home is crazy most of the time." Our friends always gave the same answer, "We start each morning with worship together. We all get up at 5:30 A.M. so we can spend at least an hour singing hymns, praying for one another, and reading the Scriptures. We seldom miss a day."

Granted, our friends were unusual people with special gifts for producing organization and order. But the real secret of their home was not their organizational talents; it was making the worship of God their central focus.

When we organize our home and marriage around the worship of the throne of God, we replicate what is going on in heaven. Our time of worship together brings earth to heaven, and God responds by bringing heaven to earth. It sounds like a plan to us.

MARRIAGE MINUTE TRUTH:

WE CAN IMMEDIATELY ENTER THE PRESENCE OF GOD THROUGH PRAISE

Primary Passage:
*Amen! Praise and glory and wisdom and thanks
and honor and power and strength be to our God
for ever and ever. Amen!*
Revelation 7:12

One of NASA's more impressive accomplishments was landing a tiny robot on the surface of Mars to sniff at rocks. The pictures sent back from the red planet displayed a barren, hostile world made up of jagged rock formations and arid mountains.

Some days God seems to be as remote to our experience as Mars is to Earth. Disappointing news arrives by mail, unexpected interruptions occur from morning until evening, and just as one child gets better, the next one gets sick. None of these events are catastrophes by themselves, yet they still can create a sense of distance between God and ourselves.

On such days how do we close the distance between heaven and earth? The Bible's answer is to enter into the praise of Christ. We are then immediately ushered into God's presence, where He reveals Himself to us. Psalm 22:3 says, "You [God] are enthroned as the Holy One; you are the praise of Israel." If God seems distant or remote to the two of you today, put this book down and begin to offer Him praise as a couple. Praise Him for His love, character, mercy, and salvation. You won't end up on a different planet, but the landscape of this one will be radically changed.

MARRIAGE MINUTE TRUTH:

GOD CAN PRESERVE US THROUGH TIMES OF TRIBULATION

. . . .

Primary Passage:
*And he said, "These are they who have come out of the
great tribulation; they have washed their robes and made
them white in the blood of the Lamb."*
Revelation 7:14

. . . .

A good friend of ours accidentally drove his truck off the Skyway Bridge in Chicago. The tractor and semitrailer he had been driving that snowy evening fell sixty feet and landed on top of him. It took firefighters several hours to cut through the mangled wreckage to reach him, but he emerged standing up. Rescuers were amazed to find inside the wreckage only enough space for his body. Everything else around him had collapsed. No one had ever survived a plunge off the bridge from that distance. In our friend's hour of greatest tribulation, God demonstrated He could preserve him.

Our friend's experience reminds us of a scene depicted in the book of Revelation. Those God has preserved out of the Great Tribulation now gather to praise Him for His keeping power.

God can preserve our marriages in other tribulations as well. When serious illness strikes, when temptation threatens our fidelity, or when our finances simply collapse, God can keep us. The key is to "wash our robes" in the blood of the Lamb, to lean entirely and completely on the saving and cleansing power of Jesus Christ. Regardless of the wreckage around us, when we commit our lives and marriages to the preserving power of Jesus, we can emerge from the debris standing up.

MARRIAGE MINUTE TRUTH:

OUR HOME SHOULD BE A PLACE OF REFRESHMENT

Primary Passage:
Never again will they hunger; never again will they thirst. The sun will not beat upon them, nor any scorching heat. For the Lamb at the center of the throne will be their shepherd; he will lead them to springs of living water.
Revelation 7:16–17b

A church in the Cincinnati area has taken a radical approach to reaching the lost. It's called kindness evangelism. Its members distribute ice-cold cans of soda at stop lights during the summer and clean the rest rooms of local businesses in the winter. When dry and thirsty motorists ask them, "Why are you doing this?" they simply reply, "We want to demonstrate God's love in a practical way."

Heaven is going to be a place of refreshment. No more hunger pangs, no more scorching thirst, no more noonday sun beating down relentlessly upon us as we do our work. Instead we will find continual refreshment in the presence of Jesus the Shepherd. He will lead us to springs of living water (reminiscent of Psalm 23).

Our homes ought to be a foretaste of heaven's refreshment. Not only can we offer one another a cup of cold water when we're hot and thirsty, but we can also hand out a cup of cool and refreshing encouragement when life's heat has worn us down. Heaven can come to earth when we make the simple effort to show God's love to each other in practical ways. Kindness outreaches ought to start with the person we married.

MARRIAGE MINUTE TRUTH:

OUR HOMES SHOULD BE PLACES WHERE SORROWS ARE HEALED

....

Primary Passage:
And God will wipe away every tear from their eyes.
Revelation 7:17c

....

*W*e never went out much as a family," a young woman told us. "My father was an alcoholic, so we stayed home and fought most of the time." Unfortunately, her story could be repeated a thousand times by those who grew up in homes where the living room became a no-man's-land and the dinner table a place of open warfare. Children raised in those battle zones learn to head for emotional cover and keep tears of anguish to themselves.

The apostle John saw a vision of heaven that is radically different from our young friend's childhood home. It's a place where God will wipe away all our tears. The sorrows of abuse, neglect, betrayal, loss, violence, sickness, and death will no longer exist. Either the memory of such painful experiences will be removed or we will be so overcome by the presence of God that such hurts will forever lose their sting.

Until we reach heaven, let's make a daily commitment to make our homes a place where hurts are healed and grief is comforted. Let's come alongside our mates in their times of loss and remembered pain. Let's offer the support and encouragement they need to go on with life. We know that as long as we are on earth there will be tears. But as long as we have each other, tears need never be shed alone.

MARRIAGE MINUTE TRUTH:

THE GREATEST COMFORT WE CAN OFFER EACH OTHER IS OURSELVES

Primary Passage:
But God, who comforts the downcast, comforted
us by the coming of Titus.
2 Corinthians 7:6

*J*oni Eareckson Tada broke her neck when she was only seventeen. During one particular stay in the hospital, the thought of her total paralysis suddenly caused her to be overcome by a suffocating sense of claustrophobia. Her tears of anguish and dread went unnoticed until she heard the door to her room creak open. In the darkness she saw the silhouette of her best friend, Jackie, crawling on her hands and knees toward her bed. Jackie took down the side railing, climbed into bed with her, put her arm around Joni, and began to softly sing, "Jesus, Man of Sorrows, what a friend. . . ."

That very moment Joni knew that she would survive her ordeal of paralysis. The love of God, which she felt had all but disappeared from her life, came flooding back into her heart through the person of Jackie.

As husbands and wives, God has called us to comfort each other with the comfort we have received from God. We don't have to be able to answer the "Why?" question for the other person when he or she is suffering. All God asks us to do is be there for our spouses. Nearness and compassion expressed to our husband or wife can bring the presence of God back into his or her life. When our spouses are nearly suffocated by sorrow or grief, let's be their breath of fresh air.

MARRIAGE MINUTE TRUTH:

WE SHOULD ACCEPT OUR SPOUSE AS GOD ACCEPTS US

. . . .

Primary Passage:
*But God demonstrates his own love for us in this: While
we were still sinners, Christ died for us.*
Romans 5:8

. . . .

*Q*uit acting like your mother and I'll accept you."

"When you apologize for your behavior, I'll consider being intimate with you again. Not until then."

What do these two statements have in common? They follow the same pattern: performance first, acceptance second. It's a formula we're tempted to use in marriage.

The problem is that it is in reverse order to the way God treats us. God doesn't demand we first meet a certain standard before He accepts us. If He did, none of us would ever be saved. He offers us acceptance despite all our problems, past sins, and character flaws. It is a free gift we neither earn nor deserve. It is pure grace based on His Cross alone.

Why is it we have such trouble extending grace to the spouse we pledged to "love, honor, and cherish" for a lifetime? Many, if not most, of our marital problems would disappear if we simply treated our spouse as God treats us—acceptance first, performance last. It's a winning formula for everyone.

MARRIAGE MINUTE TRUTH:

CONFESSING OUR PRIDE IS THE FIRST STEP IN ACCEPTING OUR SPOUSE

Primary Passage:
*Therefore confess your sins to each other and pray for
each other so that you may be healed.*
James 5:16

*T*he man on the phone was openly weeping on a radio talk show. "I need to ask my wife's forgiveness when she gets home this evening," he said with deep emotion. "For all these years I've withheld my acceptance from her because of her weight. I now see how wrong that was." He had just realized that his pride had caused him to reject his wife for years. Thousands of listeners could hear the deep contrition in his voice. It was a sacred moment.

His pride had convinced him through the years of his "right" to have a wife who fit his definition of attractive. Because she failed to meet his arbitrary standard, he had refused her the warmth and affection she so desperately desired from him.

Pride is the sin that's behind every other sin we commit in marriage. It's behind our jealousy, critical heart, gossiping tongue, lustful thoughts, angry outbursts, and rejecting behavior. We need to remember that it was pride that made the devil who he is today. The only remedy is humility. We need to confess our sin of pride to each other and humble ourselves before God. Be prepared if you take that step: You will gain a new love and a new marriage.

MARRIAGE MINUTE TRUTH:

EVEN IN OUR ANGER WE SHOULD SEEK TO BUILD OTHERS UP

. . . .

Primary Passage:
*Do not let any unwholesome talk come out of
your mouths, but only what is helpful for building
others up according to their needs, that it may
benefit those who listen.*
Ephesians 4:29

. . . .

During World War II, General George C. Marshall served as chief military adviser to President Roosevelt. Marshall was known as a first-rate soldier in the same league as George Washington, according to some historians. After the war he proposed the Marshall Plan, the incredible relief program that saved post-war Europe from chaos and the encroachment of Communism.

General Marshall once came across a junior officer angrily reprimanding and berating a private. The irate officer was just about to shred the last threads of the man's dignity and self-esteem when Marshall interrupted him. "You have forgotten, Captain, that this man too is a citizen, like yourself."

Paul tells us that even when we are angry we should say only "what is helpful for building others up according to their needs" (Ephesians 4:29). That eliminates sarcasm, cynicism, and demeaning remarks between husbands and wives. We should use only "wholesome words" to build our spouse up. If we have a tendency to let our tongues get away from us when we're angry, it's helpful to stop and remind ourselves, "This person too is a citizen of this family, like myself."

The order of the day then becomes, "At ease."

MARRIAGE MINUTE TRUTH:

AN ABSENT FATHER SETS HIS CHILDREN UP FOR DESTRUCTIVE CHOICES

Primary Passage:
*The rod of correction imparts wisdom, but a child
left to himself disgraces his mother.*
Proverbs 29:15

*I*t was in seminary we were taught the impact of a father's prolonged emotional or physical absence from a home. Left to themselves, children can develop destructive behavior patterns known as compensatory masculinity and compensatory femininity.

When a father is missing from the home because of a separation, divorce, or simply too much time spent at work, a destructive pattern begins to emerge. When boys lack a loving and involved male role model, they are left to guess at what it means to be a man. They frequently conclude that manhood is proven by engaging in early, if not predatory, sexual behavior.

Compensatory femininity occurs when a young girl lacks the love, nurture, and affection she needs from her father. She ends up "looking for love in all the wrong places," as the country western song says.

The positive side to all of this is the tremendous difference a father can make in the life of a young boy or girl. Children won't need to compensate for a missing dad in destructive ways if their dad is present and involved. Instead they will have the best chance possible to grow into spiritually positive adults. Dads, could anything be more important than this task?

MARRIAGE MINUTE TRUTH:

A LOVING FATHER MAKES A LOVING GOD SEEM MORE BELIEVABLE

. . . .

Primary Passage:
*As a father has compassion on his children, so the
Lord has compassion on those who fear him.*
Psalm 103:13

. . . .

*Y*ears ago we knew a middle-aged man who told us that he has struggled his entire life with trusting or believing in authority figures—including pastors. His own dad had left him when he was a small boy. He has never been able to trust anyone in authority as a result.

The greatest risk children face from homes where the father is absent is spiritual resentment. They are tempted to believe God is neither loving nor available. Their dad didn't care, and wasn't there when they needed him, so why should God be any different?

The Bible makes a rather dramatic statement, "As a father has compassion on his children, so the Lord has compassion on those who fear him." God Himself is willing to be compared to an earthly father. That ought to motivate every father to do everything he can, by the grace of God, to project an image of God that his children can love and respect.

The only way to counteract spiritual resentment in our children is to model the love, concern, and nurture of God in our homes. We need to live out a life filled with compassion and mercy for our kids. God's own reputation is on the line.

MARRIAGE MINUTE TRUTH:

THE TEST OF A PARENT'S SUCCESS COMES WHEN CHILDREN BECOME ADULTS

Primary Passage:
*Children's children are a crown to the aged, and
parents are the pride of their children.*
Proverbs 17:6

*R*egardless of political persuasion most would agree that former president George Bush led a remarkable career of public service. Just before he left the White House, a reporter asked him which accomplishment from his distinguished life of service he was the most proud of. He thought for a moment and then replied, "That my kids still come home to visit us." Despite his busy life lived in the glare of public scrutiny, Bush had communicated to his children they were a top priority to him.

The real test of our parenting waits until all our children are grown and gone. It's then we'll discover whether or not we successfully built a loving bond that will bring them home for a visit. The time to begin that process is now, while our kids are still tugging on our sleeves, begging us to go outside and play ball or to sit down and read them a book. If our children are teenagers it may take both creativity and persistence to get them to spend time with us. But no child, not even an adolescent, outgrows his deep-seated need for a father and a mother.

If we have done our job well, then they will someday point to us and say, "That's my Mom and Dad. They're the greatest." Won't that be a moment to cherish?

MARRIAGE MINUTE TRUTH:

THE TIME TO RESIST INFIDELITY IS BEFORE WE ARE EVER TEMPTED

Primary Passage:
For these commands are a lamp, this teaching is a light,
and the corrections of discipline are the way to life,
keeping you from the immoral woman, from the
smooth tongue of the wayward wife.
Proverbs 6:23–24

A leading pastor's journal carried the sad account of one pastor's lapse into immorality. His son happened to pick up the phone one day and heard his father talking to another woman from the congregation. He was asking her if she would like to have sex with him. Tragically, it was up to the son to alert others that his father was involved in an immoral relationship. Ultimately the pastor lost his ministry.

The time to resist the sin of infidelity is not when things have progressed to the point of proposing sexual intercourse with another person. No, the time and place to resist that sin is before we even come close to the border of transgression.

How do we prepare in advance for a temptation we have not yet encountered? Proverbs tells us we are to learn the commands of the Lord. We are to fill our lives with His teaching. We are to accept the disciplines of correction to keep us from the immoral man or woman. We are to seriously study God's Word and allow it to penetrate our hearts so that when the phone call comes, the potential lover gets nothing from us but a busy signal.

ADULTERY CAN UTTERLY DESTROY ALL THAT WE HAVE WORKED FOR

Primary Passage:
*Do not lust in your heart after her beauty or let
her captivate you with her eyes, for the prostitute
reduces you to a loaf of bread, and the adulteress
preys upon your very life.*
Proverbs 6:25–26

He was a well-respected member of our community. He had been voted back to the state legislature nearly a dozen times by his loyal constituency. Then a local newspaper reporter jotted down his license number outside a known house of prostitution. When the reporter called the legislator's office to confront him with the evidence, the politician calmly replied, "Would you lend me a hose for my car? Because if you run this story I will kill myself in the garage tonight when I get home." Fortunately the legislator did not follow through on this threat, but the man's reputation and career was ruined in just one edition of a newspaper.

We often fail to count the true cost of adultery. It can cost us not only our marriages, but our careers, our reputations, and even our very lives. In the end we have nothing of more value than a loaf of bread. Such a high price for a few minutes of forbidden pleasure. The reward is hardly worth the cost. Let's remember that when our adversary, the devil, tempts us to unfaithfulness, he has in mind our total destruction. And if he wins, he'll make sure it makes front page news.

MARRIAGE MINUTE TRUTH:

OUR CHEERFUL ATTITUDE CAN BRING LIGHT INTO THE DARKNESS OF DESPAIR

. . . .

Primary Passage:
A cheerful heart is good medicine,
but a crushed spirit dries up the bones.
Proverbs 17:22

. . . .

*W*hen Cheryl's older sister was just ten years old, she was selected to turn on the lights on the city Christmas tree. It happened on her golden birthday and was a night she would never forget. As she flipped the switch on, a towering pine tree came alive with a sea of color and dazzling light. The assembled crowd broke out in applause and appreciation.

The Bible teaches that God can use us to turn on the lights of joy and hope in the lives of others. A cheerful heart is not only good medicine for our own lives, but it can be used as an excellent tonic in the lives of those around us who are struggling with sorrow and a sense of hopelessness.

As we rejoice in the goodness of God and the blessings of Christ that we have received, our joyful hearts can spill over into the lives of others. Our spouse, our children, our friends, even our boss can be affected by the cheerfulness of our spirit.

In many ways cheerfulness is a choice. It's a willingness to focus on all that we have received instead of all that we have lost. It's actually a beautiful gift that we can give to others every day. Cheryl's sister Cathryn has had a sweet and cheerful spirit her entire life. She has not only turned on the city's Christmas lights, but she has also lit up the lives of others with her cheerful heart. You can too.

❧❧❧❧❧❧

MARRIAGE MINUTE TRUTH:

A FOOTHOLD CAN ONE DAY BECOME A STRANGLEHOLD

. . . .

Primary Passage:
. . . and do not give the devil a foothold.
Ephesians 4:27

. . . .

*O*ne of the sweetest older men we ever knew was once a complete alcoholic. He was just fourteen years old when his father poured him his first taste of Jack Daniels and said, "Here, boy. Drink this if you want to be a man."

The boy obediently downed the shot glass. From that day onward he developed a thirst for alcohol that ultimately destroyed everything meaningful in his adult life. Only an eleventh hour conversion to Jesus Christ rescued him from total destruction. It's hard to imagine, but four small ounces of whiskey forever changed his destiny. Four ounces of sinful anger can have the same impact on our marriages.

We start out taking little snipes at each other. Gradually, sarcasm becomes a way of life. Deeper resentment then settles in. Finally we can't remember the last time we felt warmth and closeness between us. The toehold became a foothold. The foothold ultimately became a stranglehold. To get free, we need to confess and renounce the sin that gave the devil a foothold in our relationship.

The next time the devil offers a shot glass of anger to sip, we need to pour it out. It's far too dangerous to swallow.

❧❧❧❧❧❧

MARRIAGE MINUTE TRUTH:

IT IS GOD'S MERCY THAT PROVIDES FOR OUR DAILY NEEDS

Primary Passage:
Then God said, "I give you every seed-bearing plant
on the face of the whole earth and every tree
that has fruit with seed in it."
Genesis 1:29

"Thank You, God, for giving us this wonderful meal that we don't deserve," the emcee at a school banquet prayed.

At the end of the banquet an irate parent approached him, "I have a bone to pick with you," she said.

He blinked at her in disbelief. "What did I say?" he asked.

"It was your prayer," she snapped back. "You said we didn't deserve the meal we were about to eat. Well, young man, I've worked hard all my life and I want you to know that I deserved this meal. I resent the fact you say I didn't."

The emcee meekly apologized, and the woman walked away obviously gratified she had put him in his place. Although she believed she had struck a blow for the right, she could not have been more in the wrong. It is only because of the grace of God, only because of His provision, and only because of His mercy that we have food to eat each day. Because of our sin, we deserve nothing but judgment. But God, rich in grace through Christ, has given us salvation and granted us all things richly to enjoy.

Tonight, before you eat supper together, stop for a moment and look at your table of food. You are looking at a banquet of grace.

MARRIAGE MINUTE TRUTH:

GOD HAS TAKEN IT ON HIMSELF TO PROVIDE FOR OUR DAILY NEEDS

Primary Passage:
God saw all that he had made, and it was very good.
Genesis 1:31

*O*ne summer we rented two small garden plots in the community garden. We even used our anniversary to plant tomatoes, green beans, corn, and a host of other vegetables. The world was about to meet two new gardening champions.

Unfortunately, as the summer wore on we found ourselves caught up in vacations, work schedules, and taking care of small children, and we didn't tend to our gardens. When we checked on them in August they were overgrown with weeds the size of small trees. Mosquitoes the size of small pigeons came swarming out of the overgrowth, and we were forced to abandon the farm.

It's good that God is a better gardener than we are. He has taken it on Himself to plant His creation with every type of seed-bearing plant or food that exists today. He is still the One who gives the earth its tremendous produce. He has pledged Himself to care for our daily needs and to feed and clothe us. He is faithful to us every season of the year, isn't He? Give God thanks for the beauty of the earth and its bounty. Our needs are ever before Him, and He delights in caring for us. Take time as a couple to praise Him today for His constant goodness and provision.

MARRIAGE MINUTE TRUTH:

GOD NEVER INTENDED
US TO KNOW DEPRIVATION

Primary Passage:
*Now the Lord God had planted a garden in the east, in
Eden; and there he put the man he had formed.*
Genesis 2:8

John Perkins is a wonderful Christian spokesman for the poor and disadvantaged. Born in rural Mississippi, John was still a young child when his mother died. Her death was hastened because she lacked basic nutrition, something as simple as a bottle of milk.

God never intended the world to work this way. He designed a world that would feed all its inhabitants. The words *deprivation, starvation,* or *malnutrition* weren't in His original Creation vocabulary. Because sin entered the world, the words *famine, hunger,* and *death* are now sadly part of everyday vocabulary.

The good news is that God is in the process of redeeming the world through Christ. The day is coming when Christ will return and once again make the word *deprivation* an unknown term. Until then, we must do all that is in our power to bring relief to the suffering, food to the starving, and hope to the destitute. Just because the world is under the curse of sin does not mean God wills for people to starve and children to die. God has commissioned us to be agents of redemption. We are to do all that we can in the name of Christ to heal this hungry and broken world.

MARRIAGE MINUTE TRUTH:

GOD'S GREATEST GIFT TO US IN THE CREATION IS RELATIONSHIPS

Primary Passage:
*The Lord God said, "It is not good for the man to be
alone. I will make a helper suitable for him."*
Genesis 2:18

*D*aniel was in his early fifties when we met him. He was well established in his career, he consistently earned trophies as a triathlon competitor, and he led weekly Bible studies in the county jail. As a hard-working single man he owned his own home, set his own schedule, and traveled wherever he liked.

To everyone's surprise, well into the sixth decade of life, he fell smashingly in love and was married in one of the most joyous ceremonies we recall.

Daniel is much like Adam. Adam had just about everything a man could ever want in the Garden of Eden. Unhindered fellowship with God, a good job, abundant resources, and total independence. There was only one thing missing in his life—an intimate relationship with another human being. Despite Adam's perfect environment, God had created a need in his heart that could only be met by a woman—Eve.

Have you stopped to consider that the greatest gift God has given you (apart from your salvation in Christ) is your relationship with your spouse? Everything else in your life could be perfect, but without him or her, something vital would be missing. Give thanks that God has met your every need, including the need for relationships.

MARRIAGE MINUTE TRUTH:

SIN IS THE REASON IT'S SO DIFFICULT TO EARN A LIVING

Primary Passage:
*Cursed is the ground because of you; through painful
toil you will eat of it all the days of your life. It will
produce thorns and thistles for you, and you
will eat the plants of the field.*
Genesis 3:17–18

*Y*oung Teddy Roosevelt moved out West after his wife and his mother died on the same day. He left behind the congestion and sorrow of New York to search for solace in the vast prairies of the Dakotas. There he invested his money in a huge herd of range cattle. Calamity struck again. A huge blizzard wiped out his entire investment with one fell stroke. He gave up and went home to New York.

Why is it so hard to make a living? Why does the clothes dryer break down just after you've paid off your son's braces? Why does the plant close just months before you were planning to purchase your first home? Why does the error on the bank statement always seem to go against you?

The answer is original sin. God's resulting curse upon the ground has introduced difficulty in our ability to make a living. Yet that curse is not God's final word. Through Jesus Christ the grace of God is at work in our lives today. In this redeemed relationship God blesses our work, multiplies our efforts, and gives us the means to survive. The wonders of His love are at work "far as the curse is found."

MARRIAGE MINUTE TRUTH:

GOD'S SOLUTION TO THE FALL OF MAN IS REDEEMING GRACE

Primary Passage:
*The Lord God made garments of skin for Adam
and his wife and clothed them.*
Genesis 3:21

*O*n the day Abraham Lincoln learned that the Civil War had ended, he walked over to the conductor of the Marine Band and asked him, "Please play 'Dixie.' I've always rather liked that song." Despite a bloody rebellion that cost the nation half a million lives, Lincoln's first gesture toward the South was one of grace.

Something similar occurred immediately after Adam and Eve's tragic rebellion against God in the Garden of Eden. Instead of inflicting a furious and vengeful judgment, God made garments out of animal skins to clothe them. Biblical scholars often note that providing such clothing required a blood sacrifice and thus loss of us. That shedding of blood was a foreshadowing of Christ's sacrifice upon the cross to cover our sin and shame.

From the beginning of time the theme of the Bible is redeeming grace. Though Adam and Eve had the hearts of rebels, God had a plan to cover them with His righteousness. Rejoice today that God has covered our sin with the merit of Christ. Rejoice that He sees both of you clothed in the holiness of Christ this very hour. God's grace is His answer to our rebellion. Grace rather than judgment has the final word.

MARRIAGE MINUTE TRUTH:

GOD REMEMBERS THE RIGHTEOUS

. . . .

Primary Passage:
*The Lord then said to Noah, "Go into the ark, you
and your whole family, because I have found
you righteous in this generation."*
Genesis 7:1

. . . .

*L*ocal folklore in the region of Mount Ararat tells of an un-
usually hot summer near the turn of the twentieth century.
Russian soldiers, who controlled the area at the time, supposedly
discovered a massive wooden boat partially exposed in melting
glacial ice. The legend says they entered the vessel and discovered
several decks with cages capable of housing thousands of animals.

Whether or not local legend is accurate, God's Word definitely
teaches Noah and his family were rescued in an ark from a
worldwide flood. "Noah was a righteous man, blameless among
the people of his time" (Genesis 6:9).

Noah's story should be an encouragement to us. God has
pledged Himself over and over in the Scriptures to watch over the
way of the righteous. The economy may be turbulent, our income
may be unsteady, and our bills may be mounting, but God will not
forget us. He will place the ark of His care and concern around
our homes. He will bring us through whatever flood threatens to
overwhelm our marriage at the moment. As the waters rise, God
also rises to the occasion. He remembers the righteous.

MARRIAGE MINUTE TRUTH:

GOD PRESERVES, RATHER THAN REMOVES, HIS PEOPLE IN DISTRESS

Primary Passage:
The waters flooded the earth for a hundred and fifty days. But God remembered Noah and all the wild animals and the livestock that were with him.
Genesis 7:24–8:1

J. C. Penney was one of the most successful businessmen in the country during the 1920s. Then came that fateful day in October, 1929, when the bottom fell out of the stock market. Discouraged and distraught over losing his wealth and his job, he eventually admitted himself to a hospital, a broken man.

He awoke one morning to hear the sound of a hospital chapel service singing the old gospel hymn, "God Will Take Care of You." J. C. Penney suddenly experienced the presence of God by his bedside assuring him, "I will take care of you." Not long after, he left the hospital a renewed person.

God doesn't always take us out of our troubles. Rather, like He did with Noah and his family on the ark, He often preserves us in the midst of our problems. We shouldn't be discouraged if our problems don't suddenly disappear when we pray about them. God doesn't usually work that way. Rather, He wants our faith to grow by believing in His promise, "I will take care of you."

J. C. Penney went on to rebuild his company into one of the nation's outstanding retail stores. More important, he went on to testify with his life of God's care. God doesn't always need to take us out of our distress. He has the power to keep us through our distress. And that's just as wonderful.

MARRIAGE MINUTE TRUTH:

GOD WILL CARE FOR HIS PEOPLE TO THE END OF TIME

Primary Passage:
As long as the earth endures, seed time and harvest,
cold and heat, summer and winter, day and
night will never cease.
Genesis 8:22

The end of the world is always a popular topic in the supermarket tabloids. Whether the subject is "newly discovered Bible prophecies" or the "unpublished writings of Nostradamus," the story is always the same—the end of the world is near. Buy the paper and get the inside scoop on how it will happen.

We, of course, do believe the world is going to end someday. The book of Revelation makes it quite clear Christ is going to return and a new heaven and earth will appear. Until that moment arrives, however, God has promised that nature itself will follow the rhythms and patterns necessary to sustain life. Embedded in this promise is also the assurance the world will not end until Christ's return.

No famine or hole in the ozone layer will cut short God's plans for the end of history. God has appointed a time when He will bring the world to a close. Christ will return to judge sin and usher in His complete rule. So don't be thrown off by sensational predictions of the end of the world. The end will come, but it will be just the beginning for all the redeemed in Christ.

MARRIAGE MINUTE TRUTH:

HARD WORK IS GOD'S ORDAINED MEANS OF EARNING A LIVING

Primary Passage:
*Go to the ant, you sluggard; consider its ways and
be wise! It has no commander, no overseer or ruler,
yet it stores its provisions in summer and
gathers its food at harvest.*
Proverbs 6:6–8

A friend of ours likes to play the lottery. He hopes that his special numbers will one day spell instant wealth and freedom. He can then say good-bye to the daily grind of getting up, going to work, and putting up with a difficult boss.

His attitude is in error. It's based on the idea that all work is a curse and all idleness is a blessing. The Bible teaches something quite different. The Scriptures teach that work is the opportunity to share in the creative initiatives God Himself has established. It's also God's ordained method for us to provide for our needs. Even before sin entered the world God gave Adam work to do in managing the Garden.

Praise God today for the meaningful and important work He's given you, whether inside or outside the home. Show the discipline, initiative, and foresight to engage in hard work like the ant mentioned in Proverbs. The ant has no boss or supervisor, but still diligently works to store provisions and to gather food at harvest. Enjoy your work, commit to God's glory, and pray for His blessing on it. It's a much better bet than the lottery.

MARRIAGE MINUTE TRUTH:

A WILLINGNESS TO WORK IS AN IMPORTANT CHARACTER TRAIT

Primary Passage:
*How long will you lie there, you sluggard? When
will you get up from your sleep?*
Proverbs 6:9

*Y*ou've seen the commercials. A camera crew jostling boom mikes and portable shoulder cameras wheels into the driveway of an unsuspecting contestant. Holding a million-dollar check the size of a toboggan, they ring the doorbell. When an unsuspecting person answers and realizes she has won, she screams, squeezes her own face on both sides, and twirls around in a swoon.

What's wrong with this picture? Is it the invasion of privacy? The ridiculously high odds against winning? Or is it the subtle, subversive message that freedom from work is true joy?

Our willingness to work is a character trait that God highly values. In the book of Proverbs the sluggard is derided for his unwillingness to get up and go to work. Scarcity and poverty, not a sweepstakes van and camera crew, is about to pull up into his driveway and surprise the lazy individual.

It's wrong to hate work. Not every job is pleasant or fulfilling; many are not. But laziness, idleness, and shiftlessness are soul destroying. Over time our refusal to work (unless we are physically or otherwise unable to work) diminishes us. So when the alarm rings tomorrow morning, let's get up and thank God we have a job. He'll be pleased.

MARRIAGE MINUTE TRUTH:

REFUSING TO WORK SERIOUSLY COMPROMISES OUR WITNESS

Primary Passage:
*If anyone does not provide for his relatives, and especially
for his immediate family, he has denied the faith
and is worse than an unbeliever.*
1 Timothy 5:8

The billionaire owner of Cable News Network, Ted Turner, was raised in a religious home and went for six years to a Christian prep school. Yet standing before a packed audience of humanists he declared, "I was saved seven or eight times, but when I lost my faith I felt better about it." He described the notion of a blood atonement on the cross as "weird, man."

Most believers would read Turner's comments as a denial of the Christian faith. It's a dangerous step that none of us who know Christ would even consider taking.

Yet the apostle Paul tells us we do exactly the same thing when we *refuse* to work and provide for our family's needs (with the exception of course of a job loss or illness or injury). We are denying the faith and are worse than an unbeliever.

Laziness, indolence, and a lack of concern for our loved ones' needs compromise our witness. It denies our faith. The good news is that when we do our best to provide for our family we are affirming our faith in Christ. Our witness does not go unnoticed. We broadcast the message that love for Christ means love for our families. It may not make CNN Headlines, but the story will be carried in full in heaven.

MARRIAGE MINUTE TRUTH:

GIVING US WISDOM TO PLAN FOR THE FUTURE IS ONE WAY GOD PROVIDES FOR US

Primary Passage:
*Joseph collected all the food produced in those seven years
of abundance in Egypt and stored it in the cities.*
Genesis 41:48–49

*E*arly in our ministry career we served an inner city church. One need we immediately noticed was that single mothers were often running out of food by the end of the month. We began a food pantry to help. One day a corporation donated 14,000 pre-packaged hot dogs (with a shelf life of ten years). We were able to come up with recipes for the hot dogs that helped families for the entire next year.

Planning for the future is one method God uses to provide for our needs. Joseph had the foresight to assemble huge quantities of grain in Egypt before the years of famine arrived. As a result he saved millions of people from starvation.

Are you preparing for the future? Or are you spending every dime you have right now?

As John Wesley would say, "Earn as much as you can, save as much as you can, give as much as you can." God is not offended by our saving or making careful preparation for the future. He views that as an exercise in foresight and wisdom. Rainy days probably will come into your lives. Do you have an umbrella?

MARRIAGE MINUTE TRUTH:

EXTRAORDINARY TIMES PROMPT GOD TO DO EXTRAORDINARY THINGS

Primary Passage:
*So the people grumbled against Moses, saying, "What
are we to drink?" Then Moses cried out to the Lord, and
the Lord showed him a piece of wood. He threw it into
the water, and the water became sweet.*
Exodus 15:24–25

*D*uring the Civil War years Dwight Moody and his wife often ministered at battlefields where the wounded still lay out in the open. On one sad occasion they arrived in Tennessee to find men from both sides dying of dehydration and hunger. They had only a little water with them and virtually no food. They held a prayer meeting through the night for God to meet this dire need.

The dawn's early light revealed a farmer driving his wagon over a hill in their direction. When he arrived they saw that the wagon was loaded down with bread. The farmer explained that during the night God had awakened him and impressed him and his wife to bake as much bread as possible and gather the rest from neighbors.

When we face extraordinary circumstances, God is prompted to respond in extraordinary ways. He often sends us help from the most unexpected places. Take a moment to think about the numerous times in your marriage that God has acted to help you when you faced extraordinary difficulties. Who did He send on a bread wagon? How did He answer prayer in an unusual way? God's love sometimes comes in a loaf, doesn't it?

MARRIAGE MINUTE TRUTH:

GRUMBLING IS THE LANGUAGE OF DISBELIEF

. . . .

Primary Passage:
In the desert the whole community grumbled against
Moses and Aaron. The Israelites said to them, "If only
we had died by the Lord's hand in Egypt!"
Exodus 16:2–3

. . . .

Chuck Swindoll tells the story of a Swedish missionary who was urged not to go to a certain country because of its oppressive heat. "Why, it's 101 degrees in the shade!" warned a well-meaning friend.

"Well," replied the missionary, "we don't have to spend all our time in the shade, do we?" We could all benefit from that missionary's example of refusing to grumble about circumstances.

It had been a scant six weeks since God had delivered the people of Israel from their four hundred years of slavery in Egypt. What was their response? Grumbling.

Chronic grumbling is the language of unbelief. Translated it says, "God, You can't be trusted to take care of me, can You? If I were in charge of the universe, I'd manage it a whole lot better than You do."

Stop and evaluate your lives for hints of grumbling and complaining. Are you upset with God for the small size of your house? The lack of vacation time? The high number of miles on your car? Come in out of the shade. We don't have to spend all our time there, do we?

MARRIAGE MINUTE TRUTH:

GOD PROVIDES FOR US ONE DAY AT A TIME, BUT TOGETHER ALL THOSE DAYS FORM A LIFETIME

Primary Passage:
*Each morning everyone gathered as much [manna] as he
needed, and when the sun grew hot, it melted away.*
Exodus 16:21

*W*hen the Israelites wandered in the wilderness for forty years, God fed them one day at a time. No doubt He could have provided forty years of food all at once if He had chosen to do so. Instead He taught them the simple truth that God takes cares of us one day at a time—but when we put all those days together they form a lifetime.

Are we tempted to complain that God hasn't paid all our bills into next year? Or that we haven't been able to put away all the money for our children's college education? If we have been diligent in following God, we don't need to worry that tomorrow's expenses aren't paid. God is prepared to meet each need as it arises, one day at a time.

We can rest in the fact God will provide us with manna tomorrow morning. Even if we have no idea how He is going to do it we can relax and trust Him. Why? God views all of time with a single glance. He's already seen the beginning, end, and middle of our lives. He's already settled the issue of how He will provide. So let's get up each day with a basket of faith in our hands—the manna will be there.

MARRIAGE MINUTE TRUTH:

GOD'S PROVISION FOR US IS A POWERFUL WITNESS TO UNBELIEVERS

Primary Passage:
Go at once to Zarephath of Sidon and stay there.
I have commanded a widow in that place
to supply you with food.
1 Kings 17:9

*H*ave you heard the preacher's story about a saintly old woman who prayed each morning for God to send her food? Her neighbor, a confirmed atheist, grew disgusted by her childlike faith in a God he didn't believe existed.

One morning he went down to the grocery store and bought her two bags of groceries. He then quietly placed them on her doorstep, rang the bell, and hid around the corner. The woman opened the door, saw the groceries, then cried out, "Thank you, Lord! Thank You for meeting my need again today!"

Her neighbor jumped out from behind the bushes. "God didn't have anything to do with these groceries," he said with a sneer. "I'm the one who bought them. See, there is no God."

The woman looked over at her neighbor, then down again at the groceries, and in a loud voice she cried out, "Thank You, Lord! You not only sent me groceries but had the devil deliver them!"

God used a Gentile woman to provide for Elijah's need during a time of famine. God's daily provision for you is a witness to the world that your God is the true God. Regardless of how they get to your doorstep, or who delivers them, God sent them.

MARRIAGE MINUTE TRUTH:

WORRY POSES A GREATER THREAT THAN TOUGH FINANCIAL TIMES

. . . .

Primary Passage:
*Therefore I tell you, do not worry about your life,
what you will eat or drink; or about your body,
what you will wear.*
Matthew 6:25

. . . .

A woman once sat on an airplane with her eyes glued to the window. Because of turbulence the left wing could be clearly seen moving up and down. The person sitting next to her, sensing her intense anxiety, leaned over and said, "I'll watch the wing for a little if you'd like to get some rest."

Worry is always unproductive. It never gives back anything of value for all the sweat, high blood pressure, and anxiety we invest in it. Jesus told us not to worry. He said it's a futile effort that won't add a single hour to our lives.

What is it that you and your spouse worry about? Is it losing your job? Paying off credit cards? Failing health? Jesus said don't waste your time on such things. Commit your present, your future, even your eternity into God's hands.

The Bible never promises that we will be spared of all trouble and ill health. Instead the promise of God is that He will walk us through the dark valleys of our life. He will never let us out of His sight for a single moment. The result? We can take our eyes off the wing even during turbulence. God's Word promises we will ultimately land safely in His arms.

MARRIAGE MINUTE TRUTH:

WORRY UNDERESTIMATES OUR IMPORTANCE TO GOD

. . . .

Primary Passage:
Look at the birds of the air; they do not sow or reap or
store away in barns, and yet your heavenly Father feeds
them. Are you not much more valuable than they?
Matthew 6:26

. . . .

*H*ave you ever watched a frightened child hang on for dear life when a parent tried to drop him or her off at a nursery or baby-sitter? The psychological term for this panic is separation anxiety. It means the child is scared to death and believes that the parent is leaving and will never return.

How do parents usually try to calm such fears? "Please don't worry, Honey. Dad and Mom love you too much to ever forget you." As adults we sometimes manifest similar childish fears. "How are we going to solve this crisis? This is it. We're finished," or sometimes, "Oh, God, where are You? Why have You abandoned us?"

Worry of this type is a serious underestimation of who God is. God will no more abandon us to drown in the deep waters of financial or family troubles than we would leave our own child in the nursery and never return.

Jesus said the antidote to worry is realizing our great value to God. Once we grasp that truth, we can stop fretting. God is coming back to get us. He promised.

MARRIAGE MINUTE TRUTH:

FAITH AND WORRY WON'T MIX

Primary Passage:
*If that is how God clothes the grass of the field, which is
here today and tomorrow is thrown into the fire, will he
not much more clothe you, O you of little faith?*
Matthew 6:30

One popular cult group teaches that God (or a god) appeared to a young princess in the form of a bumblebee. That's an unpleasant belief if for no other reason than that birds, flowers, and insects have no soul. And God is the Supreme Soul.

What is true is that God takes great pains to give the birds of the air food and to give clothes to the lilies of the field. A simple glance at nature demonstrates how meticulous and faithful God is to care for His creation and creatures. Jesus said if God so cares for such soul-less parts of His creation, how much more will He care for us human beings who bear the image of God in our eternal souls?

Can we believe God loves us more than a geranium or a hummingbird? If so, then our worries are gone. If God spends that much effort and concern taking care of birds and flowers, then it should be obvious we will be the recipients of His extravagant love and provision.

MARRIAGE MINUTE TRUTH:

OUR FIRST CONCERN SHOULD BE WITH KINGDOM PRIORITIES

. . . .

Primary Passage:
But seek first his kingdom and his righteousness, and all
these things will be given to you as well.
Matthew 6:33

. . . .

On our honeymoon we visited the Cathedral of Notre Dame in Paris. As we entered the historic church our eyes were drawn to one particular sculpture. It depicted Christ hanging from a cross with a coiled snake at the bottom. The snake was limp and lifeless. The message hit home with great force. Christ's death defeated sin, death, and ultimately Satan himself. His kingdom is victorious and on the march.

God's desire for us as couples is that we develop kingdom priorities. That means we should seek to do the will of God first and foremost every day of our lives. We aren't to be sidetracked or subverted by concerns that seem to preoccupy everyone else.

Our primary focus should not be on daily problems or the difficulties of making a living. The majority of the human race seems preoccupied with money, getting ahead, and building the good life. Personal fitness, the pursuit of pleasure, and career building are idols of the day.

God would have us give our best efforts to prayer, study of the Word, and serving Christ. He calls us to put first things first and to trust Him for all else. Christ is victorious and the snake is mortally wounded. Are your priorities reflecting that truth?

MARRIAGE MINUTE TRUTH:

GOD IS CAPABLE OF MEETING YOUR EVERY NEED IN CHRIST JESUS

Primary Passage:
*And my God will meet all your needs according
to his glorious riches in Christ Jesus.*
Philippians 4:19

*H*ouston, we have a problem here."

With those now famous words, Apollo 13 Commander Jim Lovell alerted the world the three-man spacecraft was in mortal jeopardy. On the ground, flight engineers calculated the severity of the power loss the crew had just experienced. They had less power left to get home than it takes to run a coffeemaker on earth for nine hours.

Many couples face critical shortages in their relationships. It may be a shortage of hope, forgiveness, or even love. They are in danger of being left marooned in an orbit of pain, loneliness, and anger.

Fortunately help is available. The Scriptures tell us God can meet all our needs according to His glorious riches in Christ Jesus. Whether your need is financial, job related, or a marital issue, Jesus Christ provides the answer. Because of God's vast and limitless store of love, mercy, and strength, He can deal with the power shortages in your life. The key is turning over the problems to Him and then leaving them with Him. Praise Him in advance for His answer.

You have a problem. God has an answer. Over and out.

MARRIAGE MINUTE TRUTH:

CONTENTMENT IS A CHOICE WE MAKE

Primary Passage:
I have learned to be content whatever the circumstances.
Philippians 4:11

*O*ne of our most difficult choices was to sell a new home we had built a year earlier. No, we didn't have radon gas in the basement or obnoxious neighbors living next door; we just couldn't afford it. Moving into a house half the size meant we had to swallow a great deal of our pride.

Why was that so hard to do? Materialism teaches the lie that we are what we own. It promises that whatever we lack in our self-esteem, self-confidence, or self-worth we can make up in what we own.

God offers a wonderful alternative to materialism. It's called contentment. Contentment is the choice we make to be at peace with the provisions God has placed in our lives.

Who we are is shaped by what we worship. True self-confidence or self-worth comes from worshiping Jesus Christ. He allows us to be at peace with what we own, even if God never adds anything to it. If we have worked hard and followed Christ diligently, then all we own is all God must believe that we need for right now. Do you know the best news of all? God's contentment doesn't cost us a thing—except our misery.

THE SECRET TO CONTENTMENT IS CHRIST HIMSELF

Primary Passage:
I have learned the secret of being content in any and every situation, whether well fed or hungry, whether living in plenty or in want.
Philippians 4:12

It was a most unusual college course. For thirty days each January, during the coldest month of the year in Minnesota, a history professor took students to live in what was known as "The Depression House." The idea was to replicate the difficult conditions of rural America in the 1930s. For one month the students would forego hamburgers, pizza, and tacos for a diet consisting of cornmeal, homemade bread, and beans.

The irony is that students flocked to the course. The majority were from affluent homes in which they had never known deprivation or struggle. The value of the course was that they discovered true contentment and happiness can survive even a Depression.

The secret of contentment for the apostle Paul was his relationship with Jesus Christ. He found that Christ could meet his needs in any and every situation. He wrote most of his letters while held in damp and dreary prisons. Yet he could speak of joy and contentment because he discovered that even in prison Christ is present and alive. God wants us to learn the lesson in our marriage that Christ is contentment. That's the secret to getting an "A" in the course of life.

MARRIAGE MINUTE TRUTH:

GOD IS OUR SOURCE OF INEXHAUSTIBLE STRENGTH

Primary Passage:
I can do everything through him who gives me strength.
Philippians 4:13

We have a dear friend who has suffered more of life's tragedies and unexplainable sorrows than almost any person we've ever met. One Sunday afternoon his wife had not been feeling well. She decided to take a nap. An hour or so later he went back into the house and found she had passed away in her sleep—the victim of an undiagnosed medical condition.

Our dear friend is still one of the most radiant Christians on earth. His one concern in life is to serve Christ and give unselfishly of whatever he has to others. He is an embodiment of Paul's words, "I can do everything through him who gives me strength."

How do we discover that strength Paul is talking about? First we can find strength in our prayer life. Coming into the presence of God in prayer can be a source of powerful refreshment and invigoration. Second, the Word of God can give us new energy and strength as we claim His promises for our lives. Finally, new energy comes surging into our lives when we tell others of our faith in Christ Jesus. We can do all things not through more vitamins, more exercise, or more rest, but through Jesus Christ.

MARRIAGE MINUTE TRUTH:

THE PROSPERITY GOSPEL IS A FALSE GOSPEL

. . . .

Primary Passage:
They went about in sheepskins and goatskins,
destitute, persecuted and mistreated—
the world was not worthy of them.
Hebrews 11:37–38

. . . .

*Y*ou're the King's Kids! He wants you to have the very best! So don't settle for anything less than the most expensive car you can buy, the nicest house in your city, or the finest clothes New York or Paris can produce. It's yours! Simply name it and claim it! All you need is faith!"

Have you heard of the "prosperity gospel"? It's a belief that all we have to do is claim cars, homes, furniture, and vacations in the name of Christ, and they will be ours. The only problem with this particular gospel is that's it's not taught anywhere in the Old or New Testament. It's utterly false.

Consider the examples of Paul or Jesus: neither were wealthy men. Did they lack the faith to "name it and claim it"? The writer of Hebrews points out that many heroes of the faith were destitute. Some of us, like those men and women of faith before us, will know poverty and hardship. But we will also know true prosperity—the incredible wealth that comes from knowing Christ in a deep, rewarding, and intimate way. That's the promise we need to name and claim right now.

MARRIAGE MINUTE TRUTH:

GOD CAN ACCOMPLISH HIS PURPOSES THROUGH OUR SUFFERING

. . . .

Primary Passage:
*Others were tortured and refused to be released, so
that they might gain a better resurrection.*
Hebrews 11:35

. . . .

When Clarence Jones, the founder of HCJB Radio in Ecuador, went to South America in the 1930s, he had little financial backing. He had been there less than a year when he received an electric bill that he couldn't pay. He was broke. He didn't have enough money left to broadcast a signal across his living room. It was one of the darkest days of his life. Had he somehow missed God's will for his life? Was this all a tragic misadventure?

Some of you know what it's like to hit rock bottom. You don't have a dime to your name and you have no one to turn to. Why does God allow moments like that to enter our lives?

The writer of Hebrews would comfort us with the fact we're not alone. Others who have served and obeyed God have known similar hardships. The Scriptures go on to say of these people, "These were all commended for their faith" (v. 39). In the crucible of hardship, faith was forged, a faith that earned the commendation of God.

So whatever we might be tempted to do in the face of hardships, we should not give up. God is at work in our marriages in ways we cannot imagine. By the way, HCJB today reaches millions around the world with the message of Christ. God paid the electric bill, and then some.

MARRIAGE MINUTE TRUTH:

GOD IS IN THE BUSINESS OF PERFECTING OUR FAITH

Primary Passage:
*Let us fix our eyes on Jesus, the author
and perfecter of our faith.*
Hebrews 12:2

A wall in the heart of London was built by the Romans more than two thousand years ago. Despite twenty centuries of wars, revolutions, and natural disasters, that durable wall still stands. God wants to build into our lives a faith similar to that wall. He wants to build a wall of faith that can survive the difficulties and devastations of life.

We won't enter heaven with our stock portfolio, foreign sports car, or new golf clubs. All that will have to be left behind. All that we will bring with us the moment we pass from death to life will be the maturity and character faith has produced in our lives. God values the faith that was formed when we lost our job, when we lost a pregnancy to a miscarriage, and even when we faced the final inevitability of our own death. The faith that God is perfecting in us this very day is the faith that's going to shine with celestial brilliance in heaven's light.

Many of us have had different plans for our lives than the way things turned out. If it had been up to us we would have left out a number of difficulties, sorrows, and tragedies along the way. Yet in all these things God has been perfecting our faith. Faith is all important. Don't leave home without it.

MARRIAGE MINUTE TRUTH:

IT'S NOT TOO LATE TO LOVE GOD MORE THAN MONEY

. . . .

Primary Passage:
*Keep your lives free from the love of money and be
content with what you have, because God has said,
"Never will I leave you; never will I forsake you."*
Hebrews 13:5

. . . .

*S.*I. McMillen tells the story of the famous nineteenth-century industrialist, John D. Rockefeller, who was the driving force behind the creation of the Standard Oil Company. By the time Rockefeller was thirty-three he was a millionaire, by forty-three he was a billionaire, and by fifty-three he was perhaps the world's richest man.

He loved money but paid a big price for it. He was hated by his oil workers. They hung him in effigy in Pennsylvania. He once confessed he was lonely and wanted to be loved but didn't know how. Eventually his health failed and all of his hair fell out. Doctors gave him only a year to live, and newspapers had his obituary on file.

Loving money can make us sick too. It can make us strangers to our children, keep us from our spouses, and drive us to an early grave. God has an alternative. Instead of loving money we should love the God who will never leave us or forsake us.

It's not too late to make that change in our lives. Rockefeller woke up and realized what a fool he had been. He spent the remainder of his life giving his money away to hospitals, schools, and missions organizations. Instead of dying at fifty-four as many had once predicted, he lived to be ninety-seven. He died a contented person, and so can you.

MARRIAGE MINUTE TRUTH:

THE LOVE OF MONEY IS A DEADLY SPIRITUAL VIRUS

. . . .

Primary Passage:
*For the love of money is a root of all kinds of evil. Some
people, eager for money, have wandered from the faith
and pierced themselves with many griefs.*
1 Timothy 6:10

. . . .

I Was Wrong is the title of a book written by a former televangelist who was convicted of fraud and sent to prison.

The Scriptures warn us to keep away from the deadly virus of money loving. Why? To avoid piercing ourselves with many griefs.

What are some of these griefs? The first is the disgrace we bring to the gospel. It takes only a nanosecond for the world to spot a greedy or money-loving believer. "You're just like everyone else," they cynically conclude. The gospel is disgraced as nothing more than a clever ruse to make a fast buck.

The second grief is the way we abandon God's will to chase money. We can't serve God and money at the same time. The end result is that we pursue money at the expense of serving God's will. Our lives become a legacy of "what might have been" had we chosen God as our first priority.

The final grief is the loss of our usefulness to God. God can't use someone who is in love with something other than Him. The opportunities that could have been ours are lost. It's just that simple.

Don't let the title of your autobiography be "I Was Wrong." Rather, let God entitle your life in bold letters "This Person Was Obedient."

MARRIAGE MINUTE TRUTH:

MOST COUPLES GIVE UP TOO EARLY, NOT TOO LATE

Primary Passage:
*Yet this I call to mind and therefore I have hope: Because
of the Lord's great love we are not consumed,
for his compassions never fail. They are new every
morning; great is your faithfulness.*
Lamentations 3:21–23

Almost every married couple goes through times of distress. These periods of struggle can last anywhere from a few days to several years. Most couples can identify with Jeremiah, the weeping prophet who said, "I remember . . . the bitterness and the gall" (v. 19).

Sadly, some couples never get past dwelling on the painful and bitter disappointments of their marriage. They wrongly assume that life is a straight line experience and that if yesterday was painful, so will be tomorrow, and the day after that. The result is a sense of despair and hopelessness that leads one or both spouses to believe the marriage is a mistake.

But most couples give up too soon rather than too late on their marriage. They fail to realize that God's intervention in their relationship can change their entire future. Jeremiah knew years of gloom and sorrow, but he also said, "His compassions never fail. They are new every morning; great is your faithfulness." God has the same compassion and faithful love available to both of you to start over. Trust Him at His Word and start fresh today.

MARRIAGE MINUTE TRUTH:

GOD NEVER FAILS TO ANSWER WHEN WE PRAY

. . . .

Primary Passage:
*The Lord is good to those whose hope is in him,
to the one who seeks him; it is good to wait
quietly for the salvation of the Lord.*
Lamentations 3:25–26

. . . .

*W*aiting is a difficult thing for us to do. We don't like standing in line at the supermarket, the mall, or even to get into a ball game. Our human nature sees delayed gratification as a frustration, not a blessing.

Fortunately God doesn't act on the whim of human demands. He follows His own schedule and timing. He will give us what we need when He believes we need it, not a moment before. He will give us a job transfer or promotion only when He decides a move is in our best interest. He will give us relief from a difficult relative or an obstinate neighbor only when we have learned the character lessons He had in mind for us.

How do we cope as a couple in the meantime? The writer of Lamentations tells us, "It is good to wait quietly for the salvation of the Lord." The key word is quietly. Not frantically, hopelessly, or angrily, but quietly.

The Lord will not ignore any prayer request we bring before Him. He may just ask us to wait. Like delicious fruit that shouldn't be picked before it's ripe, we shouldn't rush God's answer before it's ready. When it comes, however, it will truly be sweet.

MARRIAGE MINUTE TRUTH:

DIVORCE TAKES PLACE FIRST IN OUR SPIRIT, THEN IN OUR MARRIAGE

Primary Passage:
So guard yourself in your spirit, and do not break faith.
Malachi 2:16b

When we lived in the desert Southwest, several members of our congregation were housed on a military base. Whenever one was hospitalized or in need of a pastoral visit, we first had to gain access to the base. A sharply dressed young man or woman wearing Air Force blue with a dark beret would order us to halt. The person would approach our car, ask for identification, ask the purpose of our visit, then call the people we intended to visit to verify our identification. Only then did the sentry wave us through.

We could learn a lesson from the military when it comes to posting a guard at the gate of our marriage. We are warned to "guard yourself in your spirit, and do not break faith." Why do we need to be vigilant as to what enters our spirit? Because we dare not allow bitterness, apathy, lust, unforgiveness, anger, or unfaithfulness to enter our hearts. They are the unseen, often undetected terrorists that will infiltrate and sabotage the sacredness of our marriage vows.

Divorce happens in the spirit before it happens in the relationship. It begins when sin infiltrates our hearts. So post a guard at the door of your heart and don't be afraid to use the word "Halt!" It may save your home base.

MARRIAGE MINUTE TRUTH:

WEDDING VOWS ARE FENCES MEANT TO PROTECT, NOT IMPRISON, US

Primary Passage:
How can I repay the Lord for all his goodness to me?
I will lift up the cup of salvation and call on the name
of the Lord. I will fulfill my vows to the Lord
in the presence of all his people.
Psalm 116:12–14

When we had been married less than three years, someone attempted to burglarize our home. The person kicked at our back door but couldn't get it open. Just a few weeks earlier we had installed heavy duty deadbolt locks. Those simple security devices may have saved our lives.

The same holds true for our wedding vows. They serve to protect us, not imprison us. It's our vow to forsake all others that guards the integrity of our sexual relationship. It's the promise to stay with each other through sickness and in health that allows us to face disease or accident without fear. It's the promise to love, honor, and cherish each other that assures us our spouse won't cut and run when things get rough in life.

A life without locks or fences isn't freedom, it's danger. It's chaos. It's nothing but fear and pain. The vows we make in the presence of God will spare us much unnecessary suffering. Fulfill the vows you made in the presence of the Lord and all His people. If you keep them, they'll keep you.

MARRIAGE MINUTE TRUTH:

LIMITLESS FORGIVENESS
PRODUCES LIMITLESS LOVE

. . . .

Primary Passage:
*Then Peter came to Jesus and asked, "Lord, how many
times shall I forgive my brother when he sins against me?
Up to seven times?" Jesus answered, "I tell you, not
seven times, but seventy-seven times."*
Matthew 18:21–22

. . . .

In most marriages there is one partner quicker to forgive than
the other. This gracious soul also finds it easier than his or her
mate does to utter the words, "I'm sorry," or "Please forgive me."
Yet a healthy marriage depends on the willingness of both spouses to seek or offer forgiveness as needed.

This is not the same as constantly excusing irresponsible or
damaging behavior just because your spouse says, "I'm sorry."
That's codependent behavior. Confrontation is particularly necessary if the other spouse is engaged in a repeated pattern of self-
destructive behavior such as alcohol abuse or violence.

The time to practice continual forgiveness is when genuine repentance and sorrow are present. When the offending mate realizes the gravity of the offense and asks for pardon, Jesus says we
have no choice but to grant release.

In fact Jesus stunned everyone when He insisted we forgive
seventy-seven times (in some versions, seventy times seven times)
—in other words, to forgive without limits. Isn't that just what it
takes to keep a marriage together for a lifetime? The payoff to
limitless forgiveness is limitless love.

MARRIAGE MINUTE TRUTH:

REPENTANCE OVER PAST SEXUAL SINS IS ESSENTIAL TO FUTURE SATISFACTION

. . . .

Primary Passage:
*Grieve, mourn and wail. Change your laughter to
mourning and your joy to gloom. Humble yourselves
before the Lord, and he will lift you up.*
James 4:9–10

. . . .

"He was all over me before we were married; now he completely ignores me," confessed a tearful wife to us. Their dating relationship had progressed to full intercourse long before the day of their wedding. Now, several years later, the passion and the romance had almost entirely vanished from their relationship. What went wrong? The couple had failed to put in place an essential building block for future happiness—sexual restraint before marriage.

It's obviously too late to go back and do things differently. So what hope is there that this couple can overcome the consequences of their unfortunate past?

James offers a very hopeful word to such couples. He tells us to engage in true repentance over our past wrongdoing. We are to confess that it was wrong and let the offense of what we did reach our hearts. God has promised that as we humble ourselves before Him He will "lift us up." What does that mean?

He will remove the sting and the pain of that memory and once again bless our lives. Through His grace He will begin to undo the damaging consequences of our wrong choices. Ultimately He will restore a proper and healthy sexual relationship between the two of you.

Marriage Minute Truth:

UNFORGIVENESS IS A PRISON OF OUR MAKING

. . . .

Primary Passage:
*Do not judge, and you will not be judged. Do
not condemn, and you will not be condemned.
Forgive, and you will be forgiven.*
Luke 6:37

. . . .

*W*e were once asked to visit a woman dying of a brain tumor at a local hospital. She was the relative of members of our church. Only later did we learn that the dying woman and her brother had not spoken a word to each other for more than twenty years. When they at last met again they collapsed into each other's arms. Sadly, she had only weeks to live. They had wasted the last two decades in a stubborn standoff of prideful wills.

How many times is a similar sad scenario played out in a marriage? Offenses committed decades ago remain unforgiven. A wall of anger and resentment remains in place until tragedy strikes. Then, with only hours or days or weeks left, both partners realize how foolish their behavior has been over the years.

We need to stop and consider right now the dangers our relationship faces if we continue to judge and condemn each other. If one day stretches into two, and two days into a week, and a week into a month, could it become years until you forgive each other? Today is the day to release and forgive your spouse. Now is the time to let go. Tomorrow isn't promised. Will you seize the moment?

MARRIAGE MINUTE TRUTH:

MERCY IS WHAT WE NEED; JUSTICE IS WHAT WE DESERVE

Primary Passage:
Be merciful, just as your Father is merciful.
Luke 6:36

*W*e were making introductions at a college alumni dinner when I made a remark that embarrassed my wife. To be more precise, it hurt her deeply. As we drove home that night she explained her hurt to me. There was no question about it—I needed to ask her forgiveness. When I asked her to forgive me, she blinked back her tears, managed a smile, and then said, "I forgive you." It was an act of pure mercy on her part.

She could have said, "OK, Bob, you did help clean the kitchen the other day. And you did take care of the kids for an hour while I went out. So, all things considered, I guess I'll let this one get by." If she had forgiven me based on my merit, not her love, that would have been an act of justice, not mercy.

As married couples we can sometimes forget the difference between justice and mercy. God Almighty does not treat us according to our wrongdoing, which would be justice. Instead, He forgives according to our need—that's mercy. We should offer the same to our spouse each day.

Jesus told us we're to learn from God how to forgive. The Cross satisfied God's need for justice so God can now offer unlimited mercy. Will you let the Cross teach you how to give your spouse the mercy he or she needs?

MARRIAGE MINUTE TRUTH:

DON'T EXPECT YOUR SPOUSE TO BE PERFECT; YOU AREN'T

Primary Passage:
There is no one righteous, not even one.
Romans 3:10

*S*everal years ago a mentally unbalanced individual broke into a European art museum and sledgehammered one of Michelangelo's most famous sculptures. He was soon apprehended, but not before the arm of the sculpture lay shattered on the floor. The press interviewed the museum curators about the incident. "We can restore the sculpture," they said. "The only problem is it will never be perfect again."

Much the same could be said about us as husbands and wives. What the Bible calls original sin has shattered our lives, and we will never be perfect again—not until we reach the splendor and perfection of heaven.

Until then we need to remember that neither of us is perfect—never have been, never will be as long as we are on earth. That's why we should drop the false expectation that our husband or wife should always do everything right. The other person is going to fail just as surely as we are. Sooner or later we both will momentarily lose our temper, say something unkind, or be insensitive to the other person's needs. How should we react when it happens?

MARRIAGE MINUTE TRUTH:

QUIT EXPECTING YOUR SPOUSE TO READ YOUR MIND

. . . .

Primary Passage:
*Therefore each of you must put off falsehood and
speak truthfully to his neighbor, for we
are all members of one body.*
Ephesians 4:25

. . . .

*I*f you really loved me, you'd know what I was feeling."

"If I have to tell you what I'm thinking, I won't do it."

Have you ever said things like that to each other? It's not uncommon for hurting spouses to expect their mates to know exactly what they're feeling and why. It's also very unrealistic.

The truth is we can't read each other's minds. (That's actually a blessing. Would you want any other person on earth to have complete access to your mental data files?)

The apostle Paul offers a wonderful alternative to the impossible task of reading minds: It's called speaking the truth in love. He encourages us to "put off falsehood and speak truthfully to [our] neighbor."

When we are upset with our husband or wife we should say something like this, "Dear, when you walked ahead of me through the mall, I felt unimportant to you." Or, "When you criticized my meal, I felt unappreciated." That will end the guessing game and let the reconciliation begin in your marriage. So what's on your mind today?

MARRIAGE MINUTE TRUTH:

WE MARRY TO BLESS SOMEONE ELSE'S LIFE, NOT TO BE HAPPY

Primary Passage:
*Blessed are those who hunger and thirst for
righteousness, for they will be filled.*
Matthew 5:6

I'm just not happy anymore in this marriage. I want out."
We've heard that comment from more than one distressed husband or wife. They are usually sincere in their conviction they want out. The problem is they are sincerely mistaken.

Why? Because the purpose of marriage is not to find happiness. If happiness is the primary goal of any spouse, that person is bound to end up disappointed, if not disillusioned. No one can make us happy or unhappy.

Then why should we get married? To unselfishly bless the life of another person and to glorify God. As we choose to honor God and love, serve, and show kindness to our spouse, happiness is an inevitable by-product. But if we spend our days waiting for our partner to make us happy, we may wait a lifetime to experience the genuine article.

Jesus taught us that "blessedness" is a better goal than "happiness." Blessedness results from seeking God's righteousness. If our goal is to be righteous, in our marriage as well as the rest of life, Jesus promised we will find blessedness. We don't need a new mate to find what we're looking for, just a new goal.

MARRIAGE MINUTE TRUTH:

YOU CAN DEFEAT EVERY TEMPTATION THAT ENTERS YOUR MARRIAGE

Primary Passage:
*And God is faithful; he will not let you be tempted
beyond what you can bear. But when you are tempted,
he will also provide a way out so that
you can stand up under it.*
1 Corinthians 10:13

I don't struggle with temptation. I just give in to it." Although the poster was humorous, it conveyed the deceptive message that giving in to temptation is all but inevitable. If we know Jesus Christ as our personal Savior and Lord, we have all the resources in heaven on our side to win over temptation.

That truth applies to marriage too. God has promised that He "will not let you be tempted beyond what you can bear." For example, are you sometimes tempted to be so angry with your spouse you can't see straight? God can give you the strength to gain control of your emotions again before you do or say something you'll regret. Are you being drawn to someone other than your husband or wife? Jesus can break that growing bond of infatuation before it goes another step further. Are you starting to resent how your spouse spends money? The Holy Spirit can help you examine your own heart to dig out bitterness before it takes root.

How can we find this help in our battle against temptation? Quote this verse the next time you feel yourself tempted. It's the sword of the Spirit that can slay your every enticement.

MARRIAGE MINUTE TRUTH:

ALL OF US WILL FACE TEMPTATION THIS YEAR (1)

....

Primary Passage:
No temptation has seized you except
what is common to man . . . .
1 Corinthians 10:13a

....

We can predict one thing about your life and marriage this year with absolute certainty—you will be tempted. We all will be tempted. Why? Because we face an enemy, Satan, who is on the prowl. The Bible says that he is looking for someone to devour.

Let us speak to husbands for a moment. Given our current culture and society, it's likely that you'll be tempted in four areas: (1) sexual impurity, (2) relational neglect, (3) harshness and anger, and (4) personal idolatry. In other words you'll be tempted to lust, to ignore your wife and children, to respond in harshness and anger when your expectations are not fulfilled, and to worship your career or the things you own. The good news is that God will provide a way of escape for each and every one of these temptations. More about that in the days to come.

For now, let us encourage you that all these temptations are common to man. Even Jesus was tempted. Just because we're tempted doesn't mean we're sinful or depraved. It just means we have an adversary seeking to destroy us. To be forewarned is to be forearmed.

MARRIAGE MINUTE TRUTH:

ALL OF US WILL FACE TEMPTATION THIS YEAR (2)

Primary Passage:
*No temptation has seized you except
what is common to man . . . .*
1 Corinthians 10:13a

*Y*esterday we examined the likely areas in which husbands will be tempted in their personal lives. Today we turn our attention to the unique temptations that wives struggle with. While we are indeed generalizing, it's our observation that women will struggle with one or more of these four areas: (1) relational manipulation, (2) peacekeeping rather than peacemaking, (3) simmering anger, and (4) marital despair.

Certainly this list could be amended depending on the individual person, but wives do struggle with these issues.

They are tempted to try to manipulate their husbands into becoming the people they want them to be, rather than trusting God to make those changes. They often mask their true hurts and frustrations just to try to maintain "peace" in the marriage. They are tempted to develop simmering anger, which over time can turn into bitterness and rage. Finally, they are tempted to give in to despair, convinced that nothing will ever change and that it's useless to keep on believing. Tomorrow we see how God's involvement in our temptations is the key to defeating them.

MARRIAGE MINUTE TRUTH:

GOD IS ALWAYS INVOLVED IN THE TEMPTATIONS WE FACE

. . . .

Primary Passage:
*And God is faithful; he will not let you be
tempted beyond what you can bear.*
1 Corinthians 10:13b

. . . .

If the fact we'll be tempted in our marriage relationships this year is a certainty, so is the fact that God will always be involved. Fortunately for us God is aware of every trap, scheme, and snare the devil may set for us. He knows when and where the ambush will be set. And best of all—He has already decreed that we will face no allurement beyond our power to bear.

There's a question that begs to be asked: Why does God permit us to be tempted in the first place? Why doesn't He simply decree a hedge of protection around us that makes us immune to the "fiery darts" of our enemy? The answer to that question is difficult and complex, in some respects beyond our knowing. But this much is certain: When we are tempted, God is given an opportunity to demonstrate His faithfulness. That's right, temptation is the arena for God to demonstrate to us His faithfulness to keep us from overpowering temptation.

When the two of you find yourselves tempted in some area of your marriage, stop and ask God to reveal His faithfulness to you in defeating that temptation. It's a prayer He will quickly answer. He has promised both of you a way out. Tomorrow we learn how to discover His escape route.

MARRIAGE MINUTE TRUTH:

THERE IS ALWAYS A WAY OUT OF TEMPTATION—ALWAYS

Primary Passage:
But when you are tempted, he will also provide a
way out so that you can stand up under it.
1 Corinthians 10:13c

*A*lexander the Great was once confronted with a knot that couldn't be untied. Regardless of which end of the rope one pulled on, working with the knot only made it tighter. Frustrated and not wanting to admit defeat at the hands of the "Gordion Knot," the mighty conqueror pulled out his sword and slashed it in half. So much for the unsolvable knot.

There is no knot of temptation that God cannot untie. Regardless whether it's a sexual, financial, or emotional temptation, God can show you the way out. How does He most often do that?

His most common method is to bring Scripture you've read or memorized back to mind. Or perhaps the words to a hymn. Or some truth you recently heard in a sermon. Sometimes He will send a person or a phone call to jar you back to spiritual reality.

This much is certain: You can trust the Holy Spirit to gently nudge you in the direction of the exit door when you are tempted. The important question is this: When God shows you the way out, will you take it?

MARRIAGE MINUTE TRUTH:

GUIDANCE IS FOUND IN A RELATIONSHIP, NOT A ROAD MAP

. . . .

Primary Passage:
Trust in the Lord with all your heart . . . .
Proverbs 3:5a

. . . .

*B*efore we undertake major road trips we usually order a complete set of road maps from our travel agency. They outline the shortest or quickest route to our destination, steer us around construction areas and other detours, and indicate points of interest we might like to stop and see.

Wouldn't it be nice if we could order a similar road map for each major decision we face as a couple? Should we accept a job transfer or stay right where we are? Should we put our children in public, private, or home school? The list can go on and on.

Rarely, if ever, will God fax us a copy of a road map to show us exactly which route to take. He's looking instead for us to develop a trust relationship with Him. The word for "trust" in this verse means "to hide for refuge, be confident, sure, bold, secure, even careless." God is looking for us to so completely trust Him in our decisions that we actually become "care-less," meaning without cares.

We are to trust God with all our heart—the place where we make our decisions and form our thoughts. If you as a couple are facing a particularly big decision right now, don't seek a specific road map, but surrender fully to the will of Christ. He won't let you take a wrong exit.

MARRIAGE MINUTE TRUTH:

HE CAN CARRY THE WEIGHT
OF THE WORLD ON HIS SHOULDERS

Primary Passage:
. . . and lean not on your own understanding.
Proverbs 3:5b

A pastor in New York City used to take burdened members of his congregation on a short sight-seeing trip. They would first visit a building that displayed a statue of Atlas carrying the weight of the world on his shoulders. The troubled men and women would readily identify with the statue. They, too, carried heavy weights.

He then took them across the street to a church that had a statue of the boy Jesus holding the entire world in one hand. The pastor often saw the light go on in their eyes as they realized the solution to the dilemma they were facing.

The Bible tells us to "lean not on your own understanding" when facing a difficult decision. We shouldn't become discouraged or weighted down when we don't have the solution to our problems. God doesn't expect us to. He only asks that we put our complete trust in His wisdom and knowledge. He invites all of us who are "weary and heavy-laden" to come to Him, and He promises He will give us rest.

As a couple we can find days of peace and serenity we never imagined possible when we choose to trust God rather than ourselves. He invites us to put the full weight of our dilemmas and problems on His shoulders. He does have the whole world in His hands. Isn't that a better place for it than on your back?

MARRIAGE MINUTE TRUTH:

OUT OF INTIMACY
COMES INSTRUCTIONS

Primary Passage:
*In all your ways acknowledge him, and he
will make your paths straight.*
Proverbs 3:6

During World War II Bob's father served as a copilot. We had the joy of meeting his longtime war buddy and fellow pilot at a squadron reunion some fifty years after the end of the hostilities. "We were a wonderful team," the old pilot reminisced. "It got to the point where we didn't even have to say anything to each other. I could always count on him. We both knew what the other was thinking and knew exactly what needed to be done next."

The Bible tells us we are to acknowledge God in all our ways. The word refers to knowing someone on an intimate basis. The more we know the character of God, the better we will understand the mind of God. Once we begin to know God's mind, it becomes much easier to make decisions in life.

How can the two of you develop an intimate knowledge of God?

Absorb what He tells us about Himself in His Word. You cannot know God intimately if you do not know His Word intimately. Memorize Scripture together. Read the Word out loud to each other. Listen to tapes in the car. Add to that significant time in prayer together and obedience to what you do know of God's will. You can read the mind of God if you read the Word of God.

MARRIAGE MINUTE TRUTH:

ROMANCE IS GOD'S GIFT TO A COUPLE

Primary Passage:
Let him kiss me with the kisses of his mouth—
for your love is more delightful than wine.
Song of Songs 1:2

*W*e grew up in an era when it was so popular for terrorists to hijack airliners and take them to Cuba that a new term was invented—"skyjacking." Another sinister hijacking has occurred in our time. The popular culture claims to have invented the idea of romance or at least rediscovered it. From discount lingerie stores to steamy soap operas to racy videos found in the back of video stores, the popular culture believes it has the corner on romance.

The truth is our culture is thousands of years too late. True romance, the special attraction between a husband and wife, was God's original idea. He invented it to be free of lust, exploitation, or disappointment. In the great love poem, The Song of Songs, the writer speaks of the beautiful, powerful attraction a wife has for her husband, "Let him kiss me with kisses of his mouth—for your love is more delightful than wine."

When a man and woman come together under the blessing of God in marriage, they are free to express their love with tenderness, affection, and desire. It's based on a lifetime commitment that guarantees the mystery of romance remains just between the two of them.

So don't go looking for romance "in all the wrong places." Turn to God's Word. It was there all the time.

MARRIAGE MINUTE TRUTH:

GOD IS ABLE TO DO MUCH MORE THAN WE ASK OR IMAGINE

. . . .

Primary Passage:
*Now to him who is able to do immeasurably more
than all we ask or imagine, according to his power
that is at work within us, to him be glory in the
church and in Christ Jesus throughout all
generations, for ever and ever! Amen.*
Ephesians 3:20–21

. . . .

One of the most difficult tests in our married life came just before our last daughter was born. Cheryl developed a blood clot near her heart as the result of a feeding tube that had been inserted into a vein. The choices we faced were not good.

If we treated the blood clot, we could endanger the life of the baby. If we didn't treat the blood clot, we could endanger Cheryl's life. I called a number of friends across the country and asked them to pray for Cheryl.

That night Cheryl underwent a second ultrasound to locate the blood clot. At first it appeared on the screen in bright, bold colors. A few minutes later the two technicians were unable to locate it. The clot had disappeared! She was sent home from the hospital that same night.

We learned a valuable lesson through that experience. Never forget or underestimate the power of God at work in your marriage. He is able to do more than we ask or imagine. To Him be glory in the church and in Christ Jesus to all generations.

MARRIAGE MINUTE TRUTH:

IT IS GOD WHO INTRODUCED US TO EACH OTHER

. . . .

Primary Passage:
*Then the Lord God made a woman from the rib he had
taken out of the man, and he brought her to the man.*
Genesis 2:22

. . . .

I first noticed Cheryl when we were both students. It was the opening day of classes, and I was in the bookstore. Through the large glass windows I noticed three attractive women walking down the hallway. The woman in the middle caught my eye. She was the most beautiful girl I had ever seen. I remember thinking to myself, "That's the woman I'm going to marry."

It was several weeks before we talked for the first time, and several months before we actually went out on our first date. When I asked her what she remembered of that memorable first day of school, she said, "I don't remember ever seeing you." Oh well, love is rarely symmetrical.

The Genesis account says that God created the woman and "he brought her to the man." There it is, clear, unmistakable proof that God is in the business of bringing husbands and wives together.

Looking back over nearly two decades, it's obvious to both of us that God brought us together. In His will and timing He arranged the events that allowed us to meet. He's been doing that since the beginning of the Creation. Do you rejoice in the person God brought to you? It was His doing, and you owe Him your thanks.

MARRIAGE MINUTE TRUTH:

DON'T CRITICIZE
YOUR SPOUSE'S RELATIVES

Primary Passage:
*With his mouth the godless destroys his neighbor, but
through knowledge the righteous escape.*
Proverbs 11:9

*I*s there someone in your spouse's family that you find it particularly difficult to get along with? Let us offer some encouragement to help keep the in-laws from becoming outlaws. It's important that they not rob the two of you of your closeness and intimacy as a couple.

The most important thing you can do is to talk about your feelings with your spouse. Make certain you don't attack that family member's character. The old adage that "blood is thicker than water" is always true. Even if your spouse complains that his or her relative is a pain in the neck, don't add to the distress by making degrading, humiliating, or insulting comments. It will only create bad feelings between the two of you.

Instead, explain why your spouse's relative causes you pain or discomfort. Ask your spouse to help you know how to respond properly. Give your mate the opportunity to become part of the solution. It's also important to ask your spouse to be the person to respond to boundary encroachments or personal attacks when they occur. If it's his relative, it's his problem; if it's her relative, it's her problem—simple as that. If you approach this topic in the right spirit, it will likely gain you an ally, not an adversary.

MARRIAGE MINUTE TRUTH:

WE HAVE AN OBLIGATION TO CHOOSE OUR MATES ABOVE ALL OTHERS

Primary Passage:
*So Michal let David down through a window,
and he fled and escaped.*
1 Samuel 19:12

*M*ichal, the first wife of King David, had to choose between honoring her murderous father, King Saul, or remaining devoted to her new husband. Her father wanted to kill David, who he saw as a threat to his throne. Michal loved her new husband and chose to hide his whereabouts. She did the right thing. As a result of her unselfish and caring actions, David's life was spared from death at the hands of Saul, her jealous and hateful father.

It's often painful when we have to choose between our family of origin and our spouse. But there is a biblical basis to choosing our spouse above all others. The book of Genesis (chapter 2, verse 24) reminds us we are to leave our mother and father and family and be joined to each other. That doesn't usually require that we reject our families or refuse to have anything to do with them. Instead it implies we will always give our husband or wife first place in our life. If it comes down to a choice between our family of origin and our spouse—there is no choice. Our spouse must come first.

Hopefully matters will never come to such a painful choice. But if they do, the Word of God encourages us to do the right thing and choose our life's mate above all others.

MARRIAGE MINUTE TRUTH:

YOU NEED TO TURN TO EACH OTHER, NOT ON EACH OTHER

Primary Passage:
*Set a guard over my mouth, O Lord; keep
watch over the door of my lips.*
Psalm 141:3

A noted expert on children once said, "It's not the child with a behavior disorder that needs help. It's the parents. They are usually at their wit's end." If you've ever raised an extremely strong-willed child or one with a behavior disorder, you know exactly what he's talking about.

If that's what you're facing today, let us encourage you not to engage in the blame game. It's all too tempting when frustrations rise to a boiling point to turn on each other rather than to each other. Statements like, "If only you would be a better disciplinarian, she would behave better," or "If you wouldn't pamper him so much, he would shape up," are counterproductive. The end result is only further distance between the two of you.

Regardless of the outcome of your child's future, God wants your marriage to remain intact. Ask Him to set "a guard . . . over the door" of your lips to make certain your speech is loving and respectful to each other. Don't believe the lie that either one of you caused your child's strong-willed behavior. You two are allies, not enemies. Together you will prevail.

MARRIAGE MINUTE TRUTH:

GIVE YOUR PRIMARY ATTENTION IN LIFE TO EACH OTHER, NOT THE PROBLEMS YOU FACE

. . . .

Primary Passage:
*This is now bone of my bones and flesh of my flesh; she
shall be called woman, for she was taken out of man.*
Genesis 2:23

. . . .

*G*raphs that chart the marital happiness of a couple typically take a sharp dip during the child-rearing years, particularly the teenage years.

Once you've raised children you can understand why. It's hard to give your spouse the emotional attention he or she needs when your young toddler throws his oatmeal dish and screams for attention. And it's all too easy to become consumed with your sixteen-year-old daughter when she comes home at 3:00 in the morning.

But we need to resist the impulse to focus exclusively on our children's problems, regardless of how severe they become. We need to make a deliberate choice to set aside time each day just for the two of us to be together. When we do enjoy such respites, we need to discipline ourselves to talk about other issues besides our child's behavior or problems.

Remember, you two share something very special. You can say of your spouse that he or she is "bone of my bones" and "flesh of my flesh." Make certain your relationship is growing closer by the year so you don't find yourselves perfect strangers at the end of your child-rearing years.

MARRIAGE MINUTE TRUTH:

EVEN LIFE'S MOST DIFFICULT MOMENTS ARE TEMPORARY

. . . .

Primary Passage:
*For our light and momentary troubles are achieving for
us an eternal glory that far outweighs them all.*
2 Corinthians 4:17

. . . .

*A*s the comedian Mark Lowry reminds us, some of the most comforting words in all of the Scriptures are, "And it came to pass. . . ." After all, "Difficult times only come to pass, not to stay."

Believe it or not, the day will soon come when arguing with your children over curfew times, messy rooms, and poor study habits will come to an end. The days of painful confrontations, unresolved tensions, and frustrating behavior with your teenager will also one day pass. If there were difficult notes sent home from teachers, disappointing midterm reports, or the need for a constant reminding to do chores—these too will become a thing of the past.

Hopefully these hard years will have brought the two of you together. Out of the crucible of difficult days and anxious nights will emerge a deep bond.

Regardless of the problems you may be facing with your children this day, remember this too will pass. What hopefully will remain is the memory of how you loved your children and each other in a way that honored God and brought peace to your home.

Encourage each other with these words, "It only came to pass."

MARRIAGE MINUTE TRUTH:

CHARACTER IS A STRONGER MAGNET THAN COMPLAINING

. . . .

Primary Passage:
*Wives, in the same way be submissive to your husbands
so that, if any of them do not believe the word, they may
be won over without words by the behavior of their wives,
when they see the purity and reverence of your lives.*
1 Peter 3:1–3

. . . .

*W*hat should you do when you find your spouse isn't at the same place you are spiritually? What should you do, wife, if your husband doesn't seem as excited about faith as you are?

Let me us offer some caring advice: Don't preach to him. That behavior may only breed resistance and resentment.

The apostle Peter has wise advice for a wife who finds herself married to a spouse who is in a different place spiritually than she is. His message? Win him over by your behavior rather than your words. Chances are by now your spouse knows exactly what you believe. He doesn't need more information; he needs stronger motivation to become a believer. That motivation to investigate the things of God doesn't come from hearing more doctrine, but from observing character, love, and strength in someone who claims to know Christ.

It will take time. Maybe even years. But remember, Peter says that eventually many such husbands will be "won over without words." That's a victory to celebrate for all eternity.

MARRIAGE MINUTE TRUTH:

HEARTS OPEN TO EACH OTHER CANNOT BE SEPARATED BY DISTANCE

Primary Passage:
Make room for us in your hearts.
2 Corinthians 7:2

A friend of ours has a piece of concrete in his living room taken from the remains of the Berlin Wall. This relic of the Cold War symbolizes a barrier that once separated governments, societies, and even families. Though it eventually fell, similar emotional walls still stand in too many homes across our nation today. It's a barrier that leaves both spouses feeling so alone and isolated from each other. Perhaps no one trucked bricks and mortar into your living room and built a ten-foot high replica of the Berlin Wall. Yet there's a barrier between the two of you that leaves you both feeling alone. How can you take it down?

The key is to accept each other just as you are. That doesn't mean overlooking or minimizing serious problems. Nor does it suggest we never tell our true feelings. It just means that we choose to fundamentally accept and value the person we married. For example, have you come to resent your wife because she's overweight or resent your husband because he doesn't talk as much as you'd like? The solution is not to withhold acceptance until the other person changes to your liking. In that case you may wait an entire lifetime in misery and disappointment.

Instead you need to celebrate your spouse's strengths and minimize his or her weaknesses. In that positive atmosphere you are going to see the best come out in that other person. So open your heart to your husband or wife today. God will fill it with someone very special.

MARRIAGE MINUTE TRUTH:

HUMBLING OURSELVES BEFORE GOD IS THE START OF A NEW LIFE

Primary Passage:
And he said: "I tell you the truth, unless you change and become like little children, you will never enter the kingdom of heaven. Therefore, whoever humbles himself like this child is the greatest in the kingdom of heaven."
Matthew 18:3–4

*W*e have learned so much from each of our children. Each of the five has taught us something about the character God desires for us to have as adults. Innocence, trust, thankfulness, simplicity, and, above all, humility are so evident in tiny children. An eighteen-month-old child isn't interested in making a name for himself, accumulating wealth or possessions, or even impressing others with his education or pedigree. He just delights in being with his parents and enjoying the love and joy of the moment.

Jesus said we can learn much from small children, particularly in the realm of humility. As we look to God in simple faith for the gift of His forgiveness and salvation, completely apart from our own works, we are in a position to receive the kingdom of heaven.

This same posture of humility can transform our marriages as well. As we both attempt to simply love, accept, and serve the other person, amazing things happen. Tensions disappear, arguments decrease, and our overall joy in being married radically increases. Childlike humility brings adult maturity and grace to a relationship. As the old adage says, "The way up is down."

MARRIAGE MINUTE TRUTH:

WE ARE SAVED BY GRACE THROUGH FAITH PLUS NOTHING

. . . .

Primary Passage:
For it is by grace you have been saved, through
faith—and this not from yourselves, it is the gift of
God—not by works, so that no one can boast.
Ephesians 2:8–9

. . . .

*H*igh school chemistry teaches the importance of using exactly the right formula to achieve the right reaction. For example, hydrogen and oxygen mixed together in the right combination produces water. But carbon and oxygen mixed together in a similar formula produces a lethal gas—carbon monoxide.

The need for the correct formula holds true in spiritual matters too. On this special day, often called Reformation Day, the church celebrates the rediscovery of the correct equation for receiving eternal life. We are saved by grace through faith plus nothing. What that means is that we are saved by putting our entire faith in what Christ accomplished on the cross for our salvation. He took the penalty and guilt of our sin on Himself. He bore our punishment and the anger of God toward our sin. By placing our trust in what His atoning sacrifice did, we can immediately receive the gift of eternal life.

Someone has said that if we contribute even .00001 percent of our good works to achieve salvation, we will have destroyed the biblical formula for salvation. So remember this life-giving equation: We are saved by grace through faith plus nothing. Has this experiment been done in you yet? If not, today should be the day.

MARRIAGE MINUTE TRUTH:

TO REGAIN OUR FIRST LOVE WE MUST DO THE THINGS WE ONCE DID

Primary Passage:
*Yet I hold this against you: You have forsaken your first
love. Remember the height from which you have fallen!
Repent and do the things you did at first.*
Revelation 2:4–5

How many couples would experience significant conflict in their marriage if they showed each other the same kindness and appreciation they did during their first six months of courtship? Once we opened doors; now we slam them in anger. Then we whispered words of adoration; now we mutter under our breath. Once we noticed only their strengths and overlooked their weaknesses. Now we do just the opposite.

Jesus sadly told the church at Ephesus that it had forsaken its first love and fallen from a great height. He told it that it needed to repent, to literally undergo a dramatic change of mind and direction. He urged its members to regain their first love for Him by acting out the love they once enjoyed.

There is a profound lesson here for all married couples. If we want to be in love again we must act in love. We must make the choice to speak and behave in loving and caring ways toward each other. We must do the things we once did when we beheld each other strictly through the eyes of affection and tenderness. We can recapture our first love, and once we do we will realize that our love is fresh and new again. But we must first recapture our first attitudes and actions.

MARRIAGE MINUTE TRUTH:

WE MUST LIVE IN THE WORLD, BUT THE WORLD MUST NOT LIVE IN US

Primary Passage:
I know where you live—where Satan has his throne.
Yet you remain true to my name.
Revelation 2:13

*O*ne of the most effective missions agencies in the world was started in the bar and red-light district of Chicago. Couples preparing to take the name of Jesus Christ to the remotest regions on earth lived and worked on the same streets where prostitutes, alcoholics, and drug addicts freely roamed.

Some people are afraid of rubbing shoulders with people who are far from God. Yet Jesus made a specific point of seeking out those very people. He was known to eat in some of the worst places in the community to demonstrate God did not regard anyone based on merit, regardless of how good or bad the person's past or neighborhood.

The real danger we face is not from living in the world, but allowing the world to live in us. The worship of money, pleasure, and power does far more spiritual damage to our souls than living in a community brimming with bars, brothels, or New Age bookstores. Like the church in Revelation, we can live where Satan has his throne and still remain true to God. That requires that we get to know our neighbors, take an active redemptive role in our community, and work to solve problems in our city—all in the name of the gospel of Jesus Christ.

MARRIAGE MINUTE TRUTH:

NOT EVERYONE WHO CLAIMS TO BE A BELIEVER IS A BELIEVER

. . . .

Primary Passage:
Nevertheless, I have this against you: You tolerate that
woman Jezebel, who calls herself a prophetess. By her
teaching she misleads my servants into sexual
immorality and the eating of food sacrificed to idols.
Revelation 2:20

. . . .

*T*wo high school students were arrested by the FBI for coun-
terfeiting twenty-dollar bills. From the Internet they gained the
needed information to photocopy the money, soak the paper in
tea, and then microwave the finished product. Their amateur efforts were discovered by a gas station attendant who called the
police.

How alert are we at spotting counterfeit teachers and false doctrines? Scriptures tell us quite plainly that false prophets and
prophetesses are at work in the church. More than one Christian
marriage has been destroyed by one or both spouses buying into
unbiblical ideas or philosophies.

The Scriptures teach us to unmask false teachers by paying attention to where their teaching leads people. The church at Thy-
atira had fallen into sexual immorality and idolatry. God is never
party to such behavior.

Be on guard against new, novel, and intriguing doctrines and
those who teach them. They are both as phony as microwaved
twenty-dollar bills.

MARRIAGE MINUTE TRUTH:

OUR NAMES ARE WRITTEN IN INDELIBLE INK IN THE BOOK OF LIFE

. . . .

Primary Passage:
He who overcomes will, like them, be dressed in white. I
will never blot out his name from the book of life, but will
acknowledge his name before my Father and his angels.
Revelation 3:5

. . . .

A major public relations controversy broke out at a prestigious university that had renamed its football stadium. The name change would have been a rather routine matter except for one item: In the 1920s the board of regents had entered into its official minutes a binding resolution never to change the name of the stadium. Seventy years later, when a wealthy donor appeared who was willing to pay for the complete renovation of the stadium, the regents suddenly erased what everyone had thought was written in permanent ink.

Fortunately, we as believers in Jesus Christ don't have to worry about our name being erased from the Book of Life by board action. That assurance has implications for our marriages today. We can build our marriage and family around the eternal truth that we are citizens of heaven. We can live the lives of overcomers because we know our destiny.

Regardless of the problems and difficulties we experience on a day-to-day basis, we are assured that Christ will one day acknowledge us before His Father and the angels. Our names may never be on a stadium, but praise God they are chiseled into the Book of Life in heaven.

MARRIAGE MINUTE TRUTH:

LET'S THANK GOD FOR THE DOORS HE CLOSES IN OUR FACE

Primary Passage:
*What he opens no one can shut, and what he shuts no
one can open. I know your deeds. See, I have placed
before you an open door that no one can shut.*
Revelation 3:7–8

*Y*ears ago Bob applied for a job that we were told he had the inside track on. It seemed certain that he would be chosen. We visited the community and checked out the housing market. Bob even bought a new wardrobe for the interview. At the last minute another individual entered the competition for the same job. Despite giving the final interview our best shot, we came in number two. We were crushed. We simply couldn't understand why God would open up an apparent opportunity and then deny it to us at the last moment. We felt almost cheated.

Years later we had an opportunity to talk with the same person who had landed the job instead of us. He described the job as one of the worst experiences of his life. It had been nonstop conflict, political intrigue, and heartache for him and his wife. As we listened we quietly gave thanks to God we had been spared.

It's tempting to try to pry open doors that God closes. We've discovered it's never a good idea. God shuts doors in our face not to humiliate or punish us, but to guard and protect our lives. God's most merciful word to us can often be a simple no.

MARRIAGE MINUTE TRUTH:

STAY IN CLOSE
FELLOWSHIP WITH CHRIST

. . . .

Primary Passage:
Here I am! I stand at the door and knock. If anyone
hears my voice and opens the door, I will come in
and eat with him, and he with me.
Revelation 3:20

. . . .

Perhaps you've seen the famous painting of Christ standing at a garden door and knocking. For years it has been used as an il-lustration of Christ trying to enter the lives of nonbelievers. The painting is based on Revelation 3:20, whose context implies a far different meaning. Jesus is speaking to the church at Laodicea, to a group of believers who had grown lukewarm in their devotion to Christ. It's not so much a call for unbelievers to receive Christ as it is for believers to open their hearts to intimate fellowship with Jesus once again.

There can be periods in our marriages when Christ is virtually locked out of our hearts. It can happen for any number of rea-sons: the loss of a loved one, an extended season of financial suf-fering, too much prosperity, or even too much time given to the church. We can little by little lose our fellowship with God and become deaf to the promptings of the Holy Spirit. We need to listen today for the quiet knock of Christ on the door of our lives. Just as in the famous painting, the only handle to our hearts is on the inside. Will you please answer the door?

MARRIAGE MINUTE TRUTH:

GOD HAS PRESCRIBED
A LIMIT TO OUR SUFFERING

Primary Passage:
*Do not be afraid of what you are about to suffer. I tell
you, the devil will put some of you in prison to test you,
and you will suffer persecution for ten days.*
Revelation 2:10

We once met a remarkable man whose entire ministry was to
the brokenhearted. His experience of losing his three-year-old
son to a rare genetic disease prepared him to undertake such a
unique and badly needed ministry of compassion.

After the death of his first son he was left feeling dazed and
confused. He hung on to his faith by his fingernails. Then his next
son was diagnosed with the same rare disease. One evening, when
the boy could not be awakened to take his medicine, it was assumed he would die that night. His father climbed into bed next
to his boy and held him tightly. He wanted the boy to know
someone was next to him when the end came. Miraculously the
boy survived. Today he is headed to college.

God has prescribed limits to our suffering. The church in
Smyrna was told its persecution and imprisonment would last for
"ten days." God would not allow it to extend beyond that period
of time. None of us knows how long the trials we face will continue. But we do know that God knows. Once He declares, "No
more," then all of hell cannot take one step further. So take
courage. Whether ten days or ten years, God has His limits so that
we can bear ours.

MARRIAGE MINUTE TRUTH:

OUR MONEY IS SAFE WITH US ONLY IF IT IS SAFE WITH GOD

. . . .

Primary Passage:
Honor the Lord with your wealth, with the firstfruits of
all your crops; then your barns will be filled to
overflowing, and your vats will brim over with new wine.
Proverbs 3:9–10

. . . .

*S*omeone has said our checkbooks are our biographies. Looking over the last year's entries can tell whom we have chosen for friends, what our priorities are, and what our faith truly means to us. Our hearts are where our treasure is.

That's why our money is only safe with us if it has first been put into the hands of God. Once we've done that, we can use our dollars as instruments of honor. It begins when we take the first part of our income and give it directly to God. The Old Testament called it tithing, or giving 10 percent of what we earn directly to God's work. God certainly isn't poor, nor is heaven in a cash crisis. That's not why He instructs us to offer Him our firstfruits. He understands that money is a test of our character. What we purchase or invest in first demonstrates our real priorities and commitments.

The devil will whisper in our ears that we can't afford to tithe. We won't have enough left over for our other needs. Our own experience is that we can't afford not to tithe. If our checkbook is the biography of our life, let's make God the first and last word in every chapter.

MARRIAGE MINUTE TRUTH:

GOD HATES NEEDLESS DIVISIONS WITHIN A FAMILY

Primary Passage:
*There are six things the Lord hates, seven that are
detestable to him: haughty eyes, a lying tongue, hands
that shed innocent blood, a heart that devises wicked
schemes, feet that are quick to rush into evil, a false
witness who pours out lies and a man who stirs up
dissension among brothers.*
Proverbs 6:16–19

We were fresh out of seminary when we were given one of the most difficult assignments of our lives. There had been a cold-blooded murder for hire carried out in our city. A wealthy heir to a chain of hair salons had been gunned down in his own front yard. A lawyer had been used to hire and pay for the hit man. When the police raided the lawyer's home they found $10,000 in cash stuffed in cereal boxes in the kitchen. Sadly, the lawyer had grown up in the church we now served. His parents were still members. We received the task of calling on them to offer spiritual comfort.

Proverbs says God hates seven things. Although He hates all sin, apparently these seven transgressions particularly anger Him. The last item on this list is one who "stirs up dissension among brothers." It is a serious thing to create discord and disunity in the home. It is on God's list of hated behaviors. Let's resolve that our days will be spent as genuine peacemakers. Let's face issues, discover the answers together, and be generous with our forgiveness. Let's treat stirring up dissension as a felony and resolve to live as law-abiding spouses.

MARRIAGE MINUTE TRUTH:

WE WERE LEFT ON THIS PLANET TO WIN PEOPLE TO CHRIST

Primary Passage:
*The fruit of the righteous is a tree of life,
and he who wins souls is wise.*
Proverbs 11:30

The moment we trusted in Christ as our Savior we became fit for heaven. We could have left earth at that very moment and been welcomed through the gates of Paradise. But God chose to leave us here for a little while longer. For what reason?

The Scriptures answer that question in no uncertain terms. We were left on this planet to win other people to Jesus Christ. He has chosen us to tell the Good News of redemption to a race of fallen human beings who are headed toward an eternal night if they don't receive Christ personally.

While God has other things for us to accomplish during our short sojourn on this planet, few are as important as winning souls.

If telling the gospel of Christ to others is the primary reason we're still alive, then how much of our time should be spent in this pursuit? It's an important question. Who should we be praying for? Another vital question. Which of our immediate family members or neighbors should we begin with? Only God can answer those questions. As a couple make a list of unsaved friends or family members you are going to begin praying for. God has left us here for a reason—let's fulfill our assignment.

MARRIAGE MINUTE TRUTH:

WE SHOULD BUILD OUR LIVES WITH DEEDS THAT WILL LAST

. . . .

Primary Passage:
*If any man builds on this foundation using gold, silver,
costly stones, wood, hay, or straw, his work will be shown
for what it is, because the Day will bring it to light. It
will be revealed with fire, and the fire will test the
quality of each man's work.*
1 Corinthians 3:12–13

. . . .

*T*he dry cleaning store near our home burned down when I was just a child. My father took us over to look at the charred remains. A terrible stench hung in the air. We searched among the ashes to find something of value that perhaps had survived. No luck. The fire had been a total loss.

Some day the quality of our life's work is going to be tested. Christ will evaluate whether we invested our time, energy, and money in eternal things or whether we wasted them on our own amusements, ego needs, and pleasures.

All of us will fall into one group or the other. Those who build their lives on service and obedience to Christ will find a marvelous structure in place for all eternity. Those who spend their lives on themselves will find little to nothing of value in the ashes of their life's work. It's not too late to change the course of our lives. Today we can commit ourselves to first and foremost serving God's kingdom. And when the day comes that the fire alarm sounds in eternity, we will have nothing to fear.

MARRIAGE MINUTE TRUTH:

REWARDS ARE WAITING IN HEAVEN FOR OBEDIENT SERVANTS OF GOD

Primary Passage:
If what he has built survives, he will receive his reward. If it is burned up, he will suffer loss; he himself will be saved, but only as one escaping through the flames.
1 Corinthians 3:14–15

We are constantly besieged by incentives from phone companies to switch our long-distance carrier. The salespersons promise us everything from free airplane tickets to cash back. Although some of these offers are true rewards, others are little more than shams.

The Bible assures us genuine rewards await the person who invests his life in the cause of Jesus Christ. Please understand, we are not talking about earning salvation. That is a gift of grace and not of works. A lifetime of good deeds could not earn a single second in heaven.

Who can expect rewards when they meet Christ? The family that spent their lives in another country reaching an indigenous people with the gospel. The Christian couple that took in an unmarried expectant mother into their home to save the life of the unborn baby. The husband or wife who faithfully taught sixth grade Sunday school for ten years.

The list of works that will be rewarded by Jesus Himself is nearly inexhaustible. The principle is that God will not forget our efforts done on earth. Phone company offers will come and go, but using our lives to serve Jesus is the right choice.

MARRIAGE MINUTE TRUTH:

OUR WIVES DESERVE
OUR HONOR AND THANKS

. . . .

Primary Passage:
*The wise woman builds her house, but with her
own hands the foolish one tears hers down.*
Proverbs 14:1

. . . .

*S*usanna Wesley, the mother of John and Charles Wesley, raised seventeen children. Each day she put her apron over her head and prayed for one hour. She also spent an hour each week alone with each child. Her boys were used of God to ignite a spiritual awakening that saved England from revolution and lit a fire of revival that blazed across America. Though this particular woman was limited by her day and culture from the education and training men could enjoy, God used her to shape generations to come.

We should never underestimate the impact of a godly woman. The writer of Proverbs claims that a "wise woman builds her house." That's describing much more than the construction of a safe and warm shelter. It carries with it the idea of building lives too. A wise woman builds into her husband a sense of respect and admiration. A wise woman builds into her children a sense of self-confidence, unconditional love, and true emotional nurture. A wise woman builds into her marriage a strong sense of faithfulness and support.

MARRIAGE MINUTE TRUTH:

TRUTH DESTROYS THE POWER OF DECEPTION

. . . .

Primary Passage:
Therefore put on the full armor of God, so that when the day of evil comes, you may be able to stand your ground, and after you have done everything, to stand. Stand firm then, with the belt of truth buckled around your waist.
Ephesians 6:13–14

. . . .

At the conclusion of World War II the German people were stunned to discover how many lies they had been told. The German propaganda machine had even convinced the nation that New York City had been bombed to rubble. The evil rulers understood that a lie can be as powerful as the truth if people believe it's true.

As Christians we need to be aware that certain deceptions may be at work in our lives. If the devil can get us to believe a lie such as "God has forgiven some of your sins, but not all of them," we will end up living with years of crushing guilt and ineffectiveness for God. Why? Because we have been wrongly convinced that He's still holding something against us.

That's why filling our minds with the truth of God's Word is so vital. As a couple we need to become students of the Scriptures, memorizing and discussing them with each other. The moment a particular lie is introduced into our thinking we need to counter it with the eternal truth of God's Word. Let's not live under the influence of Satan's propaganda machine. True liberation occurs when we wrap the belt of God's truth around us each and every day and oppose the Big Lie.

MARRIAGE MINUTE TRUTH:

WE NOW WEAR THE RIGHTEOUSNESS OF CHRIST

. . . .

Primary Passage:
Stand firm then . . . with the breastplate
of righteousness in place.
Ephesians 6:14

. . . .

*J*ust before we graduated from seminary, one of our favorite professors invited Bob to visit his office. He surprised him by asking if he could take a picture to remember him by. Bob agreed. "One more thing," our friend said to him, "I'd like you to wear my robe." He stepped over and put his gray doctoral robe around Bob. Though my husband had not earned a doctor's degree, nonetheless this gracious man put his robe around him and afforded him a great honor.

Christ has done something similar for us as believers. He has clothed us in His righteousness. We could never earn such a great honor. Paul tells us we can now stand firm "with the breastplate of righteousness in place." This breastplate of righteousness is the assurance that all our sins have been forgiven. The righteousness of Christ now covers our hearts. When accusations are brought against us by Satan, we can stand against them because we are as righteous as Jesus in the eyes of God.

As a husband and wife let's claim our full position of righteousness in Christ. Despite our temporary failures and shortcomings, we can encourage each other that we wear the robe of Jesus each and every day. It makes for a wonderful picture.

MARRIAGE MINUTE TRUTH:

HUSBANDS ARE CALLED BY GOD TO BLESS THEIR FAMILIES

Primary Passage:
*Then all the people left, each for his own home, and
David returned home to bless his family.*
1 Chronicles 16:43

*O*ne of our favorite contemporary paintings is of a father kneeling beside his child's bed in prayer. As he intercedes for his child, a bright cloud of angels hovers over the bed. God dispatches unseen guardians to minister to the saints, whether young or old.

After King David had brought the ark of the covenant to Jerusalem he sent everyone home with a gift. Then he returned home with one specific purpose in mind—"to bless his family."

In the Old Testament God assigned priests to offer sacrifices and prayers on behalf of Israel. In like manner husbands and fathers were expected to perform a priestly role on behalf of their own families. Although they could not offer sacrifices as the tabernacle priests did, they were expected to lead their families in worship and prayer and instruction in God's Word.

Husbands and fathers, although we are not priests shouldn't we still pray on behalf of our wives and children? Shouldn't we bring their needs before the throne of God? Shouldn't our life of intercessory prayer be a source of God's blessing on our home? Jesus, our High Priest, continually prays on our behalf. Let's follow His example and lead our family forward on our knees.

MARRIAGE MINUTE TRUTH:

WE SHOULD GIVE THANKS FOR HOW FAR GOD HAS BROUGHT US

. . . .

Primary Passage:
*Then King David went in and sat before the Lord, and
he said: "Who am I, O Lord God, and what is my
family, that you have brought me this far?"*
1 Chronicles 17:16

. . . .

*N*ot long ago we had a family picture taken. New photographic technology allowed us to immediately see on a special video monitor what our full-color portrait would look like. As we looked at the picture of the seven of us, we were overcome by the goodness of God. When we first married there were just the two of us. Now our home is filled with the laughter, noise, and sometimes confusion of more than half a dozen people. But we are still moved to say as David did, "Who am I, O Lord God, and what is my family, that you have brought me this far?"

All of us can use a healthy dose of gratitude and wonder from time to time. We need to step back and look at the portrait of our lives and marriage. Sure there have been pain and regrets, mistakes and sorrows. But think of how far God has brought all of us. Think of the dangers we have avoided, the problems we have been able to conquer, and the suffering that we have outlived. Think as well of the blessings of health, jobs, and moments of special worship we have been able to enjoy.

Can we make a suggestion? Take a snapshot of the grace of God today by writing down all the blessings He has poured out on you and put it in your wallet. It makes a wonderful family portrait.

MARRIAGE MINUTE TRUTH:

WE SHOULD SEEK THE BLESSING OF GOD ON OUR HOUSE FOREVER

. . . .

Primary Passage:
*O Lord, you are God! You have promised these good
things to your servant. Now you have been pleased
to bless the house of your servant, that it may continue
forever in your sight; for you, O Lord, have blessed
it, and it will be blessed forever.*
1 Chronicles 17:26–27

. . . .

*N*oted author and radio host James Dobson writes of how a godly ancestor of his actively sought God's blessing on his descendants. He received an assurance from God that four generations of his descendants would serve Christ in full-time ministry. Dobson recounts with tears how God has fulfilled His promise—he is the fourth generation to serve Christ in a ministry.

Sometimes we are too timid in what we ask of God. We hold back from actively seeking His blessing on our family. And because we ask not we have not. King David was no such timid soul. He rejoiced in God's promise to bless his family and descendants in a powerful fashion. He grabbed hold of those promises and believed them for his family.

God was certainly good to His Word. Later we read in the New Testament that two descendants of David, Joseph and Mary, were given the honor of raising Jesus, the promised Christ. Let's actively seek God's blessing on our marriage, our family, and generations yet to come. His answer may last to children yet unborn.

MARRIAGE MINUTE TRUTH:

IF WE DON'T BELIEVE THAT WE ARE THE WORST OF ALL SINNERS, THEN WE STILL DON'T UNDERSTAND OUR OWN SINFULNESS

Primary Passage:
*Here is a trustworthy saying that deserves full
acceptance: Christ Jesus came into the world
to save sinners—of whom I am the worst.*
1 Timothy 1:15

Our current society is fascinated by high-profile crimes and criminals. We afford well-publicized criminals a near celebrity status. Why do we do that? Does it help us feel better about our own lives? After all, if we compare our ordinary sins with those of America's ten most wanted, don't we come out looking pretty good?

Yet the apostle Paul, perhaps the most effective Christian in the two-thousand-year history of the church, referred to himself as the "worst" of all sinners. Was he exaggerating? If we compared Paul's sins to those of Nero, who burned down an entire city, or to King Herod, who murdered most of his own immediate family, we'd be hard pressed to call Paul the "worst" of all sinners. But Paul avoided the mistake of comparing his life to others. Instead he compared his life to that of the unblemished Lamb of God. He understood that his own sins were enough to send Jesus to the Cross. In like manner our sins caused Jesus' agonizing death and made Him cry out, "My God, my God, why have you forsaken me?" When we consider what our sins have caused, the term "worst of all sinners" suddenly seems too mild a term for any of us.

MARRIAGE MINUTE TRUTH:

GOD HAS FORGIVEN US TO MAKE US AN EXAMPLE OF HIS PATIENCE

Primary Passage:
*But for that very reason I was shown mercy so that in
me, the worst of sinners, Christ Jesus might display his
unlimited patience as an example for those who would
believe on him and receive eternal life.*
1 Timothy 1:16

The end of Charles Dickens's heartwarming novel *A Christmas Carol* features a transformed Scrooge. The man who once couldn't have cared less if Tiny Tim died of tuberculosis, who went into a rage because a local charity asked for a contribution to the poor, and who snarled at giving his employee, Bob Cratchit, even one day off for Christmas, was now a new person. He bought the biggest goose in all of London as a Christmas gift for the Cratchits, he poured generous sums into the coffers of the local charity, and he took Tiny Tim into his arms with love. Dickens makes the point that the very worst of us, when changed by the power of love, has the potential to become the very best of us.

All of us who have received Christ's forgiveness and gift of salvation are like the transformed Scrooge. We, the worst of sinners, are now living examples of God's unlimited patience. When we are tempted to become discouraged by our past sins and errors we can remember this—Christ has forgiven us for a purpose. He has pardoned our sins that we might become living object lessons that God can redeem anyone. Even us. Praise God.

MARRIAGE MINUTE TRUTH:

WE NEED TO PRAY FOR OUR LEADERS FOR THE SAKE OF THE GOSPEL

Primary Passage:
I urge, then, first of all, that requests, prayers, intercession
and thanksgiving be made for everyone—for kings and
all those in authority, that we may live peaceful and quiet
lives in all godliness and holiness. This is good, and
pleases God our Savior, who wants all men to be saved
and to come to a knowledge of the truth.
1 Timothy 2:1–3

We are concerned by some Christians who seem to gloat over the misfortunes and embarrassments of our political leaders. We can understand the deep moral and spiritual differences many have with those who have been granted power in our republic. We add our voice to those concerned about the abandonment of biblical morality in our culture. Despite all of this we cannot rejoice or gloat over the personal trials and embarrassments of those in authority. It seems unloving and perhaps even a form of revenge.

Paul was no cheerleader for the Roman government of his day. It was led by cruel, immoral, and exceptionally violent men. Yet he insisted that Christians should pray, intercede, and even give thanks for their leaders. Why? So that order and peace could prevail, creating the best possible environment for the spread of the gospel. God will deal with corrupt leaders. Our assignment is to pray for them in order that all men might be saved and come to a knowledge of the truth. Forgive us, Lord, if we have cared more about politics than about prayer.

MARRIAGE MINUTE TRUTH:

HUSBANDS SHOULD RECOGNIZE WITH GRATITUDE THEIR WIVES' HARD WORK

. . . .

Primary Passage:
*She considers a field and buys it; out of her
earnings she plants a vineyard.*
Proverbs 31:16

. . . .

If you are a husband, it's a good exercise from time to time to try and follow your wife's schedule for a day. If she works an outside job, you'll quickly realize that household chores don't just disappear because she has put in eight hours at an office. If she works primarily at home, you'll soon discover how many roles she is expected to play in just one day: banker, nutritionist, counselor, interior decorator, chauffeur, educator, and the list goes on and on.

Yet the work wives do often goes unnoticed or unrecognized. Ingratitude is wrong, if not sinful. So what are two ways to express true appreciation for all the work your wife does on behalf of your marriage and family?

1. Praise her for her resourcefulness. In any given day wives solve numerous difficulties, problems, and crises. Ask what dilemmas she faced that day, then praise her for her ingenuity and resourcefulness in solving them.

2. Notice the small things. As you walk through the house, take notice of all that's right and orderly. Imagine the state of affairs if you had to manage everything. Thank her for the small things she does each day to make life so much better and easier for the two of you.

MARRIAGE MINUTE TRUTH:

GOD GAVE US A SECOND OPINION IN A MARRIAGE FOR A REASON

Primary Passage:
*She speaks with wisdom, and faithful
instruction is on her tongue.*
Proverbs 31:26

There is the old joke of the man who went to his doctor for an annual physical. "So how am I doing, Doctor?" the man asked.

"You are badly out of shape," he replied in a stern tone.

"I'd like a second opinion," the man shot back.

"OK, you've got bad breath too."

While we may not welcome a second opinion in life, God arranged marriage so that we might benefit from one. In fact husbands would be much better off if they sought out their wives' insights and wisdom before making decisions. As husbands we sometimes mistakenly believe that we don't need our wives to settle a matter. We tell ourselves we have all the information or discernment needed to decide on the best solution. Yet God gave us partners quite different from ourselves in order to give us badly needed perspectives that are often different from our own.

The writer of Proverbs had come to recognize the value of his wife's input into his life: "She speaks with wisdom, and faithful instruction is on her tongue."

We need to get into the habit of tapping our wives' insights and instincts if we don't currently do so. Before making major decisions, whether in finances, relationships, or career moves, we should seek their counsel. Seeking a second opinion may help us avoid a very costly first mistake.

MARRIAGE MINUTE TRUTH:

OUR CHURCH LEADERS DESERVE OUR LOVE, SUPPORT, AND RESPECT

Primary Passage:
*Now we ask you, brothers, to respect those who work
hard among you, who are over you in the Lord and who
admonish you. Hold them in highest regard in love
because of their work. Live in peace with each other.*
1 Thessalonians 5:12–13

It was a hot August day in the desert Southwest. We had promoted an all-church hay ride for couples and families. Several longtime residents of the region crossed their eyes at the suggestion, but out of politeness they still agreed to support the event. We were only ten minutes into the desert when we realized what a huge mistake we had made. The heat, the sand, and the dryness of the trail became nearly suffocating. One by one people put their heads down and began to pant for water like greyhounds. What had been scheduled as a one hour excursion of fun and fellowship ended up feeling like a twelve-hour forced march.

Pastors and leaders do make mistakes. They are not invincible or all wise. Yet the Scriptures command us to love, support, and respect our leaders because of their office. It is not for us to personally punish, discipline, or try to control a pastor or church leader. If such action needs to be taken, there is a scriptural process to follow. God has called us to be peacemakers in the church. Can He count on you to be your church leaders' best friends and supporters?

MARRIAGE MINUTE TRUTH:

DO NOTHING THAT WOULD LEAD TO A SPLIT IN YOUR CHURCH

Primary Passage:
*Warn a divisive person once, and then warn him a
second time. After that, have nothing to do with him.
You may be sure that such a man is warped and
sinful; he is self-condemned.*
Titus 3:10–11

Several years ago Bob wrote a book entitled, *Love in Action: Healing Conflict in Your Church.* The book encourages believers to become agents of reconciliation in their congregations. One chapter is satirically labeled, "Ten Ways to Split Your Church." Here they are:

Step One: Focus exclusively on your own desires.

Step Two: Listen to every criticism.

Step Three: Focus on your pastor's weaknesses, not his strengths.

Step Four: Speak the truth or practice love, but never combine the two.

Step Five: Store grievances for future use.

Step Six: Forgive only those who ask you to do so, and only if they deserve it.

Step Seven: Hide your own sin behind harsh attitudes.

Step Eight: Use prayer to unite discontented individuals (and spread inappropriate information).

Step Nine: Do whatever you have to, to win.

Step Ten: Remember, you are on a mission from God.

Did you get all ten suggestions? Now don't do any of them.

MARRIAGE MINUTE TRUTH:

THERE IS GREAT JOY IN SERVING OTHERS

. . . .

Primary Passage:
*And whoever wants to be first must be your slave—just
as the Son of Man did not come to be served, but to
serve, and to give his life as a ransom for many.*
Matthew 20:27–28

. . . .

*W*e will never forget our first Thanksgiving dinner in the inner city. Our little church had never tried anything quite like this before. In the city newspaper and at local schools we had advertised a free Thanksgiving meal with all the trimmings. It seemed a high risk venture at the time. What if no one came? What if everyone came? What if there was trouble or even violence?

Our dear friends Ross and Maggie helped organize the event. They and others had the faith to believe the potential rewards outweighed any possible risks involved. That night more than 245 people poured through the doors as soon as they opened. Just as the food ran out the crowds trickled off as well. The entire evening reminded us of the original Thanksgiving Feast as scores of Native Americans joined us for a sumptuous meal of turkey and the trimmings. It was both a peaceful and a joyous event.

At the end of the evening our friend Ross was so delighted with the results that he skipped across the basement floor of the church. This Thanksgiving season let's recommit ourselves to serving others. Let's rediscover the example of Jesus who came not to be served, but to serve. Let's move out of our comfort zone to reach others. Don't skip the chance to skip.

MARRIAGE MINUTE TRUTH:

GOLGOTHA IS THE HILL WHERE OUR LIVES WERE GIVEN BACK TO US

. . . .

Primary Passage:
They came to a place called Golgotha (which means The Place of the Skull). There they offered Jesus wine to drink mixed with gall; but after tasting it, he refused to drink it. When they had crucified him, they divided up his clothes by casting lots.
Matthew 27:33–35

. . . .

*W*hen our daughter was only six years old, she suffered a serious bicycle accident on a steep hill near our home. When we found her at the bottom of the hill she appeared to be dead. Through the mercy of God she regained consciousness, her injuries limited to a concussion and a broken arm. But for many years after that we could not drive by the hill without choking back tears. It represented to us a place of sorrow and pain, a place where our innocent little girl nearly perished.

Yet it also became the hill where God gave us back the life of our little girl. There we gained an appreciation of how God must have felt when He looked down upon Golgotha. There His innocent Son was subjected to the cruelest of deaths. There all the sins of the world were poured out on the innocent Lamb of God. Yet there He also gave us our lives back. This Thanksgiving season let's take another look at Golgotha. Let's remember the hill where death and mercy met—and mercy won.

MARRIAGE MINUTE TRUTH:

WE WILL ONE DAY TALK FACE-TO-FACE WITH GOD

. . . .

Primary Passage:
*And I heard a loud voice from the throne saying, "Now
the dwelling of God is with men, and he will live with
them. They will be his people, and God himself
will be with them and be their God."*
Revelation 21:3

. . . .

*W*e stood one day at the gate of a local cemetery waiting for the funeral car to return us to the church. Despite the efforts made to create a lovely, landscaped environment, the smell of death seemed to hang heavy in the air. It's a fitting image of this world. Though we enjoy a world with plants, flowers, and natural beauty, the acrid smell of death hangs in the air. It won't be removed until Jesus Christ returns to earth.

On that day the stench of death will be forever banished. The beauty and majesty of God's heaven will overwhelm us. Best of all God Himself will be in our midst. Just as He once walked and talked face-to-face with Adam and Eve, we shall be invited back to an everlasting garden to fellowship with Him.

We need to live out our marriage relationships in the awareness that all is temporary. Our jobs, homes, and even our marriages will one day pass away. In their place God will put something even more wonderful. He will give us the opportunity to live with Him. As good as things might be today, something even better is coming. It's only a matter of time.

MARRIAGE MINUTE TRUTH:

WHILE JESUS CONVICTS US, HE DOES NOT CONDEMN US

. . . .

Primary Passage:
Jesus straightened up and asked her, "Woman, where are they? Has no one condemned you?" "No one, sir," she said. "Then neither do I condemn you," Jesus declared. "Go now and leave your life of sin."
John 8:10–11

. . . .

*H*ow can you tell the difference between the voice of Jesus and the voice of our adversary, the devil? That's an important question. Our lives can become quite chaotic and miserable if we confuse the two. One test we use is this: Do our thoughts convict or condemn us?

When a woman caught in the act of adultery was brought to Jesus, the crowd was ready to stone her. They had the evidence they needed, they had witnesses to accuse her, and they had the Law of Moses on their side. Jesus studied the frenzied mob for a moment. He then asked any person who was without sin in his own life to pick up the first stone and throw it. A sense of conviction engulfed the crowd. The rush to condemn the woman fizzled out one person at a time.

That's how we can discern between conviction and condemnation. The voice of Christ in our lives will convict us of anger, lust, impatience, and harshness where they are present in our marriages. The voice of Satan demands our condemnation. Yet because of the Cross, God refuses to condemn us. Conviction and condemnation—they sound alike but they are an eternity apart from each other.

MARRIAGE MINUTE TRUTH:

THE HOLY SPIRIT IS THE BEST MARRIAGE COUNSELOR THERE IS

. . . .

Primary Passage:
*And I will ask the Father, and he will give you another
Counselor to be with you forever—the Spirit of truth.
The world cannot accept him, because it neither sees him
nor knows him. But you know him, for he
lives with you and will be in you.*
John 14:16–17

. . . .

*W*e know and respect a Christian marriage counselor who for several years had not lost a single couple to divorce. Though he's written several best-selling books and has appeared on nationally syndicated talk shows, he's still not the best marriage counselor available to couples.

The Holy Spirit is. Jesus promised that He would ask the Father and He would send a Counselor who would be with us forever—the Spirit of truth. When there are tensions, unresolved disputes, and painful roadblocks in our marriage, the first person we should turn to is the Holy Spirit. We should ask Him to show us where our actions or attitudes are inconsistent with God's Word or the character of Christ. We should invite Him to show us the truth about ourselves and reveal to us the sins we can't see. We should wait for Him to help us find answers to problems we can't solve. The best news of all is that we don't have to wait to schedule an appointment. He lives in our hearts moment by moment.

The Counselor is in. Will you see Him right now?

MARRIAGE MINUTE TRUTH:

GOOD BOUNDARIES
MAKE FOR GOOD HOLIDAYS

. . . .

Primary Passage:
*[Love] always protects, always trusts, always
hopes, always perseveres.*
1 Corinthians 13:7

. . . .

*D*o holidays put a particular stress on your marriage? If they do, join the crowd. One common stress point is going home to visit relatives, particularly difficult relatives. There's the cousin who drinks too much, the ornery in-law who doesn't think you can do anything right, or the complaining aunt who rehearses all her illnesses for you. Just the thought of being together makes you anxious, if not depressed.

Rather than letting difficult relatives ruin this season for you, why not agree with your spouse on some appropriate boundaries you'll enforce with the relatives. If someone drinks too much and becomes obnoxious, you'll both excuse yourselves from the party. If someone you're uncomfortable with corners you, the other spouse will come to the rescue. Perhaps most important, if need be you'll stand up for your spouse to your parents, regardless of the cost.

You don't have to be dreading of a "blue Christmas" this year just because of family get-togethers. Loving boundaries and protection of each other can honestly bring joy to your world.

MARRIAGE MINUTE TRUTH:

WE SHOULD CELEBRATE RELATIONSHIPS, NOT PRESENTS

Primary Passage:
*But the angel said to them, "Do not be afraid. I bring
you good news of great joy that will be for all the people.
Today in the town of David a Savior has
been born to you; he is Christ the Lord.*
Luke 2:10–11

Holidays can become a stressful time of year when money is a problem or when finances are tight. One person wants to cut back and keep things simple; the other wants to be certain it's a Currier-and-Ives Christmas complete with a brightly decorated tree, steaming hot chocolate, and a mountain of gifts under the tree.

The important thing is that you labor together in finding solutions that bring you together, not move you apart. Whatever you decide has to take into consideration the unique person and temperament you both are, as well as your financial realities. Whatever the case, don't be dogmatic or rigid. Listen, attempt to hear the other person's heart, and stay focused on the truth that Christmas is a time when we celebrate a relationship, not a holiday.

The good news is not that some item is on sale, but that unto us a Savior has been born, who is Christ the Lord. Stay focused on that truth and we guarantee you a memorable Christmas.

MARRIAGE MINUTE TRUTH:

PAINFUL MEMORIES FROM PAST HOLIDAYS CAN BE HEALED

Primary Passage:
I will repay you for the years the locusts have eaten.
Joel 2:25a

*H*olidays can be hard on a marriage for a variety of reasons. One common reason is the painful memories they can bring back, particularly from childhood. In some households Christmas signaled the beginning of an extended season of fighting and bickering. Where parents were divorced it often meant being shuttled back and forth between homes, sometimes across the country. If finances were tight it meant receiving very little for Christmas, all the while watching friends celebrate their abundance of gifts. For anyone who grew up in a difficult setting, holidays and pain likely became synonymous.

Should such hard memories continually rob the two of you an opportunity to celebrate a truly joyous holiday? Not at all. Here is a strategy to begin building happier and more fulfilling memories at Christmas. Ask God to help you celebrate His love, not the season itself. Listen to your mate's pain in a supportive and accepting fashion. Finally, go out of your way to do something unselfish for someone else. Painful memories take time to heal, but God can "restore the years the locusts have eaten."

MARRIAGE MINUTE TRUTH:

THIS SEASON DWELL ON HOW MUCH YOU HAVE GAINED, NOT LOST, AND YOU WILL HAVE REASON TO CELEBRATE

. . . .

Primary Passage:
Before the years of famine came, two sons were born to
Joseph by Asenath daughter of Potiphera, priest of On.
Joseph named his firstborn Manasseh and said, "It is
because God has made me forget all my trouble and all
my father's household." The second son he named
Ephraim and said, "It is because God has made me
fruitful in the land of my suffering."
Genesis 41:50–52

. . . .

*J*oseph was a young man who had been betrayed and abandoned by his family when he was only seventeen. After his jealous brothers had attacked him, beaten him, and thrown him into a pit, their final indignity was to sell him into slavery.

It doesn't take much imagination to understand how painful the passing of each year must have been to young Joseph. Yet in his life we catch a glimpse of how to overcome our painful pasts and memories. Based on the two names he gave his sons, it's clear Joseph had chosen to dwell on how much God had given him, not how much he had lost.

This Christmas, despite all the hurts of your past, examine your life and take inventory of all God has done for you. It can be a source of fresh joy and healing as you discover just how fruitful the Lord has made you in the land of your suffering.

MARRIAGE MINUTE TRUTH:

REST IS ACHIEVED BY
SPENDING TIME WITH GOD

....

Primary Passage:
*Therefore, since the promise of entering his rest
still stands, let us be careful that none of you
be found to have fallen short of it.*
Hebrews 4:1

....

*B*usyness is an effective thief of joy during the holiday season. We simply spend too much of our time running from one party to another, tramping through malls looking to finish our gift lists, and trying to remember who we still owe a Christmas card to. The final result is exhaustion, disappointment, and often irritability. If we're not careful, exhaustion enters our marriage. We begin to snipe, argue, or just ignore the other person in plain indifference.

There are practical steps you can take to break the cycle of busyness, overcommitment, and holiday burnout. Create margin for the two of you in order to spend unhurried time together. Limit your engagements. Say no to some invitations. Don't leave everything to the last minute. Most important, decide as a couple to spend time together in the presence of God. Sit down and read Scripture to each other. Listen to soothing and uplifting music that celebrates Christ's birth. Rather than go shopping, use the time to pray in an unhurried fashion. God rest ye merry spouses.

MARRIAGE MINUTE TRUTH:

EXPECT GREAT THINGS FROM GOD, NOT FROM THE HOLIDAYS

Primary Passage:
*Then you will know that I am the Lord; those
who hope in me will not be disappointed.*
Isaiah 49:23b

*S*everal years ago a popular song asked the question, "Is that all there is?" Do you two ever experience that same emotion once the busy holiday season passes? Despite your best efforts to make it a memorable, magical season, it often turns out to be just one more furious blizzard of activity followed by an avalanche of bills come February.

In many cases it's our unrealistic expectations that set us up for a profound disappointment once the holidays are over. The popular culture portrays images of families on sleigh rides in the country, warm and glowing parties where everyone is welcomed and no one sad, and families reveling in laughter and love in ornately decorated living rooms.

Relieve yourselves right now of the pressure to have the perfect holiday—the proverbial White Christmas in Vermont. Instead, base your expectations on who God is and His mercy, grace, and tenderness toward both of you. Celebrate the fact that God loved you last year, loves you this year, and will love you forever. You won't be disappointed. Promise.

MARRIAGE MINUTE TRUTH:

GOD HAS GIVEN US THE GIFT OF A WONDERFUL COUNSELOR

Primary Passage:
And he will be called Wonderful Counselor, Mighty
God, Everlasting Father, Prince of Peace . . .
Isaiah 9:6b

*W*ho do the two of you turn to when you need advice? Through the years we've heard some of the worst marital advice on earth given by people who claimed they were professionals in their field.

One couple went to a marriage counselor who told them it was time to divorce—they were simply causing each other too much emotional distress. What he failed to tell them is how much more distressing a divorce can actually become.

The problem we face today is an abundance of information and a famine of wisdom. You can get advice from the Internet, talk shows, and entire walls of books at popular bookstores.

But who can you trust?

The good news is that the first Christmas God didn't simply send us good counsel; He sent us the Wonderful Counselor. In Jesus Christ we have the world's only and utterly reliable guide and confidant. Through His Word we can find the guidance, direction, and answers we can't find anywhere else on earth. Regardless of the problems or tensions facing your marriage, the Wonderful Counselor's wisdom cannot fail. Do you need advice today? Now you know who to ask.

MARRIAGE MINUTE TRUTH:

LOVE DENIES US THE RIGHT TO HURT THOSE WE LOVE

Primary Passage:
This is how the birth of Jesus Christ came about: His mother Mary was pledged to be married to Joseph, but before they came together, she was found to be with child through the Holy Spirit. Because Joseph her husband was a righteous man and did not want to expose her to public disgrace, he had in mind to divorce her quietly.
Matthew 1:18–19

*W*e were sitting in a cafe one day when we happened to glance at a country western video being shown on television. The hard driving, heart pounding, female vocalist sang of her unfaithful and abusive husband in a song called "Independence Day." The scenes switched back and forth between a Fourth of July parade and the man's abusive behavior at home. The video reached its climax when the beaten and betrayed wife poured gasoline all over the house and set her husband's room on fire while he slept.

Although abuse and infidelity should never be tolerated in a marriage, hurting someone back harder than he or she has hurt you is never the answer. For Joseph, the husband of Mary, hurting her back was never on his agenda even though he did not understand the cause of her pregnancy. Love doesn't deny us the right to stand up for ourselves, but it does deny us the right to strike back at our spouse. True independence is when we can respond to provocations, small or big, with the love and righteousness of Christ.

MARRIAGE MINUTE TRUTH:

CIRCUMSTANCES MAY DECEIVE US, BUT GOD NEVER WILL

Primary Passage:
*Joseph son of David, do not be afraid to take Mary
home as your wife, because what is conceived
in her is from the Holy Spirit.*
Matthew 1:20

*D*o you sometimes let difficult or perplexing circumstances change your attitude toward your spouse? Do you assume the worst? Do you let your imagination run wild?

On one occasion Cheryl had been following me home from church on a busy expressway in another car. When we became separated at a toll plaza I pulled over to wait for her, but she never appeared. I soon began conjuring up images of a flat tire, a breakdown, or, worse yet, an accident. After nearly twenty minutes of worrying, I pulled off the expressway and called home. Cheryl answered and calmly explained a driver had cut her off and she had to take an alternate route home. I had been worried for nothing.

Circumstances can deceive us. Joseph, the husband of Mary, experienced that fact firsthand. When Mary announced she was pregnant, Joseph must have been absolutely certain she had been unfaithful. Yet God didn't allow that deception to stand. In moments when circumstances can lead you to believe the worst about your spouse, stop for a moment and ask God to show you the truth. Eventually, you may discover you were worried for nothing.

MARRIAGE MINUTE TRUTH:

GOD SENT US A SAVIOR
BECAUSE WE NEEDED TO BE SAVED

Primary Passage:
*She will give birth to a son, and you are to give
him the name Jesus, because he will save
his people from their sins.*
Matthew 1:21

*P*opular song writer and vocalist Al Denson tells the story of a man who lived in Washington State near Mount St. Helens, one of America's oldest dormant volcanoes. His name happened to be Harry Truman. By the end of the 1970s the volcano was starting to show signs of stirring. Geologists and other scientists examined the data and concluded an eruption could be imminent. They advised everyone in the area to evacuate.

Most listened, but Harry didn't. Harry was never seen again after the giant mountain exploded with the force of five hundred atomic weapons. His death was not caused by the volcano. He died because he refused to believe he needed to be saved. Many face the same danger today. They won't acknowledge their need for salvation.

God didn't send Christ into the world on a fact-finding mission, to tour the planet, or to simply hand out good advice. He sent Christ into the world because without a Savior we will perish—eternally.

Will you acknowledge your need of a Savior this Christmas? The volcano of time is rumbling. The good news is there's still time to leave the mountain and find safety.

MARRIAGE MINUTE TRUTH:

GOD HAS PROMISED TO MEET OUR MOST BASIC NEEDS

. . . .

Primary Passage:
The Lord is my shepherd, I shall not be in want.
He makes me lie down in green pastures,
He leads me beside quiet waters.
Psalm 23:1–2

. . . .

*H*olidays can remind us as much of what we don't have as of what we do enjoy. Perhaps this was the year one of you lost your job, or one of your parents, or perhaps even one of your children. There will be an empty place underneath that Christmas tree that will mirror the empty place that has been left in your heart.

So what's left to celebrate under such difficult, heartbreaking circumstances? Psalm 23 tells us that despite devastating losses in our lives our Shepherd will never leave us, not even for a moment. Through the blur of tears and the sting of pain we can still make out the figure of Jesus Christ, guiding and empowering our lives step-by-step, day-by-day.

David, the writer of Psalm 23, was no stranger to sorrow and affliction. In his lifetime he lived to see the death of his sons, betrayal at the hands of his closest friends, and his kingdom nearly torn in two by rebellion in his own family. Yet he could still affirm these magnificent words, "The Lord is my Shepherd, I shall not be in want. . . ." Though you may have lost much this last year, you have not lost Jesus, nor will you ever.

MARRIAGE MINUTE TRUTH:

GOD CAN PUT YOU BACK TOGETHER WHEN LIFE HAS TAKEN YOU APART

Primary Passage:
He restores my soul.
Psalm 23:3a

When I visited Sweden, the land of my grandmother's birth, I learned a fascinating fact that helped explain why so many people left that country in the nineteenth century. It was the customary practice to divide the farm among the children at the time of the parents' death. The practice worked well for a generation or two, then problems began to appear. As one generation succeeded another, the plots became smaller and smaller. Eventually they resembled small gardens more than expansive farmsteads. No one could survive on such meager parcels, and as a result hundreds of thousands of people left their homeland forever.

Life can divide us up in a number of ways as well. The demands of balancing your job, your marriage, your children, church commitments, and time with friends may have carved up your schedule. Or anger, unforgiveness, and bitterness may have subdivided your hearts so there's little emotional living space left to support a marriage.

The good news of Christmas is that God can restore your soul. He can enter your marriage and put back together what life has carved up. The key is turning over all your emotional, spiritual, and physical property to His management as Shepherd.

You'll find room to breathe, room to live, and room to love.

MARRIAGE MINUTE TRUTH:

GOD WILL GUIDE YOUR DECISION MAKING FOR HIS OWN REPUTATION

. . . .

Primary Passage:
He guides me in paths of righteousness
for his name's sake.
Psalm 23:3b

. . . .

*S*hould we sell our house? Change careers? Expand the size of our family? These and a hundred other decisions may confront the two of you this season. If you're not careful, the stress and intensity of making these heavy decisions will steadily erode the joy and intimacy of your relationship.

Isn't it wonderful to know that Someone understands our dilemmas and knows the direction we take? That Someone is Jesus Christ, our Good Shepherd. In Psalm 23 we receive the promise, "He guides me in paths of righteousness for his name's sake." Did you catch the last phrase? The motivation God has to direct you and your spouse in making the right decisions is to preserve His own reputation.

Why would God's reputation be on the line when we face significant decisions? Because we've publicly called Him our Savior. Now people are watching to see if this God can be trusted. When they witness dramatic evidence of God's daily wisdom and guidance at work in our lives, they are attracted to Him.

Do you two have a big decision to make? Relax. Turn it over to God. Watch how He will guide you and guard His name.

MARRIAGE MINUTE TRUTH:

FEAR SHOULD HAVE NO PLACE IN OUR LIVES

Primary Passage:
Even though I walk through the valley of the shadow of death, I will fear no evil, for you are with me."
Psalm 23:4a

*Y*ears ago my mother stopped by a donut shop for her usual morning cup of coffee. She struck up a conversation with the woman sitting next to her. To her surprise she learned that the woman spent the entire day, every day, all year sitting at the donut counter. She didn't have an eating disorder; she was simply terrified of spending an entire day in her own home. "But why?" my mother asked innocently.

"Because several years ago there was a tornado in the area and it nearly destroyed our house," she replied. "Since then, I've been afraid it would happen again and I would be killed."

Few of us live with that level of paranoia in our lives. But we all do wrestle with fears from time to time. What if my lab test comes back positive? What if our son or daughter marries the wrong person? What if my husband or wife dies prematurely?

One reason Jesus came into the world at Christmas time was to rid our lives of fear. "Fear not," He told His disciples. The psalmist tells us that even when walking through the valley of the shadow of death we should fear no evil—His love and protection is our constant companion. To take courage, take Christ.

MARRIAGE MINUTE TRUTH:

GOD PROTECTS AND
DISCIPLINES US AT THE SAME TIME

. . . .

Primary Passage:
I will fear no evil, for you are with me;
your rod and your staff, they comfort me.
Psalm 23:4b

. . . .

*S*usan had been happily married for several years. One day at a parents' meeting she met Kevin. The two of them exchanged only informal conversation. Yet at the end of the meeting Susan found herself feeling drawn toward him.

On the way home the Holy Spirit spoke to her about her feelings toward Kevin. She was forced to admit she had acted foolishly by talking so long to a man who wasn't her husband. She made a commitment that very moment to avoid such involved discussions in the future—and she kept it. What happened? The Good Shepherd's rod had driven away a potential threat to her marriage.

We can take comfort that we have a Shepherd who will guard our individual lives and marriages. He will use his staff (an instrument to retrieve sheep from danger) or his rod (a heavy stick used to ward off intruders). In either case His purpose is to love and nurture us as the sheep of His pasture.

Listen to the Holy Spirit when He prompts you about potential threats to your marriage. It's the Shepherd at work pulling us back from the brink. Whether He uses His rod or His staff, it's a comfort to know we're in the care of a loving God.

MARRIAGE MINUTE TRUTH:

EVEN OUR ENEMIES MAY SOMEDAY HAVE TO ADMIT WE WERE RIGHT IN SERVING GOD

Primary Passage:
You prepare a table before me in the
presence of my enemies.
Psalm 23:5a

A friend of Bob's from high school went on to study at a prestigious East Coast university. Bob felt called to the ministry and enrolled at a lesser-known Christian college. Bob endured several years of ridicule by his friend because his college lacked the prestige and reputation of his friend's Ivy League university.

One Christmas break the two of them got together to compare their college experiences. Bob had been interviewed by the *Wall Street Journal* when a reporter had come to campus to do a story. His friend on the East Coast had read the column and called him.

"You are more fortunate than you know," confessed Bob's friend.

"Why, because I was in the newspaper?"

"No," his friend replied, "because your life makes sense."

The Bible promises that God will one day "prepare a table" for us "in the presence of my enemies." What the Scriptures are teaching is that if we live long enough, our choice to follow and serve God will be vindicated. Don't give up or be discouraged as a couple if you have chosen to follow Christ. Your table is being set even now.

MARRIAGE MINUTE TRUTH:

TRUE JOY ALWAYS HAS THE FINGERPRINTS OF GOD ON IT

. . . .

Primary Passage:
You anoint my head with oil; my cup overflows.
Psalm 23:5b

. . . .

*O*nce a year I take my son with me to Canada to go fishing. We have repeated this same marvelous trip so many times it has now become something of a family ritual. Up there, far away from the noise, tension, and rush of the city, life seems to make sense again. Time seems to condense and elongate at the same time. Although a day goes far too quickly, there are moments out on that vast lake when time seems to stand still.

There's a word I have found to describe our summer experience—joy. It's a sense of exuberant fulfillment and serene pleasure all mixed into the same experience. Not surprisingly, when I experience joy I also experience God. That's because God is the true author of authentic joy. David wrote that God Himself anoints our head with oil and in His presence our cup overflows, a beautiful metaphor of joy.

Moments of joy come all too rarely in our lives. When they enter your marriage, savor them and remember them. If you examine them closely, you'll make the remarkable discovery they have divine fingerprints all over them.

MARRIAGE MINUTE TRUTH:

THE LOVE OF GOD PURSUES US OUR ENTIRE LIVES

Primary Passage:
*Surely goodness and mercy will follow me
all the days of my life . . . .*
Psalm 23:6a

It's a moment our family still laughs about. Actually, they still laugh at Bob about it. It began one Sunday when a friend of ours visited our church and agreed to join us for a family lunch. Through a series of mishaps she ended up in front of us on the expressway rather than following behind.

Fearing we were way ahead of her on the busy expressway, she hit the accelerator. While she was frantically trying to catch up with us, we were in fact pursuing her. The speedometer registered ninety miles per hour by the time we were able to draw alongside her vehicle and wave her over.

Our relationship with God can sometimes resemble that car chase. We lose sight of God and fear that He has pulled out way ahead of us. We accelerate the pace of our lives in a frantic attempt to catch up. All the while God is right behind us—where He has always been—pursuing us with His goodness and mercy. We need to simply slow down our frantic pace and allow His goodness and love to overtake us.

Is the pace of your life running you ragged? Has this holiday season left you breathless and joyless? Then it's time to hit the brakes, not the accelerator.

MARRIAGE MINUTE TRUTH:

THE DESTINATION OF OUR LIVES GIVES THE JOURNEY MEANING

. . . .

Primary Passage:
. . . and I will dwell in the house of the Lord forever.
Psalm 23:6b

. . . .

One of our favorite getaway spots when we lived in the desert Southwest was a seven thousand foot mountain near our city. Even when the temperature on our patio climbed to eighty-five degrees, an hour's drive up the mountain would soon land us in snow covered forests and crisp thirty-degree temperatures.

There was only one problem—getting up the mountain. The only road that led up the steep mountain was so narrow the center line actually ran right next to the guard rail (OK, it wasn't that bad, but it sure seemed that way).

The drive was demanding, harrowing, if not intimidating. So why did we make the journey over and over again? The answer was the destination. Majestic tall pines, lush green valleys, and even a ski resort graced the top of the mountain.

Following God through life as husband and wife can be much like that mountain road. The highway is often difficult, taxing, and intimidating. But the destination makes it all worthwhile: "I will dwell in the house of the Lord forever." One day we'll view our lives from the top of God's mountain and we'll never regret the drive. Care to climb in?

MARRIAGE MINUTE TRUTH:

EVERYTHING IN LIFE ULTIMATELY SERVES GOD'S PURPOSES

. . . .

Primary Passage:
*In those days Caesar Augustus issued a decree that a
census should be taken of the entire Roman world.
(This was the first census that took place while
Quirinius was governor of Syria.) And everyone
went to his own town to register.*
Luke 2:1–3

. . . .

*D*eath, taxes, wars, famines, and disease. These are the awful realities of life. Sometimes, taken together, they can suggest we live
in a world that's out of control. Maybe there is no such thing as a
moral order to the universe.

The message of Christmas doesn't deny our world is broken
and hurting. Instead it says that our sovereign God is at work even
in the midst of pain, injustice, and oppression of life—making all
things ultimately serve God's purposes.

The story of the birth of Christ is a case in point. A godless
ruler imposed an unjust tax on an impoverished people for his
own selfish designs. That's true injustice. Yet the occasion of this
unjust tax led Joseph and Mary to precisely the town that Scripture had predicted as the birthplace of Christ. God took evil and
produced salvation. Remember this Christmas that as difficult as
your hardships, struggles, and pain might be, God can make all
things serve Him.

MARRIAGE MINUTE TRUTH:

GOD HAS THE ABILITY TO PLACE US EXACTLY WHERE HE WANTS US

. . . .

Primary Passage:
*So Joseph also went up from the town of Nazareth in
Galilee to Judea, to Bethlehem the town of David,
because He belonged to the house and line of David.*
Luke 2:4

. . . .

*J*ust before Bob left for seminary he broke up with the girl he had dated over the summer. Worse yet he was heading off to an isolated rural school with an overwhelmingly male population. His love life seemed stuck in reverse and picking up speed.

The first semester he was nearly overcome with loneliness and homesickness. He found himself living in an old dormitory fourteen hours away from his closest friends and family. He seriously questioned God's wisdom in sending him to such an isolated and lonely place.

All that changed the first day of school the next year. He caught a glimpse of a young woman walking down the hallway. He believed she was the most beautiful person he had ever met in his life. An unexpected thought jumped across his mind, "That's the woman I will marry."

A year later we did indeed get married. We learned that God has the ability to put us exactly where He wants us. He won't always explain His purposes or timing to us. That's where trust enters in.

Joseph had no clue why God sent him to Bethlehem to be taxed, but two thousand years later, we sing about it in hymns and pageants. It's the miracle we call Christmas.

MARRIAGE MINUTE TRUTH:

WE NEED TO SURRENDER OUR PARADOXES TO AN ALL-KNOWING GOD

Primary Passage:
*[Joseph] went there to register with Mary, who was
pledged to be married to him and was expecting a child.*
Luke 2:5

*D*o you have a number of unanswered questions that you'd like to ask God? We certainly do. Why did all of Bob's grandparents have to die when he was so young? Why was he raised in a neighborhood that persecuted him because he was in the religious minority on the block? Why did we lose two children to miscarriages just a few years after we were married?

We don't have answers to these questions. Many times the ways of God are a deep mystery to us. At least one biblical figure knows how we feel. His name is Joseph. He loved a young woman named Mary with all his heart. They had made plans to spend their lives together and serve God with their marriage. Then one day she announced she was pregnant.

It's likely none of this made any sense to him. But he did what all of us must do if we are to follow God—he left his unanswered questions in the hands of an all-wise and all-knowing God.

Can you wait for the day when there will be no more questions, only answers? If so, you are more of a relative of Joseph than you realize.

MARRIAGE MINUTE TRUTH:

OUR DISAPPOINTMENTS
ARE GOD'S APPOINTMENTS

. . . .

Primary Passage:
*While they were there, the time came for the baby to be
born, and she gave birth to her firstborn, a son.*
Luke 2:6−7

. . . .

*T*he morning after an airline tragedy that left nearly two hundred people dead, our local newspaper carried a poignant photograph. It showed a woman clutching an airline ticket. The flight number was clearly visible—the flight number of the doomed aircraft. She had missed her plane the day of the accident. That apparent misfortune was literally a lifesaver.

It must have been very hard for Mary to give birth to her first child so far from her home and family. Nothing was familiar; there was no one there but Joseph to comfort her, and her surroundings were nothing better than an animal stable. Joseph and Mary must have struggled with a sense of disappointment. One crisis after another seemed to plague their lives. What was God doing? Yet through the pain of their unanswered questions God fulfilled His promise to give the world a Savior. A series of apparent disappointments turned out to be God's divine appointment. The lyrics of a song suggest, "When you can't see His hand, trust His heart." When disappointment threatens to overwhelm your life, stop and consider that this may be God's appointment. God only says no to us in life because He wants us to experience the joy of His yes at the right time and right place.

Are you willing to wait?

MARRIAGE MINUTE TRUTH:

GOD UNDERSTANDS
DIFFICULT BEGINNINGS

Primary Passage:
She wrapped him in cloths and placed him in a manger,
because there was no room for them in the inn.
Luke 2:7b

*W*e had our last child nine years after the birth of the next youngest sibling. It had been so long since we had been parents of a newborn that we had given away or lost nearly everything we had in the way of baby items. We found ourselves expectant parents with no baby clothes, equipment, toys, or even a crib.

Our church surprised us with a wonderful baby shower and soon we were stacking shelves with delicate dresses, woolen sleepers, and soft cotton comforters. Our good friends Dave and Linda gave us the crib they had intended to use themselves. We found the remaining items we needed at local discount stores. When our daughter finally arrived, we had all we needed and then some.

How different was the birth of Jesus. The Bible tells us His mother dressed Him in cloths, torn pieces of garments—rags, if you will. She placed Him in a manger, a feeding trough for cows and oxen.

God understands difficult beginnings. Perhaps your marriage began on an extremely difficult note too. Take heart. God can overcome difficult beginnings and use your marriage for His purposes and glory. A beginning is just that, a beginning. It's what follows that truly matters.

MARRIAGE MINUTE TRUTH:

GOD VALUES ORDINARY PEOPLE

. . . .

Primary Passage:
And there were shepherds living out in the fields nearby,
keeping watch over their flocks at night.
Luke 2:8

. . . .

*M*ark Twain once said something to the effect, "There is no such thing as an uninteresting life. Every life is a comedy, drama, and a tragedy all at the same time."

The satirist could have easily been speaking of the shepherds who lay out under the stars that first Christmas evening. Scholars believe they were shepherds who raised the flocks used for sacrifices used in the temple in Jerusalem.

Because they lived outdoors they were considered perpetually "unclean" by the more respectable elements of society. Shepherds had also developed a reputation for confusing "mine with thine," as one writer put it. Their testimony was considered inadmissible in Jewish courts of the day.

So why did God choose to reveal first to the shepherds the glorious news of the birth of Jesus Christ? The answer lies in the heart of God. He loves ordinary forgotten people, sinful people just like the shepherds, just like us. Later Jesus would grow up to say He came to seek and save the lost. The good news this Christmas morning is that God came looking for us just as we are.

Isn't that extraordinarily good news?

MARRIAGE MINUTE TRUTH:

THE GLORY OF GOD DRAWS US TO HIMSELF

. . . .

Primary Passage:
An angel of the Lord appeared to them, and the glory
of the Lord shone around them, and they were terrified.
But the angel said to them, "Do not be afraid.
I bring you good news of great joy that will
be for all the people."
Luke 2:9–10

. . . .

*I*magine the sound of a siren wailing down your street. A car screeches to a halt, and a group of armed police officers jumps from the vehicle and storms your front yard. If you are a criminal hiding from the law, it's your worst possible nightmare.

But if you're a hostage being held inside a house by a kidnaper, it's the most welcome sound of your entire life. The difference is whether you believe the police are coming at you or for you. The shepherds who caught a glimpse of the glory of the Lord's angel responded with terror. They were certain that the blazing white light of heaven spelled their destruction.

Yet that was not the angel's message. "Do not be afraid," he said, "I bring you good news of great joy that will be for all the people." That good news is that we live in an age of grace. Simply explained, we live in an era where the Cross of Christ allows God's mercy to prevail over His anger and wrath. God has not come to punish us, but to pardon us. Will you hide from or seek such blinding love and glory?

MARRIAGE MINUTE TRUTH:

GOD'S TIMETABLE MAY BE DIFFERENT THAN OURS, BUT IT'S ALWAYS RIGHT

Primary Passage:
Today in the town of David a Savior has been born to you; he is Christ the Lord. This will be a sign to you: You will find a baby wrapped in cloths and lying in a manger.
Luke 2:11–12

*W*e live in an impatient age. Cars honk if you linger too long at the drive-up window. Computers purchased two years ago have to be discarded because newer models process data so much faster. Colleges offer two year degree programs that can be completed in just one year by attending one night a week.

Imagine the patience the people of Israel displayed in waiting for their promised Savior. Nearly seven hundred years earlier Isaiah had promised, "Therefore the Lord himself will give you a sign: The virgin will be with child and will give birth to a son, and will call him Immanuel" (Isaiah 7:14).

It took seven hundred years before the angel of the Lord could announce to the shepherds, "Today in the town of David a Savior has been born to you; he is Christ the Lord."

What should you do when God's timetable does not match yours? Commit the issue to God. Trust Him to work out His plan in His time. When He does act, you'll see how right God was to do things according to His schedule, not ours. It never fails.

GRACE WILL POPULATE
HEAVEN WITH THE REDEEMED

Primary Passage:
*Suddenly a great company of the heavenly host
appeared with the angel, praising God and saying,
"Glory to God in the highest, and on earth
peace to men on whom his favor rests."*
Luke 2:13–14

The most popular hymn of all time is John Newton's "Amazing Grace." Newton was taught the Scriptures by his mother when he was a small boy. Then, after being sent away to sea when he was still a boy, he went in the opposite direction. He viewed sin as a sport and boasted he had found more ways to sin than any man he knew.

It was only during a raging storm at sea when the ship was flooding faster than the bilge pumps could handle that he began to consider God. The ship miraculously survived the storm and Newton's heart was changed. In an age when ships plied the world's oceans in search of spices, gold, rum, and, in Newton's case, slaves, he had discovered the most priceless treasure of all—the grace of God.

Grace is the unmerited or unearned favor of God toward us. The day Jesus was born the message of grace was announced by the choirs of heaven. If you and your spouse put your faith in Christ alone for your salvation, you can experience the same grace that saved John Newton. Will you take that step today?

MARRIAGE MINUTE TRUTH:

GOD INVITES YOU TO TEST FOR YOURSELF IF HIS WORD IS TRUE

. . . .

Primary Passage:
When the angels had left them and gone into heaven, the
shepherds said to one another, "Let's go to Bethlehem
and see this thing that has happened, which the Lord has
told us about." So they hurried off and found Mary and
Joseph, and the baby, who was lying in the manger.
Luke 2:15–16

. . . .

*W*hen Bob was a short-order cook at a restaurant, a customer once got up from his table and walked straight into the kitchen where he was working. He asked him to move aside so that he could peer inside the broiler to determine if he was cooking his steak just right. Satisfied that Bob was, he went back to his table and sat down. Although his behavior might have bordered on the inappropriate or even rude, he did look into things for himself. As a result left a happy and satisfied customer.

Once the angels had announced the birth of the Savior, the shepherds said, "We need to check this out for ourselves." They dropped their cards and dice and headed straight for Bethlehem. The Bible says they even "hurried."

God invites you as a couple to do just as the shepherds did. See for yourself if God's Word is true. Investigate. Probe. Question. In the end you'll discover what the shepherds did. God's Word is forever true, reliable, and trustworthy. You can stake the rest of your lives on it.

A WITNESS IS SIMPLY SOMEONE WHO REPEATS WHAT THEY'VE SEEN AND HEARD FOR THEMSELVES

Primary Passage:
*When [the shepherds] had seen [Jesus], they spread
the word concerning what had been told them about
this child, and all who heard it were amazed at
what the shepherds said to them.*
Luke 2:17–18

*A*t our first church out of seminary we were asked to attend a murder trial. In the midst of those grim proceedings a moment of levity occurred. The defense called a witness who wore a brown leather waistcoat, sported a crewcut, and wore dark-rimmed glasses. He claimed to be a one-man crime buster. He read page after page from a small notebook about how he had helped crack some of the toughest cases in the city. It turned out the man was a fraud. He simply read the newspapers and showed up at high profile court cases claiming to have inside information.

A true witness is someone who repeats what he or she has actually seen and heard. The shepherds who had gazed into the face of the baby Jesus went out and told everyone the truth. A Savior, Christ the Lord, had been born in Bethlehem. Are you willing to testify to what you have seen and heard of Jesus in your own life? It could change the eternal verdict on someone's soul.

MARRIAGE MINUTE TRUTH:

GOD MAKES EVERYTHING BEAUTIFUL IN ITS TIME

. . . .

Primary Passage:
He has made everything beautiful in its time. He has
also set eternity in the hearts of men; yet they cannot
fathom what God has done from beginning to end.
Ecclesiastes 3:11

. . . .

A twentieth-century author once remarked, "Given enough time, the most difficult experiences of our lives will become to us the most precious." It is amazing how God uses time and distance to alter our perspective. Think back on where you and your spouse were a year ago today. What problems did you face that seemed to have no solution? What mountains appeared so tall that you could never climb them? What heartaches did you carry that threatened to overwhelm you? In each case, stop and consider what God has done for you both.

Although He may not have eliminated each and every difficulty from your life, God has been at work, hasn't He? He has changed you both. Let us encourage you to continue your habit of prayer and study of God's Word together as husband and wife. There are numerous other devotional books for couples you may wish to consider. If you haven't done so yet, consider tackling a book of the Bible together. And you're certainly welcome to go through this book one more time based on the growth you've achieved.

Congratulations on your efforts. Keep up the discipline. And may God continue to make everything beautiful in His time in your marriage.

Be Sure To Read Some of the Other Great Marriage Titles From Moody Press:

The Five Love Languages
How to Express Heartfelt Commitment to Your Mate Gary Chapman
1-881273-15-6 Paperback
This bestselling book explores the all-important languages of love, helping each partner discover the best ways to communicate love and commitment to one's mate.

Loving Solutions
Overcoming Barriers in Your Marriage
Gary Chapman
1-881273-91-1 Paperback
Is your marriage failing to live up to your expectations? There is hope. Discover practical and permanent solutions and steps to take to heal your marriage.

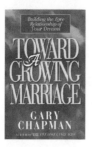

Toward a Growing Marriage
Building the Love Relationship of Your Dreams Gary Chapman
0-8024-8787-4 Paperback
Nobody said turning "I do's" into "well done's" would be easy. This well-known marriage counselor offers practical and biblical advice to help light a promising fire or rekindle one that's flickering.

Two . . . Becoming One
Experiencing the Power of Oneness in Your Marriage Don and Sally Meredith
0-8024-3445-2 Paperback
0-8024-3446-0 Workbook
Unlock time-tested secrets for building strong marriages. The practical tips in this book will help couples prepare for a marriage that will last a lifetime.

Made to Be Loved
Enjoying Spiritual Intimacy With God and Your Spouse Steve and Valerie Bell
0-8024-3399-5 Paperback
Spiritual distance from God threatens our marriages. This book will help you create a whole new atmosphere in your marriage by developing a deeper love relationship with God.

Lasting Love
How to Avoid Marital Failure
Alistair Begg
0-8024-3401-0 Hardback
Take to heart what God has told His people about creating and preserving a fulfilling marriage. Learn to guard your marriage and stand firm against anything that draws your attention from your spouse.

Loving Your Marriage Enough to Protect It (Formerly *Hedges*)
Jerry B. Jenkins
0-8024-3492-4 Paperback
An absolute must-read for every couple committed to maintaining fidelity within their marriage and faithfulness to their Lord. Exposes the causes of infidelity and provides valuable insight on how to protect your marriage from them.